TO MY PARENTS AND THEIR PARENTS

The Modern Art of Dying

The Modern Art of Dying

A HISTORY OF EUTHANASIA
IN THE UNITED STATES

❖

Shai J. Lavi

PRINCETON UNIVERSITY PRESS

PRINCETON AND OXFORD

In the United Kingdom: Princeton University Press, 3 Market Place,
Woodstock, Oxfordshire OX20 1SY

Library of Congress Cataloging-in-Publication Data

Lavi, Shai J.
The modern art of dying : history of euthanasia in the United States / Shai J. Lavi.
p. cm.
Includes bibliographical references and index.
ISBN 0–691–10263–5 (cl : alk. paper)
1. Euthanasia—United States—History.   I. Title.

R726.L3797 2005
179.7—dc22   2004057254

British Library Cataloging-in-Publication Data is available

This book has been composed in Galliard Typeface

pup.princeton.edu

Printed in the United States of America

1   3   5   7   9   10   8   6   4   2

❖ Contents ❖

❖ Acknowledgments ❖

Tʜɪѕ sᴛᴜᴅʏ began during my graduate studies in the Jurisprudence and Social Policy Program at the University of California, Berkeley. I would like to thank my teachers, Philippe Nonet, Kristin Luker, Thomas Laqueur, and Gil Eyal, who offered endless support and guidance on this project, from its inception to its completion. More than once, they provided the Ariadne thread that kept me on track. It is said in the *Ethics of Our Fathers*, "Accept a teacher upon yourself; make a friend for yourself." In the spirit of this teaching I express special gratitude to my teacher and friend, Philippe Nonet.

The Jurisprudence and Social Policy Program and its faculty created a highly stimulating intellectual environment. I would like to express deep appreciation to Malcolm Feeley, Lauren Edelman, David Lieberman, and Michael Smith. Every academic tribe has its elders. I benefited immensely from the wisdom of two: Sanford H. Kadish and Robert N. Bellah. Every book has its guardian angel. I am grateful to Meir Dan-Cohen for taking on this role.

This journey would have been an extremely lonely one if not for the friends who accompanied me on the way. I enjoyed and benefited immensely from discussing my work with Roger Berkowitz, Mark Antaki, and Karl Shoemaker, who carefully read and commented on numerous drafts of this study. I also benefited greatly from fruitful discussions with Amir Banbaji, Emmanuel Ben-Zaquen, Lawrence Cohen, Marianne Constable, Scott Heil, Barry Hoffman, Marie-Andre Jacob, Tsachi Keren-Paz, Loolwa Khazoom, Eric Klinenberg, and Joshua Price.

The work was completed during my first years at Tel Aviv University, where I joined my close friends and fellow travelers in the years to come: Yishai Blank and Roy Kreitner. I owe much to the continuous encouragement and advice of my colleagues at Tel Aviv University: Liora Bilsky, Jose Bruner, Hanoch Dagan, Daniel Friedmann, Sharon Hannes, and Ariel Porat. I offer deep gratitude to Menachem Mautner, who encouraged me to study abroad and who supported my work throughout. Finally, I wish to thank with no words and with more than words can convey Shy Abady, Sara Chinsky, and Hamutal Tsamir.

"Where there is no flour there is no Torah." I am grateful for the financial support I received as a Fulbright Scholar from the Fulbright Fund and the

United States–Israel Educational Foundation and for my one-year fellowship at the Townsend Center for the Humanities at UC Berkeley. I am especially grateful for the continuous support that I received from the Jurisprudence and Social Policy Program and the Law and Society Center at UC Berkeley, which has allowed me to dedicate my time to this study. I would also like to thank my alma matter, Tel Aviv University, for supporting my studies and work. Finally, the Cegla Super Center at Tel Aviv University has kindly given me the financial support to complete the writing of this book.

The archival work for this project took place at several different libraries and archives, and I take this opportunity to express my thanks to the following institutions and individuals: the UC Berkeley Library, especially the Inter-Library loan department; the GTU Library in Berkeley; the National Library of Medicine in Bethesda, in particular to the head of its History of Medicine Division, Dr. Stephen Greenberg; the Library of Congress in Washington, D.C.; the Library of Medicine at UCLA, especially their collection on the history of pain. I have conducted my research on the Euthanasia Society of America in its archive in Baltimore. I would like to thank Partnership for Caring and especially Karen Orloff Kaplan and Mary Meyer for allowing me to access the archive and for guiding me through it.

This book would never have become possible if not for the valuable guidance and constant encouragement of my editor, Ian Malcolm, at Princeton University Press. Working with him has been an honor and a pleasure. I would also like to thank Carolyn Hollis at Princeton University Press and Molan Chun Goldstein for their invaluable assistance.

This work is dedicated with love and gratitude to my parents Shmuel and Sara Lavi and to my maternal grandparents Menashe and Bilha Blatman. It was written in loving memory of my paternal grandparents Yehoshua and Bronia Levinsky. Their roots are my own, and my fruits belong to them.

The Modern Art of Dying

❖

The Ethics of the Deathbed: Euthanasia from Art to Technique

THE YEAR was 1818, and the Howe family had just moved to Brandon, Vermont, when the young mother fell ill.[1] Hannah was thirty years old and suffered from consumption. Lying on her sickbed, and knowing her days were numbered, she turned to her husband with a weighty question: "Do you doubt of my being prepared to die?" The question of how to die well occupied Hannah's thoughts long before she fell ill. Imagining her deathbed, she had often wished that "she might die shouting, and have an easy passage over the Jordan of death."

As her day of departure approached, she continued to grow weaker in body and could not converse much. But when she heard talk of the happy death of a certain person she smilingly began waving her hand. Her husband then asked if she felt as though she could shout. "Yes," said she, and still waving her hand, she cried "Glory! Glory! Glory!"

The final day came. Through the course of the day, she appeared as usual and her mind was clear and serene. She was surrounded by friends and supported by her husband who documented her last hour. "I took her by the hand and asked her if her confidence held out? If Jesus was precious? And if she had a prospect of heaven? She pressed my hand, and said, 'yes,' and fell asleep in the arms of Jesus without a struggle or a groan."

Early nineteenth-century Americans named this triumphant passage to death "euthanasia." For them, the word signified a pious death blessed by the grace of God.

At a young age, Dr. Arthur E. Hertzler's daughter came down with a terminal illness, most likely typhoid fever.[2] "In the saddest hour of my life, at the deathbed of my daughter," the nineteenth-century physician recalled, "on one side was the magnificent and always faithful Carrie the nurse, on the other side the incomparable Dr. Dampbell, calmly applying measures of resuscitation which he and I knew were utterly futile."

1

Futile though it was, the efforts of these professionals gave him an indescribable measure of comfort. "I know that my last conscious moments will picture that scene: nurse on one side of the bed, doctor on the other. Though scientifically futile, if my presence in a similar situation ever brought an equal amount of comfort to anyone I am sure it was more worth while than anything else I have ever done. Our mission in life is to lessen human suffering as much as we can."

"The ministers of the old days," wrote the doctor, "had an idea that something notable should take place at the moment of dissolution and seemed to think I should provide pabulum for their discourses." But quite to the contrary, Dr. Hertzler believed that "saints and sinners died alike," and that at the time of death, whatever might have been the antecedents, there was no pain.

For mid-nineteenth-century physicians, "euthanasia" meant a painless death accompanied by physician assistance.

In June 1887, Dr. Edward Thwing received a telegram summoning him to a distant city to tend to a relative stricken with apoplexy and hemiplegia.[3] Given the age of the patient—a sixty-six-year-old widow—and the severity of the attack, death was assured within a day or two. She lingered, however, for five days, speechless and comatose. Her vigorous constitution succumbed slowly. Automatic movements, such as pulling at clothes, lifting her hand to her head, and other signs of restlessness continued until near the end.

The attending physician had left the case in Dr. Thwing's hands forty-eight hours earlier, believing that the patient's life would soon be over. Recalling the case Dr. Thwing noted: "The reality of suffering I could not admit, but the appearance of it in actions, purely reflex, was painful to me. As her only surviving kinsman, I took the responsibility of administering a mild anaesthetic, moistening a handkerchief at intervals from a vial containing two drachms of chloroform and six drachms of sulphuric ether." He held the handkerchief near the nostrils, but not too close so as to facilitate the free admixture of atmospheric air, and carefully studied the facial expression of the unconscious sufferer. After two or three minutes the stertor ceased. The spasmodic actions of the arm were arrested. Respiration became easier and there was a general repose. "Euthanasia," the physician reported, "was gained and an apparently painful dissolution avoided. Fifteen minutes after withdrawing the anaesthetic, the final breath came, without the slightest spasm of the glottis or respiratory muscles, without any other physical struggle or sound."

At the autopsy, one of the five physicians present described a case where, at the request of the parents, he had administered ether to a child suffocating in membranous croup and produced euthanasia, "not less to the relief of the parents than to that of the patient."

Only during the late nineteenth century did euthanasia gain its familiar meaning: the use of anaesthetics to guarantee a swift and painless death. Soon after, attempts were made to legalize euthanasia. The first pro-euthanasia organization in the United States, the Euthanasia Society of America, was founded in 1938. Today, proposals to legalize euthanasia are still being debated throughout the country, and one form of medically hastened death, physician-assisted suicide, is already legally practiced in Oregon.

This is a study of the history of euthanasia in the United States. The question before us is, How did the notion of euthanasia as the medical hastening of death emerge as a characteristically modern way of dying? To ask how euthanasia became possible is not to seek a simple causal explanation but rather to search for the deeper historic significance of this phenomenon. Reversing Rilke's question "What kind of beings are they then, who finally must be scared away by poison?"[4] we may ask, Who is this modern man, for whom medical euthanasia has become a compelling way of dying? The answer lies in nineteenth-century changes in the ethics governing the deathbed, changes that still inform the way we die today.

What makes the medical hastening of death a modern way of dying is not simply that the time of death, in addition to the manner of dying, is determined by human will. That would make the medical hastening of death no different from suicide. Suicide is always an extraordinary act performed under extraordinary circumstances, whereas the medical hastening of death is meant to be a routinized response to a problem we all know we may face, the onset of a fatal illness. Attempts to institutionalize the medical hastening of death and legalize the practice are thus a significant aspect of the modern idea of euthanasia.

The first proposal to legalize medical euthanasia dates back to 1870, and it bears a striking resemblance to similar proposals made over a century later. These later proposals require that euthanasia be performed only by a professional physician and characteristically limit its scope to patients who are both hopelessly ill and suffering. History, to be sure, records "euthanasia" proposals prior to the nineteenth century. But these earlier proposals, made by Thomas More and Francis Bacon, differ in several important ways from those of the late nineteenth century.[5] Most notably, More's proposal does not mention physicians at all,[6] and Bacon's does not endorse active killing.[7] Furthermore, the earlier proposals emerged in the philosophical and imaginary genre of utopias. The nineteenth-century proposals were the first to endorse the medical practice of euthanasia as an actual matter of a public policy.

It is common to think of the current euthanasia debate in relation to mid-twentieth-century advances in medical technique. But the modern problem of dying, namely the condition of hopeless suffering for which euthanasia is one proposed solution, predates the technical advances that are so commonly associated with it, such as life-support systems and advanced surgery. This study, in seeking euthanasia's deeper origins and significance, begins at the turn of the nineteenth century, when the modern problem of dying and the framework for its solution first emerged. It ends precisely where most scholarship on the topic begins—in the 1960s—and shows how most of what took place in the latter half of the twentieth century can be traced back to these earlier developments. This little-known story of euthanasia is the focus of the present study.[8]

The origins of medical euthanasia, I will argue, lie in a movement of dying from the domain of religion through that of medicine and finally into the jurisdiction of positive law and public policy. It is a movement that itself is driven, following Heidegger, by what I refer to as the rise of technique and the decline of art in our world.[9]

The story of euthanasia must be understood at three different levels. First, we must know the bare facts, the tale of the individuals and the movements that promoted the legalization of euthanasia in the late nineteenth and early twentieth centuries. Second, we must trace the emergence of euthanasia as a modern way of dying by following the gradual transformation of the ethics governing the deathbed.[10] Finally, at a higher level of significance, we should reflect on the expanding technical search for mastery over death[11] and the gradual shift of dying from a work of art to a product of technique. While the first level of analysis requires no further elaboration at this point, a brief discussion of the two other levels may shed light on the structure of the study as a whole.

The Changing Ethics of the Deathbed

In less than two centuries, the meaning of "euthanasia" has changed several times, and in radical ways. Though my interest lies more in the cultural history of practices than in the history of words and ideas, the history

4

of deathbed practices can be told by tracking the unfolding definitions of "euthanasia" itself. These semantic changes capture the historic shifts in the ethics of the deathbed—understood broadly as the rules governing the conduct of dying, including religious, medical, and legal codes of conduct.

The literal meaning of "euthanasia" is quite removed from its contemporary usage. "Euthanasia" is a compound of two Greek words—*eu* and *thanatos*, which together signify a "good death" or an "easy death."[12] For centuries, this literal sense was the only one conveyed by the word. An eighteenth-century medical definition of euthanasia is "a soft easy Passage out of the World, without Convulsions or Pain."[13] This image of a good death is not foreign to the modern sensibility. But "good death" as "easy death" was exclusively a matter of divine providence or good fortune, and beyond human control. Euthanasia, in its original sense, was a death one could hope for but never be assured of.

For centuries, the deathbed in the Christian world was governed by religion, and euthanasia signified a death blessed by the grace of God. The dying person was encouraged to follow a certain course of behavior on his deathbed, which would constitute a holy way of dying and exemplify a holy way of living. These rules of conduct governing the last hour of life were put in writing and published in short manuals, known as *ars moriendi*, or "the art of dying." This mainly Protestant tradition was highly popular through the eighteenth century.[14] In the United States, it made its final public appearance in the early nineteenth century, when the art of dying itself entered its terminal stage.

In order to understand the rise of medical euthanasia in the United States, it is crucial to comprehend this moment of transition, when the *ars moriendi* tradition finally faded from view. To explore its significance, the first chapter of this study examines the way in which Methodists, the largest organized religious community in early nineteenth century America, taught Americans how to die. More than any other religious group, Methodists were concerned throughout life with forming the proper disposition regarding death. They would gather around the deathbeds of neighbors and relatives to view the final departure and to meticulously document the hour of death. The final hour was a time of great exultation, in which the dying person, surrounded by family and friends, would approach the end like a fearless soldier ready to die a triumphant death. It is precisely this way of dying that the most celebrated of all New England Puritans, Cotton Mather, termed "euthanasia."[15]

The Methodist ethic of dying contrasted most strikingly with traditional Catholic notions of death. For Catholics, dying constituted the passing over a bridge between this world and the world to come. Deathbed rituals were a *rite de passage*, preparing those who were dying for their final journey into a better world. For Methodists, however, dying belonged to this world and signified the culmination of life, which subsequently lost its unique transformative power. The art of dying became an art of holy living, and dying became a problem of life proper. It is at this turning point in the history of dying that our story begins.

In the course of the nineteenth century, a relatively short span of time, both the sense of euthanasia and the law governing the deathbed changed. The decline of the art of holy dying was captured in an 1861 edition of the *Sick Man's Passing Bell*, an *ars moriendi* book first published early in the seventeenth century. The edition has a melancholy tone and especially laments the fact that when a man is dying, both the physician and the lawyer are sent for, but the "physician of the soul stands outside the door."[16]

A new way of dying was emerging, and its most visible sign was the increasingly dominant presence of the physician at the bedside. While physicians did attend the deathbed in earlier centuries, it was only in the nineteenth century that treatment of the dying, as such, became a medical concern and medically regulated. Whereas in previous centuries the medical doctor would leave the bedside when it was clear that the patient was hopelessly ill, a new ethic developed in which the physician was expected to remain present at the deathbed. The law of the deathbed had shifted from religion to medicine.

The idea of euthanasia changed accordingly. Euthanasia now stood for the new task of the medical profession—to assist dying patients in their last hours, short of hastening death. Euthanasia no longer meant a good death but rather signified the actions taken by physicians to achieve such a death.

The second chapter attempts to understand the new role of the physician at the deathbed and how this role opened the way for a claim that physicians should not merely help the patient to die an easy death but also actively hasten death. Why, until the present day, is the task of hastening death put in the hands of physicians, whose duty and expertise are precisely its opposite—to prolong life?

This new competence of the medical profession emerged neither from new scientific knowledge nor from technical advances in medicine. On the contrary, the physician's role at the deathbed was secured long before he had any medical treatment to offer the dying patient. It is precisely because physicians did *not* have the means to cure dying patients but nevertheless felt obliged to care for them that medical euthanasia emerged as a possible solution to the problem of dying. The second chapter shows the logic of these developments, in which euthanasia lost its benign sense of easing death and acquired a much more controversial meaning as a way to bring about death.

The third and fourth chapters examine attempts to legalize euthanasia, in the sense of hastening death, at the turn of the twentieth century. Until quite recently, the act of hastening death was unquestionably forbidden by law, as well as opposed by the medical profession. A famous story is related of Napoleon's physician, Desgenettes, who refused the emperor's request that he fatally drug severely plague-stricken soldiers to keep them from falling into enemy hands. Similarly, John Keats, dying of tuberculosis, could not persuade his physician to administer an overdose of laudanum.[17] And yet it was not uncommon for physicians, in the privacy of the bedroom, to administer drug overdoses with the clear intention of bringing to an end the misery of their dying patients. What made euthanasia proposals scandalous was the fact that they turned a discreet, behind-closed-doors practice into a public affair. In attempting to make euthanasia legitimate, they also sought to bring the ethics of the deathbed under the jurisdiction of state law.

The question here, however, is not, How did the once-illegal practice of euthanasia become legal? After all, the medical hastening of death is still mostly illegal in the United States as well as around the world. Rather, we should ask, How did legalized euthanasia become a thinkable, even if not fully actualized, way to die?

The "legalization" of euthanasia entailed much more than repealing the prohibition of the practice; it called for its regulation. Whereas *decriminalization* is a removal of the legal sanction, *regulation* brings the practice under the domain of law. Proponents of legalized euthanasia viewed the law as an instrument to shape the conditions and safeguards under which euthanasia could be performed. Law was to play a central role in institutionalizing euthanasia, turning it from a discreet medical practice into a matter of public policy reform.

The power of state legislation to overrule common-law tradition was not as clear to jurists at the turn of the twentieth century as it is in the twenty-first. The general notion that the state could revise basic principles of common law to form new public policies became self-evident only at the turn of the twentieth century.[18] Early attempts to legalize and regulate euthanasia took place precisely during this time of transition in which law became an integral part of public policy. The third chapter will draw our attention to this change in the concept of law and show how the history of euthanasia is as much a history of law as it is of dying.

Chapter 4 begins where chapter 3 ends: at the point when it is already clear that law is an instrument of public policy. Euthanasia, the term as well as the practice, underwent one final change. The practice, which to this point had been a specific medical solution to the specific issue of dying, now expanded. The medical hastening of death was now offered as a possible end to all kinds of suffering, such as that of the "physical handicapped" and the "mentally retarded." Furthermore, euthanasia came to be viewed as one part of a set of practices meant to control biological processes at both ends of life. Dying was no longer only a problem of the suffering individual; it had become a broader social concern.

Chapter 4 explores the history of the Euthanasia Society of America (ESA) and the way in which the society attempted, through the use of positive law, to turn euthanasia into public policy. In particular, it examines how the ESA fought to distinguish its euthanasia proposals from those of the Nazis, who wished to terminate all "life unworthy of living."

The fifth chapter considers another means of hastening the death of dying patients, one that does not go by the name of "euthanasia." In what I call "lethal dosing," the physician injects the patient increasing doses of pain-relief medication, intending only to relieve pain but knowing that it will probably hasten death. Despite its affinity with euthanasia, lethal dosing became a mundane practice openly encouraged by the medical profession without first being legalized. The metamorphosis of dying into a product of technique is all but accomplished with the disappearance of this practice of lethal dosing from public scrutiny.

It is quite remarkable that the practice of euthanasia underwent such a dramatic evolution in little more than a century. It is hard to imagine two ways of dying as distinct from one another as the Methodist death prevalent in early nineteenth-century America and the medically hastened death advocated in the latter half of the twentieth century. Yet not only do these two deaths bear the same name—euthanasia—but also manifest humanity's same wish to transform dying into a doing, and thus to bring death under the power of art at one end and technique at the other.

The final chapter addresses a different form of taking life that will be referred to as "mercy killing." Mercy killings are performed not by the medical profession but rather by a family member, such as when a daughter kills her cancer-ridden father. Mercy killings are noteworthy in that while the law clearly prohibits the practice and the state often presses charges against perpetrators, with few exceptions most mercy killers have been acquitted. On the part of the courts as well as the general public, the act of mercy killing is neither condemned nor approved; rather, it is viewed as being beyond the scope of man-made law. This merciful act of violence is contrasted to medical euthanasia to exemplify the difficulty in regulating the taking of human life and to point out the often-overlooked limits of positive law.

Dying from Art to Technique

Ethical considerations governing the deathbed have moved from religion through medicine to positive law and public policy. These transformations do not tell the full story of euthanasia, and themselves have a deeper historical significance. There are familiar theories to understand these historical changes, of which two are worth mentioning: the disenchantment of the world, as elaborated by Max Weber,[19] and the rise of biopolitics, the term used by Michel Foucault to refer to government practices ordering biological processes.[20] On the surface, these two understandings appear to be unrelated: one explains the decline of the old world, while the other describes the rise of a new order. Often the history of dying has suffered from a narrow focus on one of these processes at the expense of neglecting the other.[21] This study accepts in principle the basic truth of both notions but seeks to expand the discussion by exploring their necessary interdependence. The inner relationship between the disenchantment of the world and the rise of biopolitics is evident if these two historical moments are rethought as one: namely, as the decline of art and the rise of technique in the modern world.[22]

Dying in the Christian world up until the nineteenth century was a work of art. The term "art" is used here in a specific sense that requires elaboration. Art is often conceived of as a sphere of cultural enterprise that centers around specifically designed art objects such as paintings, sculptures, or music. We thus expect to find art today in galleries, exhibitions, and concert halls. But this was not always the case, and the confinement of art to one sphere of human existence is a modern phenomenon that points to a general decline of art.

True art, as Heidegger observed, is known by its power to make the fullness of a life world visible through one being in that world. The Gothic cathedral is a work of art for it makes manifest in one being that which was most essential in the medieval Christian world. It is in the cathedral that Christians come together as a people to worship God and to face the truth of birth and death, this world and the world to come.

Dying, too, can be a work of art to the extent that in this one moment of life, the whole world of the dying can become present. In the life of the

Christian believer, dying was a unique moment in the course of life. Yet it is precisely this uniqueness that allowed dying to capture life as a whole. Death was a moment of truth in which the dying person and those attending the deathbed faced the ultimate truths of Christendom: immortality of the soul, sin, and God's saving grace. Like the Gothic cathedral, dying could make visible the relation between man and God, heaven and earth.[23]

By virtue of its power to reveal the fullness of a life world, art becomes a spectacle. And it is for this reason that dying, while it was performed as a work of art, drew the attention of the community of believers. The Methodists, as we shall see, meticulously documented exemplary deathbed experiences. These accounts were published posthumously in Methodist journals under the striking title "biographies." Unlike the contemporary obituary, the Methodist biography told very little about the deceased's life but instead focused in great detail on the hours preceding death. In this way, it manifested the belief that the fullness of life could be captured in the moment of death.

Most terminally ill patients in the United States today die in hospitals and other alienating environments, surrounded by strangers for whom their death is no longer a spectacle.[24] Scholars have often explained this change as a result of a death-denying attitude that has become prevalant in the United States since the late nineteenth century.[25] But perhaps the causal relation is the reverse: it is not that the change in attitude has led to the decline of the deathbed spectacle, but rather that the powerlessness of the modern deathbed to present the fullness of a life world has led to the prevalant attitude toward dying, which might be characterized less as denial and more as forgetting, a fading away of the traditional art of dying. The modern forgetting of the art of dying is accompanied by a new deathbed ethic governed by the rise of technique. But what precisely is technique?

Technique, in what follows, does not refer to particular objects, such as modern machinery, nor to particular ways of doing things, such as scientific technique. Like art, technique refers to a distinct way of viewing things, and to a distinct manner in which things appear in our world.[26] In this sense, we may think of ourselves as inhabiting a technical world, a world in which not only technical objects but also the way we die is reshaped in light of our desire for technical mastery over the world.

Technique first makes its appearance as as result of modern humanity's desire to master all aspects of life, from birth to death. However, not every will to master is an expression of modern technique. The existence of tools in every known society throughout history suggests that there is nothing novel about this human desire. And indeed, mastery by means of tools should not be confused with the uniquely modern phenomenon of technique. Unlike most acts of human mastery, which aim to order nature and human conduct with the purpose of achieving a further good, under the rule of technique, mastery becomes an end in itself and not merely a means to another end. This is what Weber has famously termed the logic of instrumental rationality,[27] which indeed is an essential aspect of technique.

Yet, to fully understand the nature of modern technique, we must go beyond the Weberian concept. Technique is not merely a certain way of doing things but rather a particular way in which things appear to us in our world. For things to come under the purview of technique, they must appear only through their potential to be ordered and lose any characteristic that stands in the way of regulation.

The modern hospital is a good example of the appearance of technique. In the modern hospital, people are treated as patients. They are hospitalized for the purpose of managing their health, which entails more than just being cured. The patient's medical condition and health is examined and diagnosed, measured and prognosed, experimented on and compared, stabilized as much as cured, assessed as much as healed. As patients enter the hospital, they lose their identity as individuals who belong to a particular life world and assume a new identity—that of a patient. Patients are stripped of any distinct identity that they have outside of the hospital, as family members, as experts in their own field, as individuals with particular customs, clothing, and food. Within the hospital context, patients are regarded only through the lens of health management. Medical personnel may care for the patient's emotional well-being as well as physical condition, but only because this is acknowledged to be an important aspect of health management. Hence, the patient's place within the domain of the modern hospital manifests the rule of technique more decisively than does the development of medical machinery or scientific method.

Technique may also be understood through its dialectical relation to art. Technique appears first in opposition to art. Unlike a work of art, it does not express the singularity of a being. On the contrary, through technique a particular entity from a life world loses its distinctive character as it is called upon and made available as one element of a technical enterprise.

While acknowledging the tension between art and technique, we should not overlook the fact that technique emerges as the realm of art declines, which suggests that these two modes of being are not only in opposition to each other but are also interrelated. The origins of technique lie dormant in art, which has always had a dual nature. Art in the sense conveyed in ordinary language as well as in its deeper significance refers both to a work of art and to mastery through craftmanship, such as when one speaks of the art of pottery or the art of war or, in the present context, the art of dying. In the rise of modern technique, art plays a transformative role. Not only does it constitute one side of the binary opposition, art-technique, but it also acts as a mediator between the two. And it is for this very reason that the story of euthanasia is less about the decline of art and the rise of technique but is more accurately the tale of how the art of dying gave birth to the technical mastery of dying. My interest, therefore, is not in glorifying the past but rather in analzying how, from the outset, technique has been inscribed into the work of art as modern humanity's destiny.

In light of the above, it may be argued that the rise of medical euthanasia was not simply a new way of mastering the dying process. After all, all deathbed ethics, even the most traditional ones, manifest the human desire to control the manner in which a person dies. The uniqueness of medical euthanasia lies in the desire for technical mastery, that is, mastery for mastery's sake alone.

This understanding of the modus operandi of technique leads to a more profound understanding of the conditions for its possibility. Regulation of the deathbed is only possible if the phenomenon to be regulated undergoes a transformation whereby it severs its connections with anything that cannot be regulated. We shall see how a radical transformation in the way people die was necessary in order to bring about regulation by state law. In this manner dying, which was traditionally experienced as a moment of transition between this world and the next, became a this-worldly event lending itself more easily to regulation.[28]

The movement of dying from religion through medicine to public policy should be seen as the gradual transformation of dying into a problem of living. This process was accompanied by new ways to govern dying. Different ethical considerations governing the deathbed—from the spheres of religion, medicine, and public policy—as we shall see, correspond to different moments in this incremental process of transformation.

Thus, we may point to three pivotal moments in the transformation of dying. First, the Methodist deathbed, governed by the Protestant ethic, turned the art of dying into a this-worldly accomplishment. In this way, the uniqueness of dying as a transitional moment was overcome and dying became a problem of holy living. Second, through the medicalization of dying, euthanasia signified medical treatment in the aid of dying. Here, dying became a bioscientific concern, where the dying person was no longer distinguishable from the sick patient. The third and final step in the rise of euthanasia as technique occurred when the problem of dying became an issue of policy making. At this point, dying became indistinguishable from a host of biopolitical concerns, and euthanasia was offered as a panacea for a variety of incurable and dependant medical conditions, including the handicapped and the retarded as well as the dying.

There is a final question to raise before we begin recording these historical transformations. What is the significance of the transformation of dying from art to technique? Or, as it is more commonly phrased, What are the ethical implications of euthanasia?

Euthanasia is an ethical question, but not in the sense that most professional ethicists would have us think. The ethical dimension of euthanasia does not lie in asking whether and under what conditions the medical hastening of death should be practiced. The proper question for a study of ethics is not, "What are we to do?" but rather, "Who have we become?"

An introduction should not offer an answer to this question but should mark the terrain of possible answers. It is commonly believed that through euthanasia modern humanity has finally managed to control death, to bring it under its will. Recall Nietzsche's advice: "*Death*. One must turn the stupid physiological fact into a moral necessity. *So to live, that one has also at the right time one's will to death!*"[29]

But have we moderns, through the regulation of medical euthanasia, truly gained mastery over dying? Perhaps Kafka's reflections on the will to death were closer to revealing the modern condition. Referring to himself and thinking no doubt of modern man, he wrote: "You, who can't do anything, think you can bring off something like that? How can you even dare to think about it? If you were capable of it, you certainly wouldn't be in need of it."[30] Today, it is far from being clear whether human action governs the technical mastery over death or whether human actions are now being regulated by technique.[31] The deeper question here is whether human beings are masters of their own destiny or whether today, perhaps more than ever before, they are helpless in facing their mortality. What is ultimately at stake in regard to euthanasia, therefore, is human freedom.

The Holy Craft of Dying: The Birth of
the Modern Art of Dying

How did euthanasia, the medical hastening of death, become a possible way of dying? Euthanasia emerged in a particular historical period, and it is through the reconstruction of this history that we seek its understanding. The challenge is to break from common wisdom, which oscillates in its search for euthanasia's origins between early antiquity and late modernity. Medical euthanasia is neither as old as the Stoics nor as recent as the mid-twentieth-century respirator. Euthanasia, as we shall see, emerged as a nineteenth-century response to the *new* problem of the hopeless suffering of the dying patient.

A possible challenge may arise: is it not the case that dying, the pain accompanying it, and the despair it gave rise to, were always a problem? And if so, why did euthanasia proposals emerge only in the latter half of the nineteenth century? Should we not insist that the problem was old, while acknowledging that its medically crafted solution was new?

Indeed, the isolation of morphine from opium in the early nineteenth century and the discovery of anesthetics in the middle of that century offered the medical profession new techniques for guaranteeing a swift and painless death. Absent such means, medical euthanasia would serve as a poor alternative to natural death. And yet it would be a mistake to see in the development of any particular technique the source of the cultural transformation in the way we seek to die. The discovery of anesthesia cannot serve as an explanation because it itself—and, more strikingly, its application at the deathbed to hasten death—requires explanation.

Euthanasia, for this reason, should not be understood only as a new means for achieving a good death but rather as a new way to envision what a good death is. Instead of *thinking of euthanasia technically*—that is, as a means—we should *think through euthanasia about the technical*. Indeed, the history of euthanasia presents the rise of dying as a technical challenge, a challenge to bring death under human mastery.

To begin this inquiry, the opening chapter tells the story of how Americans died at the turn of the nineteenth century, before an important transformation in the way of dying took place, a transformation closely related to the medicalization of death and dying. This is the story of how Americans died before dying had become a modern problem, a time during which "euthanasia" still had a very benign sense: a good death blessed with the grace of God.

To tell this story, I focus on the largest Protestant group in nineteenth-century America, the Methodists. This denomination, which originated in England in the eighteenth century, had a peculiar interest in the final hours of life and had an unmatchable influence on shaping the way Americans lived and died.[1]

The Methodist way of dying at the turn of the nineteenth century will also offer us a glimpse into the long and venerable *ars moriendi* tradition that had governed the deathbed scene for centuries.[2] This tradition reached a high point during the religious awakening at the turn of the nineteenth century[3] but soon after lost its binding power and all but vanished from the public sphere. By the end of the nineteenth century, death and dying were governed by medicine, not by religion, and the old art of dying was replaced by a medical and technical governance of death. The story of the Methodist death is the story of the last survivor of the *ars moriendi* tradition and of the transformation of dying from art to technique.[4]

But nineteenth-century Methodism has left us with more than nostalgia for days long past. In a less obvious way, the Methodists were as much precursors of the modern world as they were continuing a venerable Christian tradition. The religious awakening of the turn of the nineteenth century, which seemed to make the *ars moriendi* tradition more popular than ever, in fact carried the seeds of its demise. We will see how— embedded in the Methodist art of dying as a this-worldly attempt to master death—we may already find the seeds of the technical governance of death. Paradoxically, the Methodist art of holy dying, a rigorous Protestant ethic, set the ground for the emergence of a new technomedical spirit that would soon transform the experience of dying. The challenge before us is, therefore, twofold: to see how the Methodist death was the continuation of the old *ars moriendi* tradition and at the same time to understand in what ways it cut against that tradition to prepare the ground for a new beginning.

At the time of the American Revolution, Congregationalists, Presbyterians, Baptists, and Anglicans claimed the lion's share of church membership in America.[5] The Methodists were then just a small group of believers, but one that was about to rapidly expand. From a small community of 8,500 members in 1780, the number of Methodists in America grew exponentially to 57,630 in 1790 and to 511,150 by 1830.[6] In 1850, the Methodists' twenty-thousand churches made them the preeminent Protestant denomination in America.[7] Indeed, the Methodists represent nineteenth-century America, not only in terms of their sheer numbers, but also in the diversity of their membership, which covered North and South, rich and poor, and slaves, slave owners, and abolitionists.[8] Methodism became in many ways the most American of Christian denominations; as one scholar remarked, "Not only in its inception but throughout its development it was most in tune with the American song."[9] So significant were the Methodists of the nineteenth century that one scholar dubbed that century "the Methodist Age" in American history.[10]

The relation between the religious transformations of the nineteenth century and the emergence of a modern way of dying has been acknowledged in contemporary studies.[11] James Farrell's *Inventing the American Way of Death, 1830–1920* is the most elaborate of such attempts. However, for Farrell, as for the French historian of death and dying Philippe Ariès, the rise of the new American way of dying is portrayed in a negative way as a denial of death or, in Farrell's own terms, as "the dying of death."[12] By this, Farrell refers to the decline of dying as a significant event in the life of Americans as it had been prior to the nineteenth century.

For Farrell, dying lost its centrality in American life because it became a natural phenomenon and thus a less mysterious, supernatural, and terrifying event. He shows how the more rationalistic and scientifically inclined denominations, such as the Congregationalists and Unitarians, sought to overcome the "ignorance, superstition, and timid fanciful sentimentality" of the eighteenth-century deathbed. Under this new view, death became a natural phenomenon, and the fear of death was replaced by the joy of life. While Farrell focused on the more progressive Unitarian Church, the research in this study places the Methodists at its center. The difference in emphasis reflects a disagreement on what is most fundamental to the modern way of dying.

Contrary to this established tradition, I wish to propose that the modern way of dying is to be understood not merely in negative terms as a decline but in a positive way—as a new *art* of dying. It is this aspect of dying that is of interest here, and it is in the Methodist attempt to master death that the new art of dying manifests itself most clearly. Unlike Farrell, who sought the emergence of a new way of dying in the weakening of religion and religious belief and in a transition from Puritanism to scientific naturalism and deism, I argue that the important transformation happens earlier and precisely among the most enthusiastic religious groups. Among them we can find the modern way of dying not in denial but, to the contrary, in the most intense confrontation with death.

Our account will begin by exploring eighteenth-century Methodism and particularly the life and work of the founding father of Methodism, John Wesley, and his close peers and students. It is by focusing on the denomination's founding ideas that we can best understand the nature of what the later, more numerous, and thus more influential Methodists believed. Wesley was not only the founder of Methodism in England, but also brought it to the shores of the New Country. And although immediately after Wesley's death the Methodists separated from the Anglican Church in which he had kept them as a sect, the new Methodist Episcopalian Church remained true to his early teaching.[13] Our story, therefore, appropriately begins at sea, with the first journey of Methodists from England to the new American soil, a founding moment in the life of John Wesley and the Methodist Church.[14]

The Fear of Death

Setting sail for the New World, John Wesley was following his call to spread the word of God among the Indian inhabitants of Georgia.[15] He was accompanied on this two-year journey by his brother Charles and a group of German Moravians, who shared with them their food and mission, though not their language. On the night of Sunday, October 23, 1735, Wesley was awakened by the tossing of the ship and by roaring winds. He found himself in a deep state of fear: fear of death. In the midst of the storm, as the mainsail split in pieces and the noise of waves pouring over the decks was overcome only by the sound of terrified screams in English, the Germans calmly sang their prayers. For Wesley, in the presence of the calm Moravians, the gravity of his own feelings became even more burdensome. Later he interrogated one of them, "Was you not afraid?" the Moravian answered, "I thank God, no." And when Wesley insisted, "But were not your women and children afraid?" the mild reply came, "No; our women and children are not afraid to die."[16]

The storm from without was then matched by a storm from within. Wesley was deeply concerned with the state of his soul. Even more than overcoming pride, anger, and revenge he viewed the overcoming of fear as the ultimate proof of true belief. Any assurance Wesley may have had of his faith in Christ was now shattered. He recorded his feelings in a painfully honest manner: "[My fear] plainly showed I was unfit, for I was unwilling to die."[17]

Wesley's preoccupation with death began long before he traveled to Georgia and lasted long after it. This interest stemmed both from his existential concern with the problem of death and from a more speculative theological questioning.[18] Wesley's first public sermon, along with several of his other early teachings, focused on the question of death.[19] While his later sermons did not deal directly with death, other sources suggest that the problem kept haunting him throughout his life—as a letter he wrote in his later years to his brother Charles reveals: "If I have any fear it is not that of falling into hell, but falling into nothing."[20] Other Methodists shared this preoccupation with death. His brother Charles was drawn to it, as many of his hymns testify.[21] One of these, titled "Preparation for Death," reads:

> Thou to whom all hearts are known,
> Attend the cry of mine
> Hear in me thy Spirits groan,
> For Purity Divine;
> Languishing for my remove,
> I wait thine image to retrieve;
> Fill me, Jesus, with Thy love,
> And to thyself receive.[22]

The concern with death and dying persisted into nineteenth-century American Methodism, decades after its founding fathers tested their faith against death itself. In contrast to the medieval preoccupation with the morbid, for Wesley and the Methodists who followed him the focal point of religious meditation was *dying*, not death; the *dying* body, more than the cadaver; and the *deathbed*, rather than the grave.[23]

Methodist writings and practices give rise to several questions.[24] What role did death play in the life of eighteenth and early nineteenth-century Methodists? How can the Methodist preoccupation with death, dying, and sickness be explained? Why was the fear of death so troubling for Wesley and the Methodists who followed him? And finally, what is the heritage that the Methodists have left us in facing death and dying, fear and pain?

The Transformation of Death

The key to unlocking the Methodist relation to death lies in the writings of the seventeenth-century English bishop Jeremy Taylor.[25] Taylor's searching writings about the need to reconceive the place of death in the life of the Christian believer had an enormous influence on the theology of the young Wesley, as the latter recorded in his journal:

> In the year 1725, being in the twenty-third year of my age, I met with Bishop Taylor's Rules and Exercises of Holy Living and Dying. . . . Instantly I resolved to dedicate all my life to God, all my thoughts and words and action, being thoroughly convinced there was no medium, but that every part of my life (not some only) must either be a sacrifice to God, or to myself; that is, in effect to the devil . . . [I became] convinced more than ever of the absolute impossibility of being half a Christian.[26]

Taylor's work originally appeared in two volumes, one devoted to the rules of holy living, the other to the practice of dying.[27] Whether Taylor's work should be read as a whole (*Holy Living and Dying*) or as two separate treatises (*Holy Living* and *Holy Dying*) became a matter of serious pondering for historiographers and literary critics,[28] but need not be a concern in this investigation. Rather, what is crucial is to understand the manner in which these two books, while discussing very different aspects of religious life, nevertheless form one coherent teaching. Taylor instructs the believer to approach both death and life with unrelenting vigilance, to reflect on every moment of life to ensure that it is being lived with utter devotion to God. The believer must make his conscience his own personal inquisition.

The immediate fruit of Wesley's encounter with Taylor was his new practice of keeping a diary, in which he recorded at the end of each day his actions hour by hour.[29] The diary was meant to serve as a daily opportunity for self-reflection and to assure Wesley that every moment of his time and every aspect of his life would be dedicated to the service of God. The pages of this diary recalled the routine practices of religious life, laying out in detail the number of hours dedicated to studying, fasting, prayer, communion, spiritual introspection, visiting prisoners and the sick, and so forth. It is this highly strict and methodical practice of daily religious life that gave the Methodists their name.[30]

Taylor's writings had a clear impact on the development of the Methodists' unique way of life. His influence on their way of dying, however, is not as clear. Taylor's treatise on death was in fact a seventeenth-century Anglican response to the existing tradition of *ars moriendi*. The first manuals in English on the art of dying were published in the fourteenth century, and the tradition was revised and revitalized by the humanists, the Reformers, and the Counter-Reformers. In essence, these were practical manuals designed to assist the dying in preparing for the deathbed and the temptations associated with it. In some cases, these guides gave additional advice to bystanders on how to assist the dying patient, and in other cases they recommended special prayers that were appropriate at the hour of death.

And yet if Taylor's *Holy Dying* were no more than a practical guide for the dying person, how could it have had such an effect on the young Wesley? How could a treatise on the art of dying sow the seeds for a new way of devoted living? No doubt it could not, unless *Holy Dying* was not different in its essence from *Holy Living* and meant to offer a new look not on death but on life itself. To understand what such a teaching may have entailed, we need to make a closer examination of Taylor's work within the tradition of *ars moriendi*.

Taylor was writing within and yet against the tradition of *ars moriendi*. By the time he sat down to write his book, he had before him a rich variety of materials to rely on. And from a literary perspective, at least, it is clear that he drew upon them so that in *Holy Dying*, "[a]ll the distinctive but limited insights of the preceding two and a half centuries are caught up and merged into a single luminous vision of the nature and the meaning of Christian death."[31] And yet in much more fundamental ways, Taylor was right to complain of writing the work: "I was almost forced to walk alone."

In the tradition of *ars moriendi* that developed in the fifteenth century, the day of judgment was brought from the time of the end of the world into the bedchamber. The art of dying was concerned with the last article of life, which was viewed as a test.

> The test consists of a final temptation. The dying man will see his entire life as it is contained in the book, and he will be tempted either by despair over his sins, by the "vainglory" of his good deeds, or by the passionate love for things and persons. His attitude during this fleeting moment will erase at once all the sins of his life if he wards off temptation or, on the contrary, will cancel out his good deeds if he gives way.[32]

Books on the craft of dying were a compilation of guidelines concerning the proper way of passing this test. Focusing on the last hours of the dying person, they gave rules for appropriate conduct to be practiced and beliefs to be held before death approached. They also specified rituals and prayers that needed to be performed at the bedside by the dying person and by friends and family. In addition, such books would occasionally include suggestions on how to overcome bodily and spiritual pain, as well as rites that should be performed on the corpse of the dead.

Taylor did not break from the *ars moriendi* tradition but rather radicalized it. While *Holy Dying* addresses most if not all of these issues, it was written from a significantly different perspective. Unlike the tradition, his advice does not address *the dying* but rather *the living*, long before the first signs of approaching death appear. The practice of *ars moriendi*, according to Taylor, cannot wait for the last moment, and must be exercised throughout one's life.[33] This is the case not only because a long preparation is needed in advance but also because death is no longer seen primarily as a passage from this life to a world to come. Rather, for Taylor, facing death becomes another way of approaching life, and facing death changes from an otherworldly into a this-worldly experience.

Taylor gives death a central role in the life of the Christian believer. Death proper, according to Taylor, is *not* the separation of soul and body; neither is it the deliverance from this world to another. Basing his radical interpretation of death on scriptural proof, Taylor offers as his starting point the well-accepted belief that death entered the world with Adam's sin and that, moreover, "man did die the same day in which he sinned."[34] But in what sense, Taylor asks, may it be said of Adam that he died that same day, when he is known to have lived hundreds of years after eating the fruit of the forbidden tree? Death needs then to be construed differently, not as the going *out* of this world but rather as the manner in which man is *in* this world.

> Change or separation of soul and body is but accidental to death. Death may be with, or without either: but the formality, the curse and the sting of death, that is, misery, sorrow, fear, diminution, defect, anguish, dishonor, and whatsoever is miserable, and afflictive in nature, that is death: death is not an action, but a whole state and condition.[35]

For Taylor, death is transformed from an event taking place at the outer limit of life to the condition under which life itself takes place. This understanding of death shares, no doubt, the old Christian notion that after original sin man is afflicted by death. And yet Taylor diverged from tradition in his application of this insight to the practice of *ars moriendi*. Death is not merely a metaphor for the condition of man in a corrupted world but an actual way of living—that is, living-toward-death.

Taylor's great innovation in rethinking the relationship between living and dying had an important influence on Wesley and the Methodist approach to death. For Taylor, living and dying are not two distinct stages of human life. Rather, living and dying are two aspects of one and the same phenomenon—human existence—and these aspects give rise to distinct yet related practices. When living becomes living-toward-death and the challenge of holy dying is not a subordinate aspect of holy living but rises to the level of holy living itself, the concern with one's being-toward-death becomes a matter of constant reflection. It is this way of experiencing the relationship between life and death that in later years comes to guide the Methodist believer.

Having read Taylor at the age of twenty-three, John Wesley, a recently ordained preacher, devoted his first sermon to the problem of death.[36] The sermon as a whole is a young preacher's ambitious attempt to struggle with the weighty problem of the existence of evil. The sermon begins with a verse from the book of Job: "There the wicked cease from troubling; there the weary are at rest."[37] The reference is to Job's wish to have died at birth, rather than to have suffered the misfortunes of life. Wesley's early sermon is of special interest, because it shows the struggle between the traditional approach to death and the more radical thoughts about death as developed by Taylor.

At first it seems that Wesley is offering a conventional answer to the problem of evil and its relation to death. Evil is in the doing of wicked men, who deny God and do not fear His judgment. The righteous who suffer in this world will be saved through their deliverance to another world. Death thus emerges as the solution to the problem of evil, since to die is to flee from the shadowy existence of evil in this world to a better world. In other words, the suffering of this world is made bearable in light of the happiness of the world to come. Death, in Wesley's language, is "not only a haven, but an entrance into a far more desirable country."[38] And yet a closer examination of his sermon leads to a more radical understanding of death, which foreshadows his later, more developed, theology. Death, Wesley points out, is not only an escape from evil but also a manifestation of it. Death is not only the last moment of life but also the essence of being alive. In fact, death appears to man not only as a refuge but as the greatest of all evil and hence what he fears the most. Evil, therefore, cannot be overcome by seeking refuge in a world to come but rather must take place in *this* world, in an art of dying—which is none other than the art of living. The art of dying thus transforms itself from an otherworldly event into a this-worldly challenge.

But what precisely is the nature of the challenge to overcome death? First and foremost is overcoming the fear of death.

Fear of Death and Christian Perfection

What is so wrong about fearing death? Is it not the case that the fear of death may play a positive role in bringing nonbelievers to faith? Indeed, it was not at all uncommon at the time for preachers to terrify their listeners with descriptions of hell in order to arouse in the hearers a fear of death that would lead them back to God.[39]

The Methodists, perhaps more than other denominations, were known for their hellfire deathbed preaching. Thus, when Friedrich Nietzsche asks his readers never to forget "that it was Christianity, which made of the death-bed a bed of torture," he calls to the witness stand none other than George Whitefield, one of the leading American Methodists of the eighteenth century. Whitefield, Nietzsche writes, preached "like a dying man to the dying,"

> now violently weeping, now stamping loudly, and passionately and unashamedly, in the most abrupt and cutting tones, directed the whole weight of his attack upon some one individual present and in a fearful manner excluded him from the community. . . . Whole masses then come together appeared to fall victim to a madness; many were paralysed with fear; others lay unconscious and motionless, some were seized with violent trembling or rent the air for hours with piercing cries.[40]

There is good reason to take Nietzsche's recommendations seriously and remind ourselves that the fear of death was central to the Methodist way of dying. And yet one should not lose sight of how spreading fear of the approach of death, was complemented in the Methodist art of dying with a constant demand for a countermove in which one would overcome this fear. It was fear of death that led Wesley to realize that his faith was lacking and that he was not a full Christian and therefore not a Christian at all.[41] And it was the power to overcome the fear of death and dying that helped him distinguish the true Christian from the nonbeliever.

This radical reflection on death and dying, which already appears in the writings of Taylor and other post-Reformation writers, was developed into a comprehensive theology and a way of life by the early Methodists. As early as 1726, several days after the death of his close friend, Robin Griffiths, Wesley wrote to his mother,

> I never gave more reason to suspect my doctrine did not agree with my practice for a sickness and a pain in the stomach attended by violent

looseness, which seized me the day he was buried, altered me so much in three days, and made me look so pale and thin, that those who saw me could not but observe it.[42]

What doctrine is Wesley referring to? At this early stage of his life, this doctrine cannot be stated clearly. Wesley developed the most essential components of his theology later in his life through a continuous struggle with the problem of death. What *can* be said is that he realized that the true Christian does not fear death. For one thing, fear of death shows a strong attachment to the pleasures of this world, and an unwillingness to let go of the vain satisfactions of life. For another, it may manifest a flawed understanding of the promises of salvation. Yet, these are insufficient grounds for explaining Wesley's strong reaction to the discovery that he feared death. The problem with the fear of death is not only the vanity of the attachment to pleasures of this world (a bodily sin), nor does it originate in a weak belief in Christian dogma as such (a sin of the mind). Rather, it arises out of a much graver flaw—that of an imperfect heart.

Wesley's encounters with death and the fear of death led him to seek the true grounds of belief. This journey, a theological investigation, emerged out of his personal struggle with death. In pursuing his investigation, Wesley chose a noteworthy path. He did not confine himself to reading Christian doctrine and scripture but also studied the lives of contemporary Christians who could serve as models for true belief. The writings of the Christian forefathers could not suffice, for it was unclear to Wesley whether their teachings suited the historical conditions of his own time. Wesley used this logic of experimental theology to search for guidance from others as well as to evaluate his own beliefs. The question of true belief was a question not only for speculative thought but also of empirical psychology.[43]

In searching for models, Wesley's first choice was to turn to the Moravians' remarkable faith that he had first observed during his stormy Atlantic passage.[44] Later on, when he encountered Peter Bohler, a Lutheran and subsequently a Moravian minister, Wesley developed some of his more fundamental beliefs. The most important of these was the old Lutheran principle of "justification by faith alone." The Moravians, like other Reformers, denounced the Catholic belief that man's action was a ground for salvation. They believed that neither sins nor confessions, sacraments nor rituals could have any effect on divine grace or on the choice of the elect. Man's "good works" could not determine his destiny, declared the Moravians; faith alone had significance. Wesley and the Methodists who followed agreed with this broad view but did not join the Moravians in believing that whether a person would be damned or saved was predestined before his or her birth. The Methodists believe in the potential for universal salvation, free choice, and the need of man to prepare for accepting the gift of grace.[45] This belief is perhaps one reason for their great success in America, for it resonates with the spirit of democracy.

The Moravians had a unique interpretation of salvation, which equated justification with sanctification. Justification is a radical transformation in the life of the believer, which includes not only a forgiveness of sins (justification in the strict sense) but also a setting free "from law of sin and death" altogether, and therefore from the fear of sin and death (sanctification).[46] Justification is thus known through its fruits. The fear of death is therefore a sign that one has not been justified. In other words, for the Moravians there were no degrees of faith.[47] The slightest doubt or sign of imperfection suggested that there was no faith at all. Wesley, at least in his early years, adopted this Moravian understanding of salvation, and his own personal experience of revival was shaped accordingly.

John Wesley's experience of Christian perfection took place on May 24, 1738.[48] He was attending an evening meeting at Aldersgate Street, where one of the participants was reading Luther's *Preface to the Epistle to the Romans*. What took place there, he would not forget for the rest of his life.

> About a quarter before nine, while he was describing the change which God works in the heart through faith in Christ, I felt my heart strangely warmed. I felt I did trust in Christ, Christ alone for salvation, and an assurance was given me that he had taken away my sins, even *mine*, and saved *me* from the law of sin and death.[49]

After this transformative experience, the teaching of his Moravian mentors regarding Christian perfection—namely, the conscious certainty of the fullness of one's faith—became a truth that he could claim for himself.[50]

The Triumphant Death

When John Wesley's rivals argued against his teachings and would not yield to the force of his reason, he would say simply, as if it were proof enough of itself, "the Methodists die peacefully."[51] Yet this was not quite true. The Methodist deathbed was a battlefield, and one could die in peace only after death had been overcome triumphantly.[52]

The Methodists were not the first to face and overcome the problem of despair and fear at the deathbed. The Catholic Church considered despair prominent among the temptations facing the dying, but whereas Catholics sought to overcome despair by the hope of the world to come, the Protestant tradition emphasized the possibility of achieving a state of grace in *this* world. Thomas Becon's "The Sicke Mannes Salve" (written in the mid-sixteenth century) set the tone.

Becon's work offers ways of overcoming temptations and doubts at the deathbed. One such doubt proceeds from the Catholic teaching that "no man in this world is certain of his salvation, neither can any man say with a safe conscience and undoubted faith, I am of the number of God's elect." Becon puts the following words in the mouth of the comforter, who replies:

> This is the doctrine of the papists, both wicked and damnable. The papists in teaching this doctrine doth not only trouble, disquiet, make afraid, wound, kill, and slay the consciences of the simple people, and of such as credit their devilish doctrine; but, as much as in them lieth, they make God a liar, his holy word false, and our faith frustrate, void, and vain. Take away the certainty of salvation from any man; and to what point serveth the merciful promise of God, and the faith which apprehendeth and layeth hand on the most loving promises of God? This doctrine openeth a very path unto hell, and bringeth unto desperation.[53]

What is at stake for Becon in the art of dying is not simply the need to overcome the fear and doubt of the deathbed but to overcome them in a way that will assure salvation. He damns the Catholic approach precisely because it does not offer a guarantee of hope in this world but only a promise of, and hope for, a world to come. Becon argues that the only way to salvation is by securing its fruits in this world. We would do well to bear the objection that otherworldly hope is uncertain and therefore worthless, for it will be sounded later by the modern medical profession against any attempt by religion to comfort the dying patient.

Wesley and the Methodists who followed in his footsteps radicalized this Protestant teaching and sought the promise of salvation in an inner experience of perfection. This was contrary to an accustomed belief among the Puritans, who preceded the Methodists and believed that even the elect could not rely on purely subjective proofs of conversion. Such reliance would be presumptuous and might lead to false "security."[54] For the Methodists, it however, was precisely the "subjective" state of the soul that was to bring the fruits of salvation.

Perfection was not to be understood as perfect obedience. In relation to obedience, Wesley continued to claim: "the hope of our calling: to know that our hope is sincerity, not perfection; not to do well, but to do our best."[55] Neither was it a guarantee that sin would not rise up again, which was the basis for his constant concern about backsliding.[56] Rather, perfection was attained through a conscious certainty, in a given time, of the fullness of one's love for God and neighbor. This feeling itself was God's gift of love.[57]

The Methodist rehearsed the art of dying as an art of living. A constant examination of one's soul and disposition toward death served as a measure of true faith, and a holy life was marked by a peaceful acceptance of mortality. The hour of death thus became the ultimate test for the believer, who was confronting the sincerity of his belief for the last time.

Dying was not merely another event in the life of the Methodist; it was the culminating moment through which the entirety of life could be understood. A manifestation of this intense understanding of death can be found not only in Methodist theology but also in the day-to-day practices of dying.

The Spectacle of Dying

We may learn of the Methodist way of dying through numerous accounts of deathbed scenes that were written and carefully studied by members of the group as examples of great deaths. The hour of death was an occasion for the dying but also for other members of the community to experience the greatness of a holy death and the power of true belief. The Methodists consistently, and quite remarkably, titled these accounts (which were published in regional journals) "biographies." In striking contrast to the modern obituary, the Methodist "biography" would tell very little about the person's life, focusing instead—at times exclusively—on the person's way of dying.[58] Through a close examination of these accounts, we may gain insight on how the Methodist theology of death led to the Methodist practice of dying.[59]

Wesley was fond of collecting such accounts and copying them into his journal. Most often, these were not accounts of well-known Methodist leaders but of ordinary believers who died a holy death; for a great death, like salvation, was not the sole privilege of an "elect." When Wesley himself approached death, it was quite natural for his physician, Dr. Whitehead, to ask Wesley's close assistant, Elizabeth Ritchie, to document his last days.[60]

The carefully documented death was then printed and spread among the preachers, to be rehearsed in public as an "authentic narrative" of his death.[61] This was in accordance with Wesley's strong belief that

> [t]he last scene of life in dying believers is of great use to those who are about them. Here we see the reality of religion and of things eternal; and nothing has a greater tendency to solemnize the soul and make and keep it dead to all below.[62]

Wesley's triumphant death brought to life the principles laid down by the rules of *Holy Dying*.[63] If Taylor was responsible for the script, the performance was left to Wesley himself. He staged his death as a victory, and it was to be remembered as such. The editors of Ritchie's text emphasized (by additions to the text, marked in the following passage by brackets) the victorious nature of Wesley's death:

> . . . and then, as if to assert the faithfulness of our promise-keeping, Jehovah, and comfort the hearts of his weeping friends, lifting up his dying arm in token of [victory, and raising his feeble voice with a] holy triumph not to be expressed, again repeated the heart reviving words, "The Best of all is, God is with us!"[64]

These last words, we are told, were voiced so loudly as to be heard by all in the room. And indeed his death left this expected impression on many, as Wesley's close friend, Mrs. Rogers, recalled:

> The solemnity of the dying hour of the *great, good* man, I believe will be ever written on my heart. A cloud of the divine presence rested on all! And while he could hardly be said to be an inhabitant of earth, being now speechless, and his eyes fixed; victory and glory were written on his countenance, and quivering, as it were, on his dying lips! O could he have *then* spoke, methinks, it would have been nothing, but "Victory! victory!—grace! grace!—glory! glory! . . ." Not the least sign of pain, but a weight of bliss.[65]

What made the Methodist death a triumphant death? Whether the dying Methodist was fighting bodily pain, temptation, the fear of death, the Devil, or Death itself, the struggle was fought with an enthusiastic spirit. The deathbed was characterized by an overflow of emotions, such as "exceeding great joy," "fervour of spirit," "much zeal and affliction," "vehement rejoicing." This array of extreme emotions went hand in hand with a variety of practices that reflect the same disposition just preceding the moment of death: crying aloud, bursting into tears, calling out hymns, clapping of hands and so on. Very few Methodists approached death in utter silence.[66]

The Methodists did not die alone. Death was a public event, and dying persons chose in advance those who would accompany them in this last journey. Death took place in the presence not only of immediate relatives, the physician, and the local preacher, but also friends and neighbors. Yet it maintained an intimate atmosphere and was not open to the general public. The deathbed scene was mainly a spectacle to be seen and studied. However, often the bystanders played more than a passive role. They would commonly assist the dying person in his or her last hour. It was common for the dying person to cry out to the surrounding people, "Help me to rejoice; help me to praise God," at which all would join in prayer.[67]

The state of the soul was not the concern of the dying person alone but of his or her family and friends as well. This was partly out of care for his or her soul and partly in an attempt to glorify the dying person and God at the time of death.[68] One of the most fascinating aspects of the Methodist way of dying is the dialogue between the dying person and the surrounding bystanders. More than a dialogue, the interaction is in fact an interrogation of the soul of the dying. In place of the traditional confession of sinful acts, one encounters an inquiry into the state of belief. Even when the dying person is asked about his or her own sins, it is not primarily to arouse confession or repentance of those sins but rather to change the state of the soul and to crush any assurance in one's own doings and replace it with a belief in the mercy of God. A report made by a minister of his conversation with a lieutenant general who was a professed infidel conveys such a dialogue:

> I went in, and after a short compliment, said: "I am told, my lord, your life is near an end; therefore I presume, without ceremony, to ask you one plain question: Is the state of your soul such that you can entertain a solid hope of salvation?" He answered: "Yes." "On what do you ground this hope?" He replied, "I never committed any willful sin. I have been liable to frailties, but I trust in God's mercy, and the merits of His Son, that He will have mercy upon me." . . . I made the following reply: "I am apt to believe you are not tainted with the grossest vices, but I fear you a little too presumptuously boast of never having committed willful sin. If you would be saved you must acknowledge your being utterly corrupted by sin, and consequently deserving the curse of God and eternal damnation." He asked, "Is faith enough for salvation?" "Yes, sir," said I, "if it be living faith."[69]

The fundamental question that the dying Methodist faced was whether Christian perfection had been attained, and fear of death and dying overcome. The death of Ann Peaco reflects this Methodist confrontation with death; the last question put before her by an attending friend about twenty-four hours before her death was: "Have you any doubts?" To which, despite her weakness, she distinctly replied, "None at all."[70]

If Methodists were to die a good death, they were to die with full confidence in salvation and with a heart overwhelmed by the love of God. For this most inner state of the soul to become a spectacle, Methodist were to convey their belief with great enthusiasm in words and deeds. One can only imagine the pressure that such expectations placed on ordinary members of the community and perhaps question the sincerity of some of these accounts. And yet in thinking of the deathbed as a spectacle, the emphasis should not be placed on the disparity between appearance and reality, between the stage and real life. Rather, the Methodist deathbed bridged these gaps by demanding that life itself become a spectacle and that through the art of dying the most fundamental aspects of living would come to light. There was, no doubt, a possibility and at times perhaps even a need to create an impression, but this desire itself testifies to the more basic and general belief in the power of the deathbed to convey a fundamental truth about life.

The interrogations witnessed at the deathbed were one more instance of the art of living being reflected in the art of dying. Similar forms of interrogations took place during the Methodist weekly class meetings. In those gatherings, a group of church members (usually twelve to fifteen) would conduct a similar inquiry into the inward as well as outward life of each of the participants. One by one, members were required to respond to direct and personal questions. "Had they experienced forgiveness of sins? Did they enjoy continuous communion with God? Did they maintain a private prayer life? If they were heads of families, did they pray in their familie? Did they drink 'drams?' Attend dancing? Horse-races? Other worldly amusements?"[71]

Alongside the interrogation of the dying person, it was common for the dying to pose questions to visitors about *their* condition of faith. The demand for assurance became the center of such questioning in the case of William, a nine-year-old boy and Lucy, his sister two years older.[72] Lying on their deathbeds, the children are visited by friends and neighbors, who come to pay their last visit and observe the remarkable belief manifested by these two youngsters. William was particularly motivated to question his visitor's on the state of their faith. In his questioning we encounter the import of the Methodist demand to overcome death in this world rather than in a world yet to come. The dying boy asks his visitor,

"Has Christ pardoned your sins?" He said, "I hope He has." "Sir," said Billy, "hope will not do; for I had this hope, and yet, if I had died then, I should surely have gone to hell. But He has forgiven me all my sins, and given me a taste of His love. If you have this love, you will know it, and be sure of it; but you cannot know it without the power of God. You may read as many books about Christ as you please . . . but if you read all your life, this will only be in your head, and that head will perish. So that if you have not the love of God in your heart, you will go to hell."[73]

The Methodists died in the company of friends and family. Nevertheless, at least in one significant way the Methodists did die alone. Despite the company surrounding the bed, Pascal's words, "*on mourra seul*," still held. The responsibility of dying a righteous death lay with the individual Methodist, and on him or her alone. The prayers of those surrounding the deathbed were not prayers *for* but *with* the dying person. While a minister might be present at the deathbed, his role was minimal. He did not offer absolution, nor did he serve as a confessor for the dying. Even sacraments, while not abolished by Methodism, were rarely a part of the deathbed ritual. In fact, strictly speaking, there were no ritual practices at all. This is not to say that there was no structure to the hour of death but rather that the recurring patterns emerged, paradoxically, in a spontaneous way.

The Protestant reformers of the Catholic Church abandoned reliance on the rituals of the deathbed long before the Methodists, who followed in their steps. In Becon's *ars moriendi*, the dying Epaphroditus asks, "Yea, but How shall I resist the devil?" And the comforter's response may be read as foreshadowing later objections that the medical profession will launch against practitioners of alternative medicine:

Not as the superstitious papists were wont to do, with casting of holy water about your chamber, with laying holy bread in your window, with pinning a cross made of hallowed palms at your bed's head, nor with ringing of the hallowed bell, or such other beggerly, superstitious, popish, and devilish ceremonies.[74]

Moreover, given the unique Methodist theology, the last hour of life had special weight. Unlike the Catholic, who believed in a purgatory where sinners could still be saved from the fires of hell, the Methodist had to determine his destination before death. To that extent, the deathbed was a person's last opportunity to receive salvation. On the other hand, the Methodist danger of backsliding was unknown to the Calvinist, who believed in predestination. In the Methodist view, one had no guarantee that a backslide from a previously achieved state of perfection would not occur on the deathbed, so one's belief needed to be reaffirmed up to the last minute.

An interesting debate had arisen between the two Wesley brothers regarding when sanctification occurred. Charles believed that sanctification should be expected only at the threshold of death.[75] Early in his career, he spent a long week in prayer with condemned prisoners who were to be executed. He accompanied the group of ten men to the gallows in the death cart and also witnessed their execution. Charles recalled that "[n]one showed any natural terror of death: not one showed any struggle for life." He had never seen "such calm triumph" and noted in his *Journal* that "that hour spent under the gallows was the most blessed hour" of his life.[76]

John, on the other hand, held that grace could come at any time as a gift from God, and later in his life he even believed it could come about in gradual increments. Even so, he was willing to concede that it was more likely to happen at the deathbed. As a contemporary scholar pointed out,

[I]n the normal course of Christian life, Wesley believed, the gift of perfect love is deferred until the "moment of death" (*articulus mortis*). In the face of death a man is forced into a mood of "seriousness," if he is ever likely to be. It was therefore neither accidental nor morbid that Wesley should be so deeply interested in the ars moriendi, with so avid an interest in reports of "triumphant deaths" of all sorts. However, there is no good reason why a man may not come to be utterly earnest while still alive. Thus the gift of perfection is to be sought and expected—but never scheduled or advertised.[77]

Thus, even according to John Wesley, the deathbed scene was an important place for achieving Christian perfection. Conversely, Christian perfection was the ultimate answer to the fear and despair to which death gave rise. The Methodists believed that "the bed of affliction and the chamber of death are proper places to look for the triumphs of true believers—Here is no disguise; but all is real."[78] However, the uniqueness of the Methodist way of dying lay not in the overcoming of fear and despair as such but rather in the precise way in which the triumph over death took place.

The only guarantee for salvation was faith. Maintaining faith in the face of death became the ultimate challenge of the dying Methodist. Salvation was granted not by the good works of the dying person throughout life, nor by those of the clergyman at death. What the Methodists sought was more than a declaration of faith but an *assurance* of faith, a this-worldly manifestation of salvation. This demand for assurance, or Christian perfection, was sought not in the objective reality, such as in worldly success, but rather in an inner experience of the soul. Salvation manifested itself in a specific emotional state or disposition of assurance and triumph. Salvation was assured not by a cold knowledge of Christian dogma but rather by a true experience of faith; not by a dead faith but by a living faith that could overcome death.

There could be no true victory over death without a struggle against it. Often the opponent was personified in the character of the devil, or Satan, who tempted the dying person. In a letter published in 1797 in the *Arminian Magazine*, the recent death of John Patrick, a Methodist from Yorkshire, is described by his friend.[79] Patrick was a convert to Methodism and, like many, turned to God only when sickness had seized him. Through the help of a friend who prayed with him, he sought God's mercy and eventually recovered from his illness. Then one day, during his work at the mine, the noxious gas caught fire and he was wrapped in a sheet of flame from the explosion. While "flesh was dropping from him in pieces, his first work was to fall upon his burnt knees, and praise the God of Heaven."[80] His struggle with death is described in details. When he arrived home he cried out, "Glory be thy Name! Thy Will be done! Thy Will be done!" We are told he had one "sore conflict with the Satan" on his deathbed. Satan tempted him to fear that God did not love him, because he permitted this severe affliction. And yet he answered the enemy: "What! give up my Saviour! turn my back on my Saviour! No: I'll praise my Saviour."[81] He is then described as one who "triumphed over the fear of death, having the Love of Christ in his heart, and Heaven in his view." Overcoming the devil and the fear of death was achieved by casting aside doubt and allowing oneself to be filled with love and joy. On their deathbeds, Methodists demonstrated in words and in action that they did not fear the approaching death and that they triumphed over their fears.

The victorious death is often a victory not only over the fear of death but, in a sense, over death itself. A remarkable case of a triumphant death and a victory over Satan was that of Caster Garret from Ireland.[82] As he was approaching death, "Satan made his last effort against him. For, all of a sudden he cried out aloud, 'I am undone! undone! I have lost my way! The Lord is departed from me! O, it was all lies I was telling! God has shewed me that I am a great sinner!'" But with the help of his friend who encouraged him not to despair, for it was "the enemy who wants to destroy your confidence," Garret overcame his fear and called out "God is faithful and just!"[83] Then, giving a stamp with his foot, he said, "Satan! I stamp thee under my feet!" and finally celebrated his victory and cried out, "The terror is gone! The sting of Death is gone! O death, where is thy sting! O grave where is thy victory! Blessed be Jesus who hath given me the victory! O I feel his love in my heart."[84]

To confront death face-to-face rather than let it sneak up by surprise, one needed to know enough time in advance that death was approaching. The Methodists never accepted the old saying that neither the sun nor death can be looked at directly. They wished to stare death in the eye. As Mrs. Beresford's telling behavior was reported by her close friend, "[s]he after asked if I saw no more appearance of death in her face yet. When I told her there was, she begged I would indulge her with a looking-glass; and looking earnestly into it, she said with transport, 'I never saw myself with so much pleasure in my life.' "[85] To have a victory over death meant on the one hand to remain indifferent to it, while on the other to celebrate its arrival.

It was John Donne, not a Methodist himself, who probably took the idea of looking death in the eye to its extreme. His death too was reported in one of the early issues of the *Arminian Magazine*,[86] not too surprisingly, since it was common for the magazine to publish great experiences and remarkable deaths of non-Methodist Christians as well. Before his approaching death, Donne requested that his picture be drawn. In preparation for this picture, he asked a carver to build a wooden coffin giving him the exact measures of his body. When it was ready he took off his clothes, put on a white winding-sheet, and entered the box, placing his hands as dead bodies are laid: fit to be put into the grave, his eyes shut. When the picture was finished he asked for it to be set by his bedside and continued to study it hourly until his death.

Overcoming Pain

The triumphant death was also a victory over bodily pain. An external manifestation of this victory was that Methodists seldom complained about bodily suffering. Theirs was not entirely a Stoic reaction to pain, since the dying person would often groan and moan in pain, which would only make the want of complaint ever more apparent. An account of a young Irish woman suffering from a terminal illness appeared in Wesley's journal in December of 1760.[87] When the woman was spitting a large quantity of blood, one of her surrounding visitors said, "You are in great pain." She answered, "I think little of it. My Blessed Redeemer suffered greater pain for me." And when pain was too great for the thirteen-year-old John Wooley, he cried out to God, "O Saviour, give me patience! Thou hast given me patience, but give me more. Give me Thy love, and pain is nothing. I have deserved all this, and a thousand times more; for there is no sin but I have been guilty of."[88]

But the Methodist concern with pain went beyond this limited aspect of the body. Their true worry was that of *spiritual* pain. The young Billy, who was heavily afflicted in his body, told his sister, "I had been very ill. But I do not mean in my body, but in my soul: I felt my sins so heavy that I thought I should go to hell."[89] The more significant pain was not that of the body but that of the soul, which was none other than experiencing one's distance from God. The pious Mrs. Beresford, mentioned earlier, was not at all concerned with her bodily pains but felt the true pain of the heart. As she told her visitor, "[i]f you had felt what I have done this morning, it would have killed you. I had lost sight of God."[90]

Wesley's sermon "The Trouble and Rest of Good Men" deals directly with the question of pain and dying.[91] It returns to original sin in order to introduce a new aspect of the problem of pain. "[W]hen sin was conceived," writes Wesley, "it soon brought forth pain; the whole scene was changed in a moment. He [Adam] now groaned under the weight of a mortal body and—what was far worse—a corrupted soul." After the Fall, God left man remedies for recovering from this sickness. "The whole world," according to Wesley, "is indeed, in the present state, only one great infirmary: all that are therein are sick of sin, and their one business there is to be healed. And for this very end the great Physician of souls is continually present with them, marking all diseases of every soul, and 'giving medicine to heal its sickness.' These medicines are often painful, too. Not that God willingly afflicts his creatures, but he allots them just as much pain as is necessary to their health."[92]

In Wesley's vivid metaphor, the world is a hospital, God is the physician, and the medicine he prescribes is pain. Pain, for Methodists, was far from being intolerable, not only because it was seen as a necessity of human life after the Fall but also because it had a purpose. Suffering had the power of redeeming from sin, of awakening one to acknowledge one's sinfulness and to seek grace. The same idea appears in the account of Mrs. Beresford's death: "Her pains were great; but she bore all with invincible patience and resignation, and often said, 'I find it good for me to be afflicted; in His time I shall come out thoroughly purified.'"[93]

Medicine and Religion

Methodists sought triumph over dying in salvation and believed that the true price of defeat was eternal damnation, not death. However, the Methodist emphasis on the well-being of the soul rather than that of the body did not signify a clear separation of body from soul, medicine from theology. On the contrary—for early Methodists, body and soul were inseparable. Nowhere did this close relation become more apparent than in the Methodist practice of medicine and its place in their religious life.

Wesley was no less a physician than a preacher, and he offered healing side by side with salvation.[94] One of the central duties of the Methodist was to visit the sick, not only to counsel the soul but also to treat the body. Part of the work of the Methodist was thus to learn what he or she could of the limited medical knowledge of the day—a duty that in practice also led many to appear more knowledgeable than they in fact were.

For Wesley, as well as for other Methodists, religion and medicine were interrelated. Therefore, to a large extent, his theological views bore on his medical teachings. Early in his life, Wesley published a book on medicine under the title *Primitive Physic*.[95] The book comprised a list of ordinary medicines prescribed in ordinary language for a variety of illnesses. The remedies varied from drinking water for preventing hysteric fits to the use of electric shocks for curing gout. This short, highly eclectic booklet was criticized widely, even at the time, for its lack of scientific basis.[96] If this was so, it was precisely because its author resisted any form of systematic theorizing in medicine. For him, the whole knowledge of medicine could be summarized in simple variations on the formula: "such a medicine removes such a pain."[97]

Wesley's medical advice can be seen as a critical reaction against eighteenth-century medicine, which attempted to lay new foundations for the old Hippocratic science. Wesley believed that the medical profession of his time was so overly committed to philosophical abstraction and scientific systematization that it had forgotten the only important question in medicine: namely, effectiveness. Countering the medical establishment of his time, Wesley returned to the "primitive" practices of medicine as he found them in traditional societies, in which medical knowledge was gathered through empirical trial and error and was transmitted from one generation to the next. Wesley was particularly impressed when, during his journey to America, he found this way of practicing medicine among the indigenous inhabitants of the land.

It is important to understand Wesley's medical views in relation to the medical knowledge of his time. Yet, perhaps, it is even more important to see the less apparent connection (for Wesley does not make these references explicit) between his medicine and his theology. In fact, the title *Primitive Physic*, as well as the methods of the book can be fully understood only in light of Wesley's own theology.

According to Wesley, the power of human beings to alleviate their suffering was grounded in scripture. Sickness and death were brought upon humanity as punishment from God after the Fall. Yet along with the expulsion from Eden, God made a promise: "In the sweat of thy face shalt thou eat bread."[98] This promise granted the sons of Adam and the daughters of Eve the power to lessen the pains and inconveniences entailed within mortal life.

The kinship between medicine and theology went even further. Wesley believed that since God was the source of the power to heal, the power was accessible to everyone. He thought that physicians had obscured this with their highly abstract and technical theory and with their ultimately ineffective treatments. His own medical tract was an attempt to set things right by teaching people God's simple and effective remedies in plain language. Frequently, Wesley's complaints about physicians paralleled his complaints about papist authority, "Physicians . . . began to be held in admiration, as persons who were something more than human."[99] Wesley's account of medicine makes it easy to understand his analogy between the physician and the priest and how his attack against medicine of his time was similar to that of the Reformers against the Church. Implicitly but unmistakeably, Wesley was drawing a list of surprising parallels between priest and physician, the corruption of the church and the corruption of the medical profession, the primitive church and the primitive tribe, and finally, the simplicity of scripture and that of *Primitive Physic*. As Wesley made clear, for the early Methodists the art of healing was part and parcel of the art of holy living and dying.

Decline of the Art of Holy Dying

The Wesleyan tradition was carried on in America decades after Wesley's death. The Methodists who followed him to America brought with them the fundamentals of his theology, which they struggled to perfect in the years that followed.[100] The leaders of the American Methodist Episcopal Church, Francis Asbury and Thomas Coke, organized the American church according to Wesley's principles while adapting them to the needs of both the settled communities and the frontier.[101] Asbury, Coke, and numerous others carried on Wesley's belief that Methodist leaders had a duty to prescribe medical remedies for the sick. But by the 1830s, several transformations were starting to take place that dramatically altered the Methodist way of dying.[102]

Perhaps the most apparent change was the separation of medicine from theology and physician from minister. A division of labor was established in which the minister was expected not to interfere in the works of the physician. Methodists generally decided either to preach or to practice medicine, but not to do both. And as one scholar observed, by the 1860s, clear lines of demarcation existed between these once united professions."[103] This change was partially because many physicians had joined the Methodist ranks but also because of new attempts to establish medicine as a modern—that is, independent—profession.

By the early 1860s, the editors of the *Christian Advocate* had taken a stand against ministers who endorsed and advertised untested treatments to laypeople, referring to it as "unwarrantable interference with an honorable profession."[104] Along the same lines, the popularity of Wesley's own writings on medicine diminished. *Primitive Physic*, one of the most popular medical books at the beginning of the nineteenth century, was revised to conform to new medical positions and then eventually dropped out of circulation.[105]

A further change took place in the structure of the deathbed scene. Within the Church itself, objections were raised against the premise that a triumphant death involved overcoming an otherwise great fear. Late nineteenth-century Methodists minimized the terrors of death and claimed there was no need to overcome fear because there was nothing to fear.

The tradition of saints dying in bliss and sinners dying in terror was being overtly questioned. One Methodist said in 1882 that "dying persons probably were unconscious of what they or others said, that alleged deathbed visions were 'doubtless subjective,' and that the terrors of sinners were due to the widespread fear of eternal punishment that pervaded communities at the time."[106]

In a similar fashion, late nineteenth-century Methodists began questioning the deathbed interrogations as "intrusive curiosity" about the last words of the dying. "We are to be judged by how we have lived," wrote one Methodist, "and not by how we have died." This view assured the dying that it was all right simply to die quietly, without feeling any guilt about the inability to "enter with intense earnestness into the prayers offered at the sick room."[107]

"A new attitude toward death had by 1875 already begun to appear," noted one Methodist scholar. "Wesleyan journalists began to deplore the excesses of the older deathbed piety, which they viewed as unduly productive of 'terror,' and to place their accent on 'hope.' " However, this new hope was markedly different from both the Catholic hope in a world to come and the Methodist this-worldly assurance. It is precisely the emergence of this new hope at the deathbed that, as we shall see, marks the transition from the Methodists' *ars moriendi* to the scientific and medicalized modern art of dying.

Euthanasia and the Methodist Legacy

For the early Methodists, dying was a work of art. They contemplated their death throughout life, constantly examining the state of their soul, seeking assurance of the love of God in its fruits: a fearless death. When the hour of death came, Methodists, being conscious of their mortality, were prepared to bring their life to closure. Since the art of dying was an art of living, dying was part of life; but more essentially, since the art of living was an art of dying, death was life's fulfillment.

As a work of art, triumphant death became a spectacle for the Methodist community, family, and friends. They came not only to watch how someone lived and died but also to partake in the art of dying—interrogating the dying patient on the state of his or her soul, writing and rewriting the last words of the departed. The Methodist life was completed in death, and the story of one's life was appropriately told as the recital of one's dying.

The deathbed became a microcosm of Methodist life, a moment in life that captured its entirety. In it, the relation between the Methodist believer, God, and the Methodist people unfolded. Through it, the truth of the Methodist world was brought to life.

It would be anachronistic to ask why the Methodists of the turn of the nineteenth century did not contemplate medical euthanasia as a solution to the problem of dying. Methodists on their deathbed faced radically different challenges from those faced by modern patients. To these challenges of the nineteenth century, euthanasia could offer no solution. A good death for Methodists was not a painless death but rather a death in which pain was overcome. Neither was a good death a hurried departure, for Methodists took their time to face death and acknowledge its possible terrors. While death was not rushed, neither did Methodists passively await death. An elaborate set of practices was followed, practices designed to lead Methodists in their triumphant victory. Euthanasia, by medically hastening death, would rob the dying of the opportunity to face death and overcome it.

For euthanasia to emerge as a solution to the problem of dying, the whole context of the deathbed would have to transform once again, allowing a new art of dying to emerge. In this new art, the ideal of a good death would alter, religion and medicine would part ways, and priest and physician would divorce. Death would no longer be the culmination of life, and pain would yield not to a triumphant death but to the powers of technique.

Yet the Methodist art of dying was already hinting at the rise of technique. In several important ways, the Methodist death prepared the ground for the new art of dying. Underlying the art of holy dying lay the Methodist wish to gain mastery over death. The wish to command death lies at the very heart of any art of dying and in itself cannot distinguish the Methodists from their predecessors. What is striking, however, about the Methodist death as a radical representation of nineteenth-century America is the attempt to overcome death in *this* world.

The doubt, hope, and fear that characterized the pre-Reformation *ars moriendi* were no longer acceptable for the Methodist believer. The believer wished to secure the experience of dying with a this-worldly assurance of salvation. What before was dying as an art now became a skill or expertise—a certain way of dying—that could secure a this-worldly disposition of certainty in the human power to master death. It was this close affinity between art and technique that set the Methodist art of dying as a transitional moment in which dying transformed from an art to a technique. And it was on the basis of this transition that euthanasia, soon to be understood as the medical hastening of death, became possible.

Medical Euthanasia: From Aiding the Dying
to Hastening Death

Introduction

THE Birmingham Speculative Club was a small society of professionals and businessmen who met periodically in the British midland city to discuss the problems of the day. A collection of their essays published in 1870 includes a discussion of women's rights, colonialism and its breakdown, and educational inequality. More than a century later, one cannot help but appreciate the persisting relevance of these problems to our own time while simultaneously noticing that the solutions the writers offered tend to be far less compelling today.[1]

However, one article in this long-forgotten collection is an exception to this rule. It is a piece titled "Euthanasia," written by Samuel D. Williams, an otherwise unknown businessman.[2] Its author proposes a solution to the problem of dying patients suffering from unbearable pain. He writes that:

> In all cases of hopeless and painful illness it should be the recognized duty of the medical attendant, whenever so desired by the patient, to administer chloroform—or such other anaesthetic as may by and by supersede chloroform—so as to destroy consciousness at once, and put the sufferer to a quick and painless death; all needful precautions being adopted to prevent any possible abuse of such duty; and means being taken to establish beyond the possibility of doubt or question, that the remedy was applied at the express wish of the patient.[3]

Williams's proposal was the first to advocate euthanasia, the medical hastening of death, in the modern age.[4] While euthanasia was generally opposed by the medical establishment as well as by the general public, several leading physicians openly supported legalization of the practice. In 1906, there were even attempts to pass bills legalizing euthanasia in Ohio and Iowa; although these attempts were eventually defeated, they mark a demand for a new way of dying that would persist into the twenty-first century.[5]

Indeed, most present-day attempts to legalize euthanasia share the basic structure of these earlier proposals: first, identifying the problem (namely, that of the terminally ill, suffering patient); second, designating the medical profession as responsible for solving the problem; and third, using lethal narcotics to hasten death as the solution.[6] However, unlike their nineteenth century precursors, more-recent proposals in the United States tend to assign physicians the more limited role of passively prescribing lethal medication rather than actively administering a lethal injection.[7]

Strong opposition to the medical practice of euthanasia emerged in response to Williams's proposal.[8] The possibility that physicians would help to shorten the life of patients provoked a fervent attack from most mainstream practitioners. Euthanasia was rejected not only on moral grounds but also because it challenged the most fundamental principle of medical practice: the sacred duty of the medical profession to prolong life, not to shorten it. The leading journal of the American Medical Association denounced Williams's proposal for requiring "the physician to don the robes of an executioner."[9]

While most physicians found Williams's solution unacceptable, they were all too familiar with the problem that hastening death was intended to solve. As we shall see, the condition of the terminally ill patient became a growing concern for the medical profession sometime before euthanasia emerged as its possible solution. Moreover, the proposed practice of euthanasia shared certain elements with the ordinary treatment of the dying: that is, not only recognition of the problem but also the logic underlying its solution. Rather than constituting a radical break, euthanasia was a radicalization of ordinary medical practices.

The history of the term "euthanasia" hints toward the same direction.[10] Until the eighteenth century, the term was still used in its traditional and literary sense—as "a good death," commonly understood as a natural death from old age. Williams was probably the first to use the term in its contemporary sense, denoting the active shortening of life. However, the meaning of euthanasia occurred in a third and more prevalent sense among physicians throughout the greater part of the nineteenth century: that of medical treatment to aid an easy death, short of killing. Euthanasia signified the emergence within the medical profession of a new concern with the problem of dying, and with the medical responsibility to treat the dying.

To understand the modern conception of euthanasia as the medical hastening of death, we must first understand euthanasia as medical treatment in aid of an easy death.[11] This chapter, therefore, investigates the emergence of the medical treatment of the dying patient and asks how dying became a modern problem and how euthanasia—in both its senses—became its solution.

The two defining elements of the modern problem of dying, as Williams's proposal intimates, are hopelessness and pain. One may wonder whether there is anything particularly modern about these concerns. Clearly, dying has always been characterized as a hopeless condition that is often accompanied by excruciating pain. Nevertheless, if we wish to view pain and hopelessness as key elements in the present-day problem of dying, it is because these elements have gained a unique significance in the modern age. It is the particular way in which suffering and despair, viewed in the *ars moriendi* tradition as temptations, were reintroduced as the medico-technical problems of pain and hopelessness that distinguishes the modern art of dying from its predecessors. And it is precisely because hopelessness and pain reemerged as modern concerns that new solutions such as euthanasia could be offered to overcome the problem of dying.

In addition, what becomes apparent from the early euthanasia proposals is that only the combination of these two elements justifies the hastening of death. Pain alone, unbearable as it may be, cannot justify the shortening of life, nor can the despair of dying in itself legitimize the hastening of death. Rather, it is the combined occurrence of pain and hopelessness alone that can justify the practice of euthanasia. Their concurrence is so central to the justification of hastened death that more than a century later and in the very different context of advanced medical technique, the same two conditions appear in nearly all attempts to legalize physician-assisted suicide.[12]

The discussion will therefore proceed by examining separately the two different if related problems of dying: hopelessness and pain. In both cases, the discussion will focus on how dying became a problem (whether of hopelessness or of pain) and how this problem was managed within the ordinary practice of medicine. In this regard, we will give attention to the emergence of a medico-technical drive in the treatment of the dying patient. This drive, which originated in the ordinary medical treatment of the dying, made euthanasia possible.

The early euthanasia proposals were clearly linked with broad social and cultural changes in attitudes toward death and dying. This chapter, however, will center on the medical context, and from this the broader social and cultural implications may be drawn. This point of departure is justified not only because euthanasia was defined from the outset as a medical practice and responsibility but also because, more important, the logic of euthanasia—from diagnosis of a terminal illness to treatment—was formulated in light of the medical knowledge and practices of the time. While euthanasia is an extreme solution to the problem of dying, it is no more than that: an extreme application of the ordinary treatment of dying patients, part and parcel of the emergence of a new medical and technical way of dying. The history of euthanasia will, therefore, serve as a window through which we can explore the transformation of dying from an art to a technique.

A final introductory remark: in recent years, we have become accustomed to thinking of physician-assisted suicide and other means of choosing death as reactions to the modern reality of death. Particularly, we have come to think of them as attempts to escape the iron cage of medical technique, which condemns dying patients who are invaded by tubes, respirators, and dialysis machines to suffer the artificial prolongation of life. However, as we have shown, euthanasia emerged in the nineteenth century as a solution to the problem of dying—long before the development of the technical machinery that is so commonly associated with the practice. This is not to suggest, as some historians have, that the practices of hastened death are divorced from the question of technique.[13] Rather, it is to emphasize that they are not dependent on any particular technical achievement—or, stated more positively, that they are grounded in a deeper logic of technique that governs all modern medical practices. Hastening death is more than a reaction to modern technique. It is also, in a more telling way, its fulfillment.

The Problem of Dying, I: Hopelessness

Prior to the nineteenth century, reflections on dying were all but absent from medical discourse. To the extent that physicians discussed death in the eighteenth century, the discussion centered on the determination of actual death and on the moment of death. It had very little to do with the process of dying itself.[14] The clearest manifestation of these concerns in the eighteenth century was a fascination with premature burials. With the disappearance of the rampaging fear of apparent death around the middle of the nineteenth century, a new concern not with death but with dying gradually formed.[15]

Traditionally, there was little room for the physician at the deathbed. It was common medical practice for physicians to withdraw their care from an incurable patient, leaving the dying in the trustworthy hands of the attending family, friends, and clergy.[16] Many physicians held to the simple belief that if there was nothing they could do to cure the patient, their place at the bedside was superfluous. Thus, they would willingly step aside to allow the deathbed rites to be performed. Even when there was no clear distinction between the religious minister and the medical doctor, as in early Methodism, the shift at the deathbed was clearly in the direction of the salvation of the soul, not the healing of the body. If any treatment was to be offered, it was only the minimum relief of pain that was necessary to let the dying confront death properly.

By the early nineteenth century, the absence of the physician from the deathbed was no longer acceptable. The widespread medical practice of abandoning the deathbed of an incurable patient was becoming highly questionable. A new responsibility of the medical profession at the deathbed emerged and first announced itself in early attempts to codify professional medical ethics. This new genre of writing, which became popular during the late eighteenth century, was intended to establish the responsibilities of physicians to their patients in order to secure the good reputation of the medical profession—a reputation that was threatened by the proliferation of quackery.[17] In 1817, one such etiquette read as follows:

> Let me here exhort you against the custom of some physicians, who leave their patients when their life is despaired of, and when it is no longer decent to put them to further expense. . . . Even in cases where his skill as a physician can be of no further avail, his presence and assistance as a friend may be agreeable and useful both to the patient and to his nearest relations.[18]

Despite the apparent inability of medicine to offer cure or treatment to the dying patient, a new medical duty emerged calling physicians to action. This new responsibility of the medical profession was to remain with the dying patient to the very end, despite the fact that all the *materia medica* in the physician's possession was of no avail. But what duty *could* the physician fulfill at the deathbed? This new duty of care that was spreading among physicians of the nineteenth century was summed up in one word: euthanasia.[19]

Admittedly, the use of the term "euthanasia" to discuss the responsibilities of the physician at the deathbed can already be found in Francis Bacon's writings on the duties of the medical profession in the seventeenth century. In his work "Advancement of Learning," he proclaims

> the office of a physician [to be] not only to restore health, but also to mitigate the pains and torments of diseases; and not only when such

45

mitigation of pains, as of a dangerous symptom, helps and conduces to recovery; but also when, all hope of recovery being gone, it serves only to make a fair and easy passage of from life.[20]

Bacon, however, limits the role of the physician to the treatment of the body. Consequently, he refers to medical euthanasia as "outward euthanasia," or "the easy dying of the body," distinguishing it from euthanasia proper, "which regards the preparation of the soul."[21] For Bacon, *outward* euthanasia is still subordinate to *inner* euthanasia and, in any event, does not yet take its place. As we shall see, the nineteenth-century resurrection of the division between body and soul placed more than the mere care of the body in the hands of the medical profession.

The first modern discussion of euthanasia to approach the subject not merely as medical *treatment* of the dying but also as medical *care* for the dying appeared in a formative article published in 1826 by Carl F. H. Marx.[22] Marx, one of the leading German physicians of the mid-nineteenth century from Göttingen, dubbed this new treatment of the dying with an old name.[23] Thinking through the goals in "Medical Euthanasia," he asks:

> What can be done so the passing from life may be gentle and bearable? Why should not man, with his intellect mastering so many problems, find and produce some skillfull contrivance for the care of the dying?[24]

Though Marx offered a much more modest solution to the problem of dying than Williams did, this brief passage contains, in a concentrated form, intimations of a new approach to the treatment of dying. First, dying has become a problem not only of treating sickness but also of caring for the dying. Second, this problem can be overcome by the skillful, technical mastery of dying. Third (and as a consequence of the second implication), the medical profession has the ability and hence the responsibility to resolve the problem of dying.

But what should we make of the medical attempt to solve a problem that is, perhaps in principle, unsolvable? How was the problem of dying redefined so that physicians could claim possession of a medical solution? Or, more concretely, what precisely was this new treatment that Marx, along with American physicians of the nineteenth century, had in mind?

One central aspect of the treatment of the dying patient was the relief of pain. Indeed, the alleviation of pain became central to the treatment of the dying patient and was closely related to the practice of euthanasia. (We shall return to this subject in the second part of this chapter.) Another possible task of physicians at the deathbed was to protect the patient from any additional discomfort that did not arise directly from the medical condition.[25] Thus, the physician would be responsible for preventing the possible development of bedsores and other inconveniences that were not related directly to the disease. While this task was of apparent significance, it did not require any specialized medical knowledge. In fact, any adult attendant at the deathbed, such as a family member or a nurse, could be as efficient in meeting these needs. Therefore, it is difficult to understand why the physician would be called to attend the deathbed for such ordinary duties, and it is likewise hard to see in these treatments the emergence of a new science of dying.

What, then, could be a unique contribution of the physician to the dying patient? The question becomes more pressing once we recall that nineteenth-century medicine made no real progress in its capacity to treat the dying patient. With the exception of the replacement of opium with its alkaloid, morphine, in the second half of the nineteenth century, the capacity of the medical profession to treat dying patients was no different during most of the nineteenth century than it had been during the previous century. Not until far into the twentieth century did radical changes take place in medicine's power to treat the dying patient, relieve pain, and prolong life.[26]

What we are seeking, therefore, is not any specific treatment or effective therapy that could be offered to the dying but rather a more fundamental transformation in the approach of the medical profession toward the hopelessly ill patient. Despite the hopelessness and the inevitable decline associated with dying, and perhaps precisely because of it, the medical profession followed a deeper calling to continue treatment and maintain hope in the face of death. One might even say that the new role of the physician at the bedside was to *minister* hope in the face of approaching death. "For with encouragement and with promise," Marx believed, "he will bring spirit to the dejected, hope to the fearful, confidence to the despairing."[27] It is this new disposition of hope that characterizes the treatment of the dying patient and the modern art of dying. While its appearance did not hinge on any significant advancement in medicine's power to alter the conditions of dying, it was precisely this disposition that motivated the medical profession to seek and apply new techniques for the care of the dying in years to come.

The Ministry of Hope

Early in the nineteenth century, Thomas Percival, the first to institute a modern code of medical ethics in the English-speaking world, raised the issue of the physician's duty to care for the patient's state of mind.[28] Percival based this duty on the belief that the mood of the sick patient could have an effect on his bodily constitution.

> For, the physician should be the minister of hope and comfort to the sick. . . . The life of a sick person can be shortened not only by the acts, but also by the words or the manner of a physician. It is therefore, a sacred duty to guard himself carefully in this respect, and to avoid all things which have a tendency to discourage the patient and to depress his spirits.[29]

The new role of the physician at the deathbed, according to Percival, is the ministering of hope. At times, this ministration is more important than any particular medicine that the physician can offer the patient. This is especially true at the deathbed, when truly no cure can be offered. Physicians of the nineteenth century began to argue that irrespective of the physician's involvement with suffering, disease, and death, the medical profession had a duty to minister hope. Beyond any particular treatment that the physician could perform, he should embody hope in his own persona.

> The expression on the physician's countenance should be cheerful; he should greet his patient with smiles, or in more serious maladies, at least with placidity. Even the important questions regarding symptoms and feeling should not seem serious to the sufferer.[30]

This cheerfulness, which Walter Dendy, a nineteenth-century American physician who coined the term "psychotherapeia," identifies with hopefulness, is not merely a personality trait required of the physician.[31] Rather, it is based on the certainty and confidence that the physician, *as* a physician, can instigate. Hope, in other words, is not merely a subjective mood but is conceived as part of the traits a physician should have.

To further clarify this new identity of the medical profession as a cheerful and hopeful profession, we can contrast it with the changing perception of the role of the clergy at the deathbed. As mentioned earlier, physicians tended to relinquish their responsibilities at the deathbed, leaving the treatment of the dying in the hands of the clergy. Then, early in the nineteenth century, young physicians were reproved for such behavior and were reminded that not only were they capable of caring for the dying but also that they might be even more suitable for the task than the clergy. Marx warns his colleagues:

> Whoever refuses his part in this duty [administering some kind of higher comfort] and assigns it solely to priests deprives himself of the most noble and rewarding aspect of his work. Where the priest, administering the sacraments, comes to the bedside to soothe the longing soul with the last solace of religion and comfort, who will not see the patient's deep shock when he faces this quasi-harbinger of death?[32]

Not so with the physician. The physician will not raise such terror, for he is associated with hope for a cure, not with the inevitability of death. Of the two, the minister of hope rather than the minister of fate should accompany the sick in his last hour. From the medical viewpoint, the presence of the priest at the deathbed could offer nothing but fear and terror. The possibility of saving the soul that was so intimately related to the *ars moriendi* was not denied by the medical profession but was rather deemed irrelevant. For the latter, regardless of one's religious belief, the only hope that the clergy could offer was a hope in a world to come. In this world, the presence of the minister at the deathbed could mean only one thing: imminent death. Therefore, only medicine could offer real hope—that is, this-worldly hope—grounded in the powers available to medical science and technique.

But what were these powers? Other than a vague notion of hope, offered in the persona of the medical doctor, what possible content could there be to the hope ministered to the dying patient? What were its medical grounds? The answer to this question gradually changed throughout the nineteenth century and is related to changes in medicine's perception of its own power.

Hope: From Heroic to Conservative Medicine

Early nineteenth century American medicine was dominated by what has been known as *heroic medicine*.[33] This medical ethos, developed by the notable Philadelphia physician Benjamin Rush, demanded the use of extreme medical measures such as bleeding and purging in the treatment of most diseases. Medical orthodoxy during the early nineteenth century believed that it was better to make mistakes in the treatment of a patient than not to treat at all. This categorical imperative of medical therapeutics was applied to all patients, even those who were highly likely to die.[34]

The hope that the physician could offer the dying patient was, for Rush, nothing less than full recovery. This hope was ministered to the sick even when the chances of recovery seemed very slim.

> Avoid giving a patient over in an acute disease. It is impossible to tell in such cases where life ends, and where death begins. Hundreds of patients have recovered, who have been pronounced incurable, to the great disgrace of our profession. . . . It is not necessary that we should decide with confidence, at any time, upon the essence of a disease.[35]

The notorious practices of early nineteenth-century heroic medicine have been well documented. They included bloodletting, as well as the excessive use of emetics and purgatives such as calomel, arsenic, and other poisons. While today it is clear that these excessive treatments caused great harm and brought little cure, if any, they were used then because of their capacity to bring about immediate and drastic effects. These effects were not only physical: the power of the physician to alter the condition of the dying patient increased the confidence and hope of the patient.

While Rush's radical approach characterized the early nineteenth century, it could still be found in the latter half of the century. As one physician wrote in 1882:

> Never be too sanguine of a patient's recovery from a serious affliction, and never give one up to die in acute disease unless dissolution is actually in progress; and above all else, never withdraw from a case . . . because the patient is very ill. Even after he is unable to swallow, or if food taken into the stomach is not assimilated, continue your efforts with inunctions of cod liver oil or of glycerine and quinia, rectal alimentation, etc., until he is either better or the breath is out of his body.[36]

The most straightforward explanation for such behavior was that one could never determine with certainty whether the patient was truly dying. For

> *nature*, by a crisis, or a vicarious function, or a compensatory process, may turn the scale and let the life-power rally and gain control over the disease at the last moment, and had you given him up you would be disgraced, while some other doctor, or a homoeopath, or an old woman who had stepped in, would get all the glory.[37]

While the possibility that by some miraculous turn of events the patient may recover from his ailment seems a plausible ground for continuing treatment, it does not fully explain the grounds of the modern physician's ministry of hope. After all, as the writer himself admits, any practitioner of alternative medicine or "old woman" would follow the same course of action.

Furthermore, the hope for a cure could not explain the persistence of care for the dying, since such drastic treatment was carried on even when the physician himself was assured that there was no chance that the medication provided would be of any avail—so much so that physicians often prescribed medication even when it was clear that its power to cure was highly questionable. Rush himself, deliberating the curative power of hope, admitted, "I have frequently prescribed remedies of doubtful efficacy in the critical stage of acute diseases, but never till I had worked up my patients into a confidence, bordering upon certainty, of their probable good effects."[38] For the new physician, it was important to maintain the dying patient's hope in the power of medicine, regardless of its final outcome.

In the eighteenth century, and probably long before, physicians knew that deceiving the patient to foster a belief in the power of medicine can have a therapeutic value. But there were clear limits on such uses. Wyndham B. Blanton, who wrote a comprehensive book on medicine in the eighteenth century, wrote:

> if the appearance of doing something be necessary to keep alive the hope & spirits of the patient, it should be of the most innocent character. One of the most successful physician I have ever known, has assured me, that he used more bread pills, drops of colored water, & powders of hickory ashes, than of all other medicines put together. It was certainly a pious fraud.[39]

What distinguishes the nineteenth century practice of *heroic medicine* from its eighteenth-century predecessor was not only the use of much more extreme and dangerous measures but also the expanding circle of deception, which now seemed to include not only the dying patient but also the self-proclaimed "heroic" doctor.

By the 1830s, the popularity of heroic medicine was in decline. Physicians such as Jacob Bigelow, a Harvard Medical School professor, were criticizing as futile and at times damaging the practices common to heroic medicine, such as overdosing, bleeding, and purging.[40]

As an alternative, Bigelow developed the notion of natural healing. His method was based on the idea that many if not most diseases are "self-limited." Such diseases have a natural course of development and cannot benefit from therapeutic intervention. In many cases the self-limited disease will be cured by nature, but even in those cases where the natural course of the disease leads to death, there is nothing that therapeutic medicine can do to alter its course.

It may seem that medicine's self-perception of its power was shifting from hope to despair and that in the place of heroic medicine one could now find only the pessimism of medical nihilism. But mid-nineteenth century medicine did not completely lose its belief in its therapeutic powers, and specifically in its capacity to treat the dying patient. By the mid-nineteenth century, a new school of medicine, labeled by its contemporaries as "conservative medicine," dominated the medical field. Conservative medicine sought a more grounded belief in the power of medicine, one that would avoid both extremes of either all-powerful or all-impotent medicine. Among its advocates were several of the most prominent American physicians of the period, two of whom played a central role in the history of euthanasia, Oliver Wendell Holmes and Worthington Hooker.[41]

These nineteenth-century American physicians struggled with the problem of dying and sought medical grounds on which they could offer hope to the dying patient. But how could the medical physician become the minister of hope, when it was medicine itself that was now openly acknowledging that in most cases the dying patient was incurable? What these physicians came up with was a new breed of hope—one that did not deny the dying patient's incurable condition in the name of the all-powerful capacities of medicine but that would at the same time refrain from undermining the new role of the physician at the deathbed as the minister of hope.

The scientific grounds for such an approach were laid down by Worthington Hooker, one of the leading physicians of the mid-nineteenth century. Hooker received his education at Harvard Medical School and, after several decades of medical practice, joined the Yale Medical School. In 1849, he published the only monograph on the subject of medical ethics written by an American physician in the nineteenth century.[42] In this highly influential book, Hooker devoted several chapters to the discussion of the natural influence of the mind on disease, and in particular the role of hope in treatment.

Hooker, rejecting the prevailing materialist approach, believed that while the mind was not an "epiphenomenon" reducible to the body, it was nevertheless connected to it. Like other physicians of his time, Hooker believed that there could not be any sickness of the body, however slight, that did not produce some effect on the mind, and that similarly, the mind always had an influence on the state of the body. The care of the body therefore should always be accompanied by care of the mind. The physician should always express hope for the condition of the patient, for any expression of despair may have fatal impact. The physician of the body, in other words, must become the healer of the soul.

The hope that the physician was to inspire in the patient should be neither a groundless optimism nor, as it had been in the past, a manipulative effort to deceive the patient. Precisely in this way, the hope ministered by the physician differed from that exerted by the quack. This distinction was particularly important at a time when medical orthodoxy was trying to establish its professional boundaries. Physicians of the mid-nineteenth century were forming professional organizations to secure public recognition in their professional capacities. The American Medical Association, which was established in 1847, launched a war against quackery and excluded from its ranks homeopaths and other nonorthodox practitioners. Similar distinctions were drawn in day-to-day practice. Specifically with respect to the treatment of the dying, the medical profession sought to offer a scientifically grounded hope that would win the confidence of the dying patient and counter the deceitful practices of nonorthodox sectarian groups.[43] Hooker explains:

> The quack always gives assurances of a cure to those whom he undertakes to dupe; for, besides being incompetent to estimate the degree of danger in any case, he is unable to inspire confidence in his measures except by a strong appeal to the hopes of the patient. And some physicians imitate the quack in this particular.[44]

One of the many deceitful strategies of the quack doctor was to first give a disparaging diagnosis of the patient's condition, and then match it with an excessive confidence in the powers of the drugs that he could offer. For the quack, this seemed to be a win-win situation. Either his dire prediction would come true or, if it did not, he could take credit for the recovery.[45]

The physician, like the quack, had to minister hope. And though the physician might benefit from raising false hopes, and at times a deceived patient might enjoy temporary comfort, such practice was highly criticized. This was not only because of the moral objection that the end (a hopeful patient) could not justify the means (deceit). Nor could the physician's duty to express scientific hope be explained solely as an attempt to distinguish the honorable medical profession from the unprofessional quacks. More important, the *kind* of hope that the physician was expected to minister to the dying patient was essentially different from the kind provided by the quack. The task of the physician was not merely to create a feeling of hope but to secure one based on the scientific healing powers of medicine. As another mid-nineteenth century physician remarked,

> Above all, the physician . . . should ever assume a perfect confidence in his own judgment. Confidence, the conviction that the resources of professional science and wisdom are at hand, impart a charm even in moments of danger, and especially on the sensitive mind and weakened body of the dying.[46]

While ministering hope makes perfect sense in treating the ordinary patient, it becomes much more problematic when an incurable patient is involved. When applied to the case of the hopelessly ill patient, the general course of action recommended by Hooker and other nineteenth-century physicians seems to run, so to speak, into a dead end. Nevertheless, like others of his time, Hooker believed that neither patient nor physician should lose hope even in these extreme cases. Hooker's observation on hope presents a paradox in the nineteenth-century treatment of the dying, a paradox resulting from the tension between the medical responsibility to minister hope and the knowledge that certain dying patients were medically hopeless.

It may be helpful to explore a central aspect of this paradox to gain a clearer view of its complexity. The tension between hopelessness and hope had immediate practical implications when physicians were confronted with whether to inform the dying patient of his fatal condition. Understanding how this tension was handled will also help us understand the role that hope played in the treatment of the dying.

Intelligent Hope

If the physician knows that the patient is dying, should he reveal the truth to the patient? The very raising of this question points to a new relation of knowledge between physician and patient. In earlier days, the patient was the first to know of his approaching death.[47] The warning came quite often through natural signs and a spontaneous realization, rather than through a supernatural premonition. By the nineteenth century, however, access to this knowledge had shifted from the patient to the physician.[48] One might expect that the physician, therefore, would pass on this information to the patient. But this was not the case—at least not entirely.

"It is often said that if the physician, on the whole, taking into view all the circumstances of the case, thinks that a patient is going to die, he ought frankly to tell him so. . . . This is by no means true."[49] This view, expressed by Hooker in the mid-nineteenth century, was becoming more and more popular among the medical profession. Concealing the truth of dying became, in fact, one of the new responsibilities of physicians toward their dying patients. But how should we understand the reluctance of physicians to reveal the truth of dying to the incurable patient?

Too often, this phenomenon has been conceived as "the great lie," as if the physician were withholding information from the patient and attempting to deceive him.[50] This "lie" has been interpreted as part of the allegedly more general modern phenomenon of the denial of death. The physician did not inform the patient of his approaching death, so the argument goes, because the reality of death had to be repressed and denied. It is important to see how this repressive hypothesis is not only inaccurate but, more decisively, one-sided in its presentation of the new attitude toward death.[51] It portrays the new approach to death purely in negative terms—as lies, conceit, and denial—when those are precisely what the medical profession was trying to overcome. The challenge before us is to reconstruct a positive understanding of what the physician was attempting to achieve. For this purpose, we shall focus on the emerging role of the deathbed physician as minister of hope, a role quite different from denier of death.

The repressive hypothesis, despite its apparent appeal, does not capture the full complexity of the new way of dying. Far from denying death, the physician could and often did inform the patient of his approaching death. The only change was that this knowledge should not come directly from the physician himself. As Thomas Percival wrote:

> A physician should not be forward to make gloomy prognostications, because they savor of empiricism, by magnifying the importance of his services in the treatment or cure of the disease. But he should not fail, on proper occasions, to give to the friends of the patient timely notice of danger when it really occurs; and even to the patient himself, if absolutely necessary. This office, however, is so peculiarly alarming when executed by him, that it ought to be declined whenever it can be assigned to any other person of sufficient judgment and delicacy.[52]

While Percival, who wrote early in the nineteenth century, still allowed for the possibility that in extreme cases the physician would inform the patient of his condition, later in the century, a gradual change would take place. The medical custom that physicians should never announce impending death became so dominant that it trumped the patient's need to know that truth, and so engrained that concealing the truth of dying from terminal patients was still a common practice well into the second half of the twentieth century. And though fleeting, this moment of transition in which Percival rejects direct disclosure but stops short of complete concealment is important. It demonstrates that the fundamental question posed by the modern way of dying is not whether the patient should know of his approaching death—he was not denied this knowledge—but centered on the seemingly impossible task of inspiring hope while being frank that death was inevitable. Here lay the paradox: medical treatment and what became so central to it, the categorical imperative to minister hope, had to take place irrespective of the fact that the patient was hopelessly dying.

The temporary and ultimately unsatisfying solution was to distinguish between the patient-physician relation and the relation between patient, family, and friends. While the gloomy subject of death was barred from the former context, it was allowed within the latter, so that within the nonmedical interaction between the patient and his close ones the reality of death could be present.

The patient, according to Hooker, could know with absolute certainty that his death was approaching and nevertheless believe that hope was at hand. Hooker recalled a respected friend whom others considered to be blind to his approaching death because "he talked of hope and relief now and then almost to the last." "And yet," Hooker testifies, "from day to day, he was making such preparations, even to the framing of his will, as showed that, on the whole, he believed this to be his last sickness."[53]

What is the nature of this schizophrenic condition that is so highly praised by the medical observer? Knowledge and belief seem to have been set apart. We speak of knowledge and belief here, but by no means does belief signify the nonrational opposite of scientific knowledge. Nor is the patient, as a carrier of this hope, to be contrasted to the physician, who is seen as the guardian of true knowledge. Dualistic thinking is not the point, here; we should not think of the matter as simple oppositions of truth and deceit, physician and patient, science and faith. Both physician and patient alike are caught between the certainty of death and hope in the power of medicine, and together they seek faith not in groundless belief but rather in the true power of medicine.

And yet, this seemingly irresolvable paradox between hope and fate could be settled if the incurable condition of the dying patient would not be immediately interpreted as medical failure and impotency. Even if full cure was out of reach, some treatment that may alleviate pain or even prolong life could still be available. *It was not hopelessness as such that was rejected, but only hopelessness as helplessness*, namely, as the inability to continue medical treatment of any sort.

Thus, for Hooker, the reason why hope should become the prevailing cast of the physician's mind is that hope stimulates action, "while despondency is prone to inaction, and leads to no efforts except those which are hurried, fitful and confused."[54] It is a sign of modern technique that even when it cannot promise salvation, it is satisfied with partial results. Even though it may not offer a cure to the dying patient, it celebrates small victories and a continuous deferment of death.

> The hope of the physician should be an intelligent hope. It should be based upon just and definite conclusions. It should be discriminating, and should be varied in its degree according to the character of each individual case. . . . Hope may thus be indulged in relation to the different stages of a case, without regard to the final event of it, which may be so distant and so clouded in doubt that no calculations can be made in regard to it. . . . This in many cases is much better than to come to him every day with the simple expression of the hope that he will at length recover. In the tedium of his confinement, if it be a long one, he soon tires of looking far ahead to the bright fields of convalescence, but finds relief in the time and spots lighted up of hope by the way—the oasis thus made in the desert of sickness.[55]

Euthanasia and Overcoming Hopelessness

Euthanasia, the ministering of hope to the dying patient, should be seen as a new art of dying, rather than negatively, as a denial of death. In this new art, hope becomes a way of facing death, and it is precisely when the approach of death is most evident that the need for hope is greatest. The dying patient is never to be abandoned, and physician and patient alike should always believe in the power of the medical profession to do something for the dying.

While, chronologically, the administration of hope emerged as a solution to the problem of hopelessness, logically the same set of mind and practices gave rise to both hopelessness as a problem and to hope as its solution. It was out of the medical profession's desire to offer treatment to the dying that hopelessness—at least in its modern sense as helplessness—emerged as the *problem* of dying.

TABLE 1
Dispositions of the Deathbed

	Pre-Reformation	*Post-Reformation*	*Modern*
Bad death	Hopelessness as despair	Fear and doubt	Hopelessness as helplessness
Good death	*Hope*	Faith and assurance	*Hope*
Domain	Otherworldly	This-worldly	This-worldly

But what precisely was modern about the problem of hopelessness, and about hope as its solution? Were fear and despair not always part of the temptations of the *ars moriendi* tradition, and was hope not always offered at the deathbed, as Cicero's old adage, "where there is life there is hope," suggests?[56] As intimated, the transformation from the traditional art of dying to the modern medico-technical death entailed more than the transfer of responsibility from the clergy to the physician; it involved transformations of the very nature of care itself.

What were these transformations?

The history of the art of dying can be told as the story of the varying dispositions that surrounded the deathbed. These dispositions, which are always more than mere psychological states or attitudes, colored the entire regime of caring for the dying.[57] While the expression of specific states of mind and the rejection of others are an important part of all notions of a good death, a psychological emphasis would reveal only a small part of the history of the deathbed. Dispositions are what organized the death scene as a whole and included not only the patient's state of mind and the attitude of physicians but also the rituals of the deathbed and medical treatment. Most important, the distinction between a bad death and a good death was made on the basis of these varying dispositions.

We encountered one moment of this historical transformation in the previous chapter. The Methodists, as part of the Reformed tradition, substituted Christian perfection and absolute assurance for what they viewed as a superstitious hope for another world. In this chapter, we have seen how the rise of medical euthanasia is a further move in the same direction—that is, away from the unreliable promises of otherworldly salvation.

While it may seem at first (table 1) that pre-Reformation Catholicism and modern medicine both offered hope at the deathbed, these "hopes" were radically different. The Catholic priest could offer salvation only in a world to come; in this world, the dying patient would have to await death patiently, with little that could be done to alleviate his condition. Modern medicine, following the lead of the post-Reformation, was seeking assurance in a this-worldly mastery over death. The hope offered by the physician was radically different from the otherworldly hope offered by the priest. Hope in this sense signifies the emergence of a technical drive in the medical treatment of the dying, which calls for action even in what is known to be an ultimately hopeless condition.

In the final instance, modern medicine was much closer to the this-worldly assurance of salvation offered by the Methodists than to the yet-to-come redemption offered by the Catholic Church. True, medicine could never truly triumph over death. It could not offer any form of assurance, and its promises were always limited in scope, that is, hopeful. But this was a new form of hope, and it is precisely the limit imposed on hope that marks the shift from the traditional art of dying to modern technique. The new hope offered by medical technique acknowledges the limits of its power while restlessly seeking to overcome these limits to achieve mastery over death. Precisely for this reason, modern physicians rejected the false promises offered by nonorthodox medicine, which always promised more than it could actually deliver.

The new hope was not for a cure, but for an end to helplessness. Even if medicine could not promise immortality, it insisted on its power to win small and reliable victories. It is always the desire of medicine to offer some hope to the dying patient, even when all seems to be doomed. Indeed, this defines the modern art of dying.

This limitation was seen not as a weakness but, to the contrary, as a strength. "The importance and usefulness of the medical profession," a nineteenth-century physician explained, "instead of being diminished will always be elevated exactly in proportion as it understands itself, weighs justly its own powers, and professes simply what it can accomplish."[58]

Modern medicine could not guarantee salvation. Physicians who found themselves facing the dying opted for a more tangible and limited hope. This hope was not the promise of a world to come, but a this-worldly guarantee that, as long as life persisted, could be renewed indefinitely. It is this modest megalomania that distinguished the medical practices of the latter half of the nineteenth century from heroic medicine in the first half. Though the call not to lose hope was already introduced by Benjamin Rush in the early nineteenth century, Rush's heroic medicine did not take into account the inherent limits of medical practice. It was only in the second half of the nineteenth century that mainstream physicians understood their limits, particularly in the treatment of the dying, and constructed a more subtle understanding of their power, which was not to cure but to offer intelligent hope.

In the age of medical therapeutics and technique, hope became a call for action. Awaiting death was no longer fitting for the modern science of dying, which demanded that something be done. Not only was awaiting a state of uncertainty but it was a state of indifference. Oliver W. Holmes, arguably the most notable American physician of the mid-nineteenth century, expressed this notion when he declared, "No human being can rest for any time in a state of equilibrium where the desire to live and that to depart just balance each other."[59] As long as the patient is in good mind and hopeful, he will not be bothered by inconveniences. But when hope of cure or improvement are gone, "every incommodity stares out at him, each one of them packing up his little bundle of circumstances and calling him to move to his new home, even before the apartment is ready to receive the new bodily tenant."[60]

Though Holmes was by no means advocating euthanasia, his telling metaphor demonstrates how the modern impatience about awaiting death gave rise not only to euthanasia as the medical treatment of the dying patient but also to euthanasia as the medical hastening of death. Doctors believed that death should follow as soon as hope was gone. So if medicine could not create hope, it should hasten death.

The overambitious desire shared by patient and physician to profess hope at the deathbed was the origin of the medical hastening of death, a last resort to the problem of dying. The modern deathbed is simultaneously the place where all hope is lost but also the place where a final effort is made to overcome helplessness by hastening death.

At times, the dying could be comforted with the promise of partial or temporary recovery. At other times, or for other people, this was not sufficient, and a new call for action was made despite the apparent hopelessness of the situation. In the same way that dying was defined as a problem of technique and as the apparent incapacity to cure, so the solution to the problem became technical—that is, faith in the ability of medicine to prolong life or, when such an attempt fails, to provide a good death. Medical technique was summoned to save the patient from dying, not by curing him, but by bringing his life to an end.

Thus we find the same logic behind the prolonging of life and the hastening of death.[61] In both, the treatment of the dying becomes a duty; in both, the determination of the time of death shifts from the providence of nature to the intercession of technique.[62] Finally, both share an optimistic belief in the power of modern technique to master death and replace the traditional *ars moriendi* to become the modern art of dying.

The case of the dying patient in the mid-nineteenth century is interesting precisely because it shows that even before the emergence of twentieth-century life-prolonging technology, the disposition of hope giving rise to action was at work. Hope, in other words, was not the consequence of the growing power of medicine but rather the other way around. It was this new disposition toward dying that gave rise to a constant search for action and to impatience toward what was seen as a merely passive waiting for death.

Having established the emergence of a medical-technological drive to treat the dying patient, we will consider the way in which pain became the central focus of this treatment in the second part of this chapter. As we have already argued, it is only the combination of these two aspects of dying—hopelessness and pain—which leads to the apparent solution of medical euthanasia.

The Problem of Dying, II: Pain

The treatment of pain underwent a remarkable transformation in the course of the second half of the nineteenth century.[63] Morphine, the potent active constituent of opium, was first isolated in 1806. Then, in the late 1840s, the discovery of ether and chloroform revolutionized the medical scene. Surgery, amputations, and dental operations no longer had to be accompanied by excruciating pain. Still, for a variety of reasons, not all physicians immediately accepted the use of anesthetics. Some found it unsafe, while others believed that pain was a necessary component in recovery. Religious belief in the redeeming power of pain supplied a further objection to the use of sedatives.[64] Nevertheless, by the end of the nineteenth century, anesthetics and other analgesics were commonly used to relieve the pain of surgery and obstetrics. More generally, the hope that pain—perhaps the greatest of nature's evils—could be overcome was no longer a mere flight of enlightened imagination.

The treatment of the dying patient and the relief of the pangs of death, however, were much less developed. The composer Hector Berlioz, whose sister was dying from breast cancer, accompanied by horrible suffering that drew heartrending screams from her day and night, complained that

> not a doctor dared to have the humanity to put an end to this martyrdom by making my sister inhale a bottle of chloroform. This is done to save a patient the pain of a surgical operation which lasts a quarter of a minute, and it is not [used] in order to deliver one from a torture lasting six months. . . . The most horrible thing in the world

for us, living and sentient beings, is inexorable suffering, pain without any possible compensation when it has reached this degree of intensity; and one must be barbarous, or stupid, or both at once, not to use the sure and easy means now at our disposal to bring it to an end. Savages are more intelligent and more humane.[65]

Williams's proposal to hasten the death of terminally ill, suffering patients emerged from a similar concern with the pain of dying. "Death by disease," he wrote, "is always death by torture, and the wit of man has never devised torture more cruel than are some of Nature's methods of putting her victims to death."[66] The suffering of dying was devastating, and the medical profession was gradually seen as responsible for freeing the dying from such torture.[67] The question before us is, How did the painful death become a peculiarly modern problem and the hastening of death become its solution? As in the case of hope, we may assume that pain was always a problem at the deathbed, but the precise way in which it became a problem in the nineteenth century may shed light on why and how euthanasia emerged as its possible solution.

Two possible explanations for the modern problem of pain must be ruled out from the outset. One explanation sees the source of the problem in the advancements of medical therapy. The growing medical capacity to prolong life, along with significant changes in the causes of death, have often been offered as an explanation for the increase of pain in dying. Indeed, throughout the course of the twentieth century, patients have been dying more often from slow and painful killers such as heart disease and cancer than from the swift and painless ailments of the nineteenth century such as influenza, cholera, and pneumonia.[68] Under these new circumstances of death and dying, so the argument goes, there is an ever-growing need for new solutions to the problem of pain.

There is little doubt that medical and technological advances have indeed revolutionized the experience of dying, resulting in a prolonged and at times highly painful death. And yet the problem of pain in dying, as we shall see, predates these developments and cannot be explained by them. Thus, even if it is true that dying has become more painful, there is no correlation between this change and the emergence of pain as a medical and social concern. More important, the problem of pain cannot be explained as the mere increase in the intensity of pain because, as we shall see, the modern problem of pain lies much deeper than in its magnitude.[69]

Another common explanation for the growing problem of pain is that it is not pain itself but our perception of it that has made the pain of dying an unbearable experience.[70] According to this interpretation, the growing sensitivity to pain is another instance of the "civilizing process" by which Western societies have become less comfortable with extreme experiences in general, and pain in particular. This thesis, thematized in Norbert Elias's famous civilizing-process argument, was already a common thought in the late nineteenth century.[71] In 1892, an article in a leading medical journal claimed that "in our process of being civilized we have won, I suspect, intensified capacity to suffer. The savage does not feel pain as we do: nor as we examine the descending scale of life do animals seem to have the acuteness of pain-sense at which we have arrived."[72]

Perhaps we have become more sensitive to pain. Indeed, it is not hard to imagine that an eighteenth-century Methodist who lived in a rural village had more frequent encounters with bodily suffering than a mid-nineteenth-century resident of an urban town who enjoyed the comforts of modern life. And, to continue this speculation, if both were afflicted by a similar disease, one may have suffered more than the other. But the modern problem of pain goes deeper than variation in degree and involves a more fundamental change in the place of pain in our world—so much so that one is tempted to say that pain itself, regardless of degree, became a problem and had to be eradicated, not merely alleviated.

Moreover the modern problem of pain, as we shall see, became manifest not merely in bodily sensitivity, but also in a growing cultural sensitivity to pain. Pain became a problem for the suffering body, but also for ethics, law, and medicine. This concern was reflected in the way life in general and a new way of dying in particular was designed to avoid it.

The Painless Death

With the advancement of medical knowledge and pain-relief medication, the suffering of the dying became a burning problem for laypeople such as Williams and Berlioz. Therefore, one might expect to find a similar concern, and perhaps an even higher awareness, among the medical profession. Yet, quite contrary to what one would assume, the chilling image of pain in dying reflected in popular culture contrasted starkly with the medical account of the very same phenomenon. Within the medical profession at the turn of the century, there was an almost unanimous opinion that dying was altogether painless!

In 1887, a British physician named William Munk published his book, *Euthanasia; or, Medical Treatment in Aid of an Easy Death.*[73] The dying, Munk claimed, suffer no pain. "The process of dying and the very act of death is but rarely and exceptionally attended by those severe bodily suf-ferings, which in popular belief are all but inseparable from it."[74]

Munk's belief was not merely an idiosyncrasy. In fact, most physicians of the time shared his opinion that death was not painful. Since no one who died could report back, the only reliable evidence came from those who faced death but eventually recovered. And indeed, to support the claim that dying is painless, a new genre of near-death experiences was develop-ing. The purpose of such accounts was to prove that those who faced death but were saved at the last moment did not suffer any pain.

One case, told in detail by Munk and others, is the story of Admiral Beaufort, who, as a youngster on board a ship in Portsmouth harbor, fell overboard. Unable to swim, he was soon exhausted by his struggles and sank below the surface. "From the moment that all exertion had ceased," recalled the admiral, "a calm feeling of the most perfect tranquility super-seded the previous tumultuous sensations—it might be called apathy, cer-tainly not resignation, for drowning no longer appeared to be an evil. I no longer thought of being rescued, nor was I in any bodily pain." Fortu-nately for him, after two long minutes, he was saved. Surprisingly, he re-called, "instead of being absolutely free from all bodily pain, as in my drowning state, I was now tortured by pain all over me."[75] As a rule, con-cluded Munk, the urgent symptoms of disease subside when the act of dying begins, "[a] pause in nature, as it were, seems to take place."[76]

Similar stories are told of the explorer David Livingstone, whose hand was devoured by a raging lion. He assured his listeners that "he had no fear or pain, and that his only feeling was one of intense curiousity as to which part of his body the lion would have next."[77]

Munk, as mentioned, was not the only physician of his time who at-tempted to uproot the common belief that dying was painful. In the first decade of the twentieth century, Sir William Osler, a leading physician of his time, conducted more systematic research to prove a similar point.[78] By studying the dying process of about five hundred patients, he demon-strated that only ninety showed evidence of pain or distress. Of the five hundred, Osler claimed, "the great majority gave no sign one way or the other; like their birth, their death was a sleep and a forgetting."[79]

Not only was death considered painless, but some physicians argued that death might even be pleasurable. "Even the death which is caused by violent means, as they are termed, by noxious vapours or gases, drowning, hanging, decapitation, may be not only painless, but pleasurable."[80]

There is something very striking in these accounts, not so much con-cerning the medical facts themselves, but rather in the picture of dying they attempt to portray. For Munk, Osler, and other physicians of the turn of the twentieth century, it became important to demonstrate that dying—popular beliefs and traditional wisdom notwithstanding—is painless by nature. To make such a bold claim, an ambiguous distinction had to be drawn between dying and illness, and the process of dying had to be confined to the very short span of time immediately preceding death. What, then, was the logic behind this highly dubious line of argument?[81] One thing seems clear, the conviction that dying was painless does not suggest that the pain of dying was not a problem but, on the contrary, proves how problematic the pain of dying had become.

Pain: Sense and Sensibility

It was hard to challenge the opinion that dying is painful, even if the claim is limited to the last hour of life, since such a belief was deeply anchored in Christian metaphysics.[82] Pain in general, and the pain of dying in particular, has had a privileged place within Christian belief. The belief in the redeeming virtues of pain, the idea that suffering individuals were closer to Christ, that their anguish could be offered in penitence for earthly sins, or even that God put only his elected few through terrible trials were all recurrent themes throughout Church literature.[83]

What was true about pain in general was especially true for the pain of dying. Recall the Methodists, for whom dying was the peak of life and a holy death marked a holy life. Dying was an intensified life experience, and the pain accompanying dying was therefore expected to be the most tormenting of all, as death was the moment when the soul was torn away from its corporeal body.

For Catholics especially, the suffering caused by pain should not be relieved because the patient had to maintain his lucidity until his confession could be heard and extreme unction was administered. This remained true (albeit for different reasons) within the Protestant tradition, which maintained very high, even if less ritualistic, demands on the dying person. A good death was not a painless death but one in which pain was suffered with resignation.

Even after pain was divorced from sin, evil, and punishment (what one, following Roselyne Rey, may call the demoralization and de-Christianization of pain), it could still have a purpose.[84] The medical profession found a justification for pain in the natural rather than supernatural world. Pain had a positive role: it was seen as a warning or an alarm signal, enabling one to feel one's existence and be alert to the dangers challenging the body. It

65

even functioned as a kind of advantage by diverting one away from a harmful lifestyle, warning of the approach of illness, and inviting a change before it was too late.

In the specific context of therapeutics, physicians treated pain as an instrument of diagnosis. Although at times it might be difficult to interpret the significance of pain, especially in the case of children, pain was seen as a symptom of a disease—as a sign of a pathological condition underlying it.[85] "Pain of itself," as an early nineteenth-century physician put it, "is not a disease, but only the effect of disease; its absence, when it ought to exist, is a greater proof of disease."[86]

Pain had other functions, as well. In addition to serving as an alarm, pain acted as an invaluable deterrent from experiments of a dangerous or injurious nature. Furthermore, the sense of pain helped create a condition of voluntary immobilization—an essential factor in bringing about a cure.

Yet it did not work to apply the apparent truths about pain in general to the pain of dying. When one is dying, there is no longer any need to alert the body to its condition. Thus, the pain and torment so commonly associated with dying were becoming more and more questionable. A new sense had to be given to pain—or else pain had to be eradicated. The medical profession now faced the question, To what extent could pain still be justified, shown to have a function in the natural order?

An article from 1899 titled "The Natural Right to a Natural Death" foreshadowed the contemporary right-to-die debate:

> The century which is about to close and whose children we are (for though we may share the life of the twentieth, its spirit we never can) has ennobled the world by bringing back the human mind to a more rational conception of God, and of his dealings with our race. One of the best results of this is that death has lost half its terrors for the present generation.[87]

The emergence of the scientific understanding of the death process made the pain of death unnecessary. Death was seen as a natural phenomenon; it had lost its enigmatic power. This is not to say that Americans stopped fearing the torments of hell—far from it—but from then on, death and dying could be viewed, and often were, as merely natural processes. Modern man, dressed in the white coat of the medical physician, could accept neither the agonizing pain of eternal damnation nor the pain of the deathbed.

To be sure, the belief that death could be painless was a very old one. The paradigm of such dying was *natural death*, a death of old age. The natural death was counterposed to death from violence, accident, or disease. It was conceived as eternal sleep, a painless slipping into death. Natural death was a gift bestowed on those who were most deserving or most fortunate. Painful death was the rule; natural death, the exception. A painless death was desired by many and so acquired the name "euthanasia"—literally, "a good death." As far back as the days of the Roman emperors, one may read of the desire for, and the rarity of, such a dying. As Suetonius, Augustus Caesar's historian, reported, "So often as he [Caesar Augustus] heard of a man that had a quicke passage, with little sense of paine, he wished for himselfe that Euthanasie."[88]

The new science of dying, however, transformed this ancient understanding. By claiming a common mechanism for all forms of death, it announced in effect that all deaths are natural (that is, according to the laws of pathology) and therefore painless. Important distinctions between the modes of dying were not overlooked, but the basic structure of dying had to transcend such distinctions. Whether caused by heart, lung, or brain failure, the underlying structure of dying remained the same. All dying proceeded in a sequence of three stages, the first of which was the disappearing of senses, then the delirium of the intellect, and finally the decline of heat generation and blood circulation.[89]

The age-old analogy between death and sleep changed in a very telling manner. The basic characteristics of sleep were ascribed to all modes of dying, not only to natural death.[90] Furthermore, the analogy of death to sleep did not merely expand but shifted. The crux of the analogy was not that death was akin to sleep but rather that dying was a *falling* asleep. And since both meant being unconscious, therefore both were painless.

> Death and sleep personified have been styled, poetically, twin sisters. You, as physicians, will soon learn how frequently death comes to the bedside with attractions not in the least less winning than those which make the visits of sleep so acceptable. The act of dying is not a state of physical anguish, but a state of absolute insensibility, or of pleasurable experiences.[91]

Finally, and perhaps most important, the relation between sleeping and dying was transformed from a poetic analogy into a scientific comparison. Several experiments on animals as well as observations about humans pointed out the close physiological affinities between sleep and death. It was now held that the phenomena of sleep and dying differed merely in "duration of enervation."[92] In light of the comparison with sleep, dying too was understood as a result of a loss of energy and a fading out.

Such a death [natural, from old age] occurs when the machine is actually worn out, has performed its perfect work, has run its allotted time without injury, break, or cessation, and is at last laid aside as no longer available.[93]

The traditional view that unnatural death could be caused not only by depletion but also by excessive stimulation seems to have given way to a more unified vision of death as exhaustion. Death was in fact considered as "an intense degree of debility." Even if dying was not as tranquil as sleep, it entailed a gradual loss of capacities.

[A]nd as sleep relieves us from the ordinary stimulants of the day, the insensibility thus induced, relieves us from the sufferings of the disease, which, although it is not, like sleep, preceded by the grateful feelings of repose, is preceded by a gradual diminution of those sufferings.[94]

The emerging image of dying was as a process of decay. The process of dying was depicted as a fading out. Dying took place in stages, and the dying person became less alive. Dying was often painless because it was nearly always preceded by a loss of consciousness. This view was connected with the strong notion that to live was to have pain, and that therefore the less one was alive, the less pain one felt.

There are striking differences between the Christian death, particularly the Methodist death, and the modern way of dying. In the modern version, death is no longer lived as a momentary triumph of mortals over their mortality, but is rather a shadow gradually pulling the dying patient into the darkness of sleep. The hour of dying, once a climatic moment of a culminating life, became an undignified departure, in which dying patients gradually lose their humanity.

In this scheme, pain was intelligible only as a sign of life and hope. As we saw in the case of the drowning admiral, pain receded when dying began and returned only if and when recovery became possible. Pain was a sign of life, and the pain of dying no longer made any sense. The problem of pain, therefore, was not intensity but intelligibility; not sensitivity but sensibility.[95] The emerging senselessness of pain forms the foundation by which the need for euthanasia can be understood. But before we return to the problem of euthanasia, it is worth noticing one interesting consequence of pain falling into senselessness.

The Phantom of Pain

Both theory and empirical observation led scientists of the nineteenth century to the firm conclusion that dying is painless. One question, however, remained unanswered: What should one make of the common belief that dying involved an insurmountable experience of pain? It was not merely a question of popular belief opposing scientific observation; this belief had its own logic and proof. Since death is often preceded by a long and painful illness, it was thought that the culmination of suffering occurs at the final moment, when respiration and pulsation cease. The last hour was perceived as a climax of pain, a supreme moment of suffering, both bodily and mental. It was often characterized (for what seemed a valid reason) as the "agony of death" and the "struggle for existence." Anyone who was present at a deathbed scene could hardly arrive at a different conclusion. The sight of the dying person and the patient's tormented body stood as irrefutable testimony to the suffering incurred. How could one ignore the evidence of pain manifested in the body of the dying, given the spasms, convulsions, restlessness, and tormented cries?

The emerging scientific view, rather than ignoring the horrifying sights of the deathbed, claimed the power to penetrate the mystifying clouds surrounding it. According to this view, beyond the mere appearance of pain and suffering lay the truth of scientific knowledge. "The nearer we approach the dying stage," proclaimed a leading Maine physician in 1891, "the more we throw upon it the light of science, the *less* we find of the bodily sufferings which in the popular belief are all but inseparable from it, and are emphasized in the terms 'mortal agony and death struggle.' "[96]

According to these nineteenth-century physicians, the common belief that dying was painful resulted from a misinterpretation of the phenomenon of dying. Correcting this misguided impression required a correct reading of the dying body, and a new semiology was developed for this purpose.

One needed very little imagination to infer from the bodily image of the dying the horrific pains accompanying death. One could see death approaching in the face of the dying. The nose sharp and pinched; the eyes hollow and sunk in the orbits; the ears pale, cold, shrunken, and with their lobes inverted; the face pallid, livid, or black—together these made up the celebrated *facies Hippocratica.*

To this frozen depiction, which captured the gloominess of the dying scene but fell short of conveying the suffering it seemed to involve, the modern physicians added a more animated, futuristic image:

[T]he glazed half-closed eye; the dropped jaw and open mouth; the blanched, cold and flaccid lip; cold clammy sweats on the head and neck; a hurried, shallow respiration on the one hand, or slow, stertorous breathing with rattle in the throat upon the other; a pulse irregular, *unequal*, weak and immeasurably frequent; the patient prostrate upon his back; and sliding down towards the foot of the bed; his arms and legs extended, naked, and tossed about in disorder; the hands waved languidly before the face, groping through empty air, fumbling with the sheets, or picking at the bedclothes.[97]

The scientific method was put to work, and the body was dissected by the scientific gaze. One by one, the minute movements of the body were taken apart and analyzed. Each movement had its own physiological logic, its own mechanical causation. Theoretically, at least, each one of these motions could be reproduced in a different context, which involved no pain.

For example, perhaps the most distressing of the dying phenomena are the convulsions. To isolate the convulsions from the dying process, one could show that similar convulsions occur at other times, and that in such cases they do not indicate pain. Epilepsy was a good example of precisely this point. The convulsions of epilepsy, which may persist for hours and seem most horrific to spectators, are not painful at all. Indeed, upon recovering from epileptic convulsions, the patient professes unconsciousness of all that has occurred. Furthermore, convulsions can be produced artificially, and such experiments also indicate no suffering of pain. Experiments on animals offered similar evidence. For instance, when a frog is decapitated it can be made to jump with considerable agility and precision, even without a head, leading to the inevitable conclusion that

convulsions, which so often attend the process of dying, are accepted in evidence of suffering, when in fact they are the reverse, for they imply a loss of consciousness and sensibility, and therefore, of the capacity to feel pain. They are automatic, and in all essential respects like the convulsions of epilepsy, of which the subject is wholly unconscious.[98]

The groans that accompany the convulsions—that is, the voice of the dying patient—were also discarded as proof of pain, for the same groans accompany the administration of ethereal vapor. In this case, the patients are unconscious not only of pain but even of their whole existence:

It may very rationally be asked if groaning and writhing of the body be not proof of suffering? No. In partial apoplexy groans are unconsciously uttered; and those who have groaned deeply when submitted to operation during the influence of aethereal vapour, have declared their utter unconsciousness of pain,—the sensation was often agreeable. Even the convulsive throes of the criminal on the gallows may be involuntary, and uncombined with consciousness.[99]

Likewise the sudden opening of the eyes:

Sometimes, immediately preceding the very act of death, the eyelids are raised, and a look of recognition of those around seems to be permitted to the dying man. . . . "It is consolatory to know," says Sir Charles Bell, "that this does not indicate suffering, but increasing insensibility."[100]

To sum up the picture:

The convulsive attempts at respiration, the twitching of the limbs and their tetanic stiffening, the clammy moisture, and the ashen hue, the dilating pupils, the rattle in the throat and the last long sigh or groan, are the mechanical changes of death only; quite without knowledge on the part of the dying, quite without pain, quite without all discomfort.[101]

Pain, which originally emerged from the unity of the bodily movements, had vanished. The body, reconstructed from its assembled parts, was a scientific proof that the whole was never more than the sum of its parts. The new body was a machine, an automaton, in which convulsions simply indicated the loss of nerve control, sighs and groans simply indicated the instinctive operation of the lungs, and pain indicated a failed communication that reached a deserted post.

When it occurs at death, it is probably simply the announcement that the manipulator, the controlling agency at the great central battery, the brain, has at last deserted its accustomed post, and that, as a consequence, the nerves are expending their little remaining energy without their leader in great disorder.[102]

It was an old belief, now no longer attainable, that the true suffering of the dying often exceeds its outward representations, for it may be too late for the victim to make known to surrounding spectators the true extent of the torment experienced. This belief was now reversed: the outward representation always *exceeded* the true suffering, because it was too late for the body to inform the brain of its tormented experience. "Possibly this cessation [of pain] may occur but a few moments before death, too late for any signal to that effect from the patient."[103]

Euthanasia and Killing Pain

We are now prepared to return to Williams's proposal and attempt to bridge the gap between the medical claim that dying was painless and the emerging concern among the laity with the pain of dying. Distinguishing between the lay understanding and the scientific gaze only partly explains the contrasting views about the pain involved in dying. While the early supporters of hastening death were nonphysicians, and while the medical profession was unanimous in believing that dying was painless, the problem of the pain of dying did not escape the medical profession. Even Osler could not help but notice that ninety of his five hundred patients did suffer from pain, and no physician would deny Berlioz's complaint that a dying process that lasted six months could be painful.

The problem of pain in dying, as perceived by most physicians around the turn of the twentieth century, was not its intensity but its very existence. The problem was how to make sense of pain and, consequently, how to reconcile the well-established medical claim that dying was painless with the occasional existence of pain in dying.

Munk explained that while dying is painless by nature, it may become painful because of physiological or pathological conditions that precede or accompany it. The role of the physician is to assure that any such suffering—which is always external and accidental to the dying process—is mitigated. Munk offered several methods for overcoming pain, but clearly the most effective is opium. In his eyes, opium is "worth all the rest of the *materia medica*."[104]

While physicians at the turn of the century rejected the Christian metaphysics of pain and dying, they were in fact proposing their own theodicy. The underlying assumption that governed the medical understanding and treatment of pain was that pain had a purpose and in general could be medically justified. Pain that served no function and could not be justified should not and could not exist. Unjustified pain was a medical enigma that carried its own rituals: namely, technological practices fit for removing pain.

Throughout the twentieth century, relieving the dying patient from the terrible torments of the deathbed has become not only the duty of the medical profession but even its true calling. In the words of Albert Schweitzer, "We must all die. But that I can save [a person] from days of torture, that is what I feel as my great and ever new privilege. Pain is a more terrible lord of mankind than even death himself."[105]

The suffering caused by dying became a paradigm of senseless pain, but this did not mean that physicians facing the dying remained powerless. True, medicine as a science could not explain the occurrence of pain at the deathbed, which is why the problem of pain was often ignored by the medical profession of the nineteenth century. Nevertheless, the limits of scientific understanding could not serve as an excuse for the lack of treatment. As one author wrote, "[O]ur inability to construct a perfect theory of Pain cannot be an apology for ignorance of known methods of coping with it. It is no shame that some of those methods are empirical; the question is, are they successful?"[106]

As in the case of hope in the face of hopelessness, here too we find the emergence of a technological drive that overcomes even the maxims of scientific knowledge. On the one hand, physicians as scientists have the vocation to understand pain, to treat it as a symptom of disease, and to use it as a means for diagnosing sickness. Since from a scientific point of view the pain accompanying dying made little sense, the conclusion drawn from medical knowledge was that dying was painless. This is not to say that physicians did not see that dying was often painful; but these cases, though statistically significant, were deemed by science as exceptional.

On the other hand, the vocation of physicians as practitioners was not to understand pain but to relieve it. While this distinction between science and technology was true in regard to pain in general, the pain of incurable diseases was what—for the first time in modern science—totally separated the question of relieving pain from the question of curing the disease. From a technological point of view, pain became a syndrome rather than a symptom. Pain became a disease in its own right. This meant that a technological drive to relieve pain could arise independently of the desire to cure the patient. In its extreme this led to the idea that the pain of the dying should be relieved, even if the price was hastening the death of the patient.

As distant as these two approaches may seem from each other, in the last instance both rest on the same grounds. Both are supplementary reactions to the same phenomenon: namely, the falling of pain into senselessness. It is the senselessness of the pain accompanying dying that, on the one hand, led the medical profession to conclude that dying could not be painful. And on the other hand, it was the very same senselessness that led to a growing intolerance to the pain of dying and a wish to eradicate such pain, even at the price of shortening life. Thus the senselessness of dying led both to the scientific assertion that dying *could not* be painful and to the technological call that it *should not* be painful.

Therefore, it should come as no surprise that in Williams's proposal to hasten the death of incurable patients, we find an attempt to reproduce a natural death, according to the new understanding of dying as a loss of vital powers, as a form of drowsiness. The use of anesthetics such as chloroform was designed to mechanically reproduce this ideal of natural death in which pain is no longer necessary, and therefore no longer bearable.[107] Pain became senseless precisely because the only sense that it had was given to it by the medical machinery aimed at annihilating it.

Legalizing Euthanasia: The Role of Law and the Rule of Technique

Introduction

THE PREVIOUS CHAPTER traced the emergence of euthanasia, the deliberate hastening of death, as a medical response to a crisis in the treatment of the dying patient. The hopelessness of cure and the meaningless suffering of pain led some physicians and laymen to promote euthanasia as a solution to the problem of dying. Euthanasia's origins are in the medical context, as a treatment of a medically defined condition. However, it did not remain within the confines of medical discourse and practice for long.

Soon after Samuel Williams, Lionel Tollemache, and other advocates proposed euthanasia as a medical treatment, the question of its legal status emerged. In 1906, the first attempts to legalize euthanasia took place in Ohio and Iowa. A further attempt to legalize euthanasia was made in Nebraska in 1937. In the following year, the first American euthanasia society was founded: the National Society for the Legalization of Euthanasia. This society, as its name suggests, set as its main objective the legalization of medically hastened death. The following two chapters will discuss in detail these early attempts to legalize euthanasia, along with their historical significance. Our aim is to understand what the emergence of euthanasia as a legal question entailed.

The move to legalize euthanasia may seem, at first, as the most obvious consequence of its emergence as a medical solution to the problem of dying. Since supporters of euthanasia viewed the practice not only as permissible but also as an undeniable duty of the medical profession, it was only natural that they would strive to revoke the legal ban on its practice. Legalization can be seen, from this point of view, merely as an attempt to remove the legal barrier that prevented physicians from performing medical euthanasia.

This account of legal intervention is lacking in several ways. First, it perceives law in *negative* terms, as an impediment, and overlooks the constructive role of law in the regulation of euthanasia. Second, it thinks of law as a *binary* system—either permitting or prohibiting the practice of euthanasia—ignoring the new and more intricate ways in which legal regulation operates. And finally, it views law as *external* to the medical practice of euthanasia, neglecting the ways in which the treatment of the dying patient became infused with legal concerns.[1]

As we shall see, the attempt to legalize euthanasia concerned more than removing the legal prohibition. Advocates of euthanasia assigned a constructive role to the law. Their effort was to devise a law that would set the conditions under which medical euthanasia could be administered. Such laws resembled bureaucratic (or administrative) guidelines and included forms to fill out, certificates to attain, schedules to meet, and other procedural requirements necessary to achieve the desired outcome: a well-regulated, quick, and painless death. Thus, proponents of euthanasia assigned a new role to the law, beyond its traditional judicial function to permit or prohibit certain acts. The new task of law was a medicolegal one and entailed regulating the treatment of the dying.

This move to regulate death by legalizing euthanasia should be understood in the broader context of legal reforms during the nineteenth century. As recent studies in American legal history have shown, the century was marked by the decline of the traditional common-law system and the rise of a new legal regime that was based on legislation rather than on precedent and on administration rather than on adjudication.[2] The new legislation served the emerging interest of the state in regulating a growing number of public domains, including public economy, public safety, and public health. It would be a mistake to think that these different spheres of public life were not ordered in some legal fashion before the move toward legislation. But the ordering under the common-law system differed dramatically from the newly emerging form of governance characteristic of the modern regulatory state. The common law was based on case-by-case adjudication, which lent to it an ad hoc character and a commitment to legal precedent that limited its capacity to transform and fundamentally reconstruct the social order. Not so with the modern regulatory state, which strives to restructure existing practice on the basis of new rationales and scientific knowledge, and aims to bring under its administration an expanding range of human conduct.[3]

One may wish to think of the deathbed at the turn of the twentieth century as a meeting point between law and medicine. At this encounter, both medicine and law transformed in a way that enabled a synthesis between the two, giving rise to a new medicolegal logic. This new constellation of science and law set the ground for the state to regulate the process of dying as one among many aspects of public health. To understand the significance of this historical moment in the development of euthanasia, it is essential to follow the different stages of this dialectic transformation of medicine and law: first, as we have done in the previous chapter, the shift within medicine and the rise of dying as a medical problem and euthanasia as its solution; second, a shift within law that will be explored in this chapter, entailing a movement away from common law toward an emerging medicolegal regime; and finally, in the chapter to follow, the combination of these two moments in the development of the state as regulator of public health. This development as a whole captures nothing other than the transition of dying from an art to a technique.

One final remark before we proceed. The attempts to legalize the medical hastening of death that we will examine in this chapter took place during the first decades of the twentieth century. These attempts—no more than a handful—failed. During the first half of the twentieth century in the United States, euthanasia remained an unfulfilled dream for a relatively small group of advocates, and a preposterous, at times horrifying, possibility for others. For most Americans euthanasia was simply not an issue, and for all practical purposes they viewed these early attempts as altogether insignificant.

True, these bills may seem at times as no more than figments of the legal imagination of one advocate or another. But it is precisely the way in which laws regulating euthanasia were imagined that is of interest for us. The limits of the law, here as elsewhere, are the limits of its imagination. And while the old euthanasia bills did not pass, new ones are formulated daily, sharing with the old proposals, if not the letter of the law, its spirit.

Euthanasia as Murder: The Problem of Translation

Early on it became clear to both advocates and opponents of euthanasia that the law was the main obstacle standing in the way of institutionalizing medical euthanasia. In 1879, reviewing the euthanasia debate, a leading medical journal concluded:

> The greatest difficulty [more than ethics or religion] was encountered in the legal aspects of the subject. According to all codes of civilized men, the law was distinct and clear, "thou shalt not kill." In the present state of society the practice of Euthanasia could only be regarded as the practice of murder. . . . Until there was a change in the laws and in society, there would be no possibility of making recommendations upon the practice of euthanasia.[4]

The legal status of euthanasia is stated here in clear and distinct terms. Euthanasia violates one of the most fundamental principles of the legal system: the sanctity of life, prohibiting the unjustified taking of human life in any form. Since from a legal point of view euthanasia is intentional and premeditated killing, it is, prima facie, murder. The scarce cases in which the taking of life is permitted or even commanded, such as in capital punishment and in war, seem to have nothing in common with euthanasia and, moreover, are probably as old as the prohibition itself.

As much as it was clear that euthanasia was illegal under the common-law tradition, it was equally clear that this obstacle could be overcome. True, the criminal-law tradition that banned euthanasia was centuries old; but legislation could override tradition, and the legislator could, if he so wished, change the law. One of the first American jurists to discuss the possibility of legalizing euthanasia was Clark Bell. Though not supporting euthanasia, he pointed out that

[u]nder our civilization, no power is given by the law to end even such a life [stricken with a suspension of all the faculties of consciousness, living on, unconscious of suffering, or of the value of life], but the inherent right of society to regulate its affairs, in its own best interests, must be conceded to be broad enough, to justify any legal enactment . . . authorizing the termination of human life in such cases.[5]

These accounts portray a clear, perhaps even trivial, relation between euthanasia and the law. Simply stated, euthanasia is prohibited under existing law, but it can be legalized with proper action. Two premises seem to be at work here. First is the proposition grounding the prohibition: namely, that euthanasia is murder. Second is the assumption grounding its legalization: namely, that legal intervention is no more than the removal of a legal barrier. Yet what at first might seem (and in fact appeared) to euthanasia advocates and opponents as a simple matter turned out to be a much thornier predicament.

What is at stake in understanding the legal controversy and struggle over euthanasia is the need to realize the complexity of these two aspects— the legal prohibition of euthanasia and the significance of legal intervention. In particular, we need to take into account the ways in which both these aspects were undergoing important historical changes precisely at the time that euthanasia was emerging as a social and legal concern. The first part of this chapter adds layers of complexity to the overly simplistic understanding of euthanasia as murder, by showing historical transformations in the legal guardianship of life. The second part addresses the question of legal intervention and the specific role of law in the institutionalization of euthanasia.

We begin by asking how is it that law, more than religion and medical ethics, posed the "most difficult" problem regarding the regulation of euthanasia? Any answer to this question will also shed light on why the law became the central arena in which the euthanasia struggle took place.

Religion clearly posed a challenge to the institutionalization of euthanasia. And though the religious objections were often more vocal than their legal counterparts, the binding force of religion on society was less compelling.[6] Advocates of euthanasia, as well as many opponents, viewed religious arguments as parochial, both because they did not fit the changing times—specifically, the advancement of science and medical practice—and because they depended on accepting the premises of faith, which were not shared by all and therefore could not serve as a basis for policy making.[7]

Medical objections, on the other hand, while having the aura of expertise and the support of modern science, were much less unequivocal about euthanasia. The medical profession was divided within itself. While most members of the medical profession objected to the institutionalization of the practice, others (as we have seen) gave it full support. Within medicine there was much more room to discuss the possible benefits of euthanasia and to weigh them against its dangers. Even if euthanasia was not accepted by physicians, the problem it meant to solve, as well as the logic underlying this solution, was all too familiar to the medical profession.

From the legal point of view, the circumstances that made the shortening of life at least an arguably justified medical procedure were, in principle, invalid. For the physician, the practice of euthanasia could be justified on the following grounds: since the patient is hopelessly dying, there is nothing the physician can do to prolong life. The obligation of the physician to prolong life is therefore removed. Furthermore, since the patient is suffering from excruciating pain, the physician has the responsibility to relieve such suffering using all available means. The result is the medical hastening of death. While from a medical point of view, euthanasia could mean little more than a final act of palliative care, from a legal perspective it was no different from murder. The law's verdict on the matter was unequivocal.

Criminal law, as it had developed in the common-law tradition, made no distinction between the life of a dying patient and any other human life. Shortening life by a few minutes or by a few years was equally considered murder. Moreover, the fact that the patient was suffering from intolerable pain could serve as no justification for the action, since motivation under common law could only affect the severity of punishment, not culpability itself. The medical responsibility to seek the relief of pain could not legally justify shortening the life of a dying patient.[8]

The medical understanding of euthanasia was initially untranslatable into legal terms; the language of euthanasia appeared alien to the legal mind. If euthanasia were to be considered as anything other than murder, it would have to be redefined using the appropriate legal vocabulary that would distinguish euthanasia from ordinary killing. Legalizing euthanasia was therefore more complicated than merely allowing the practice to take place; it involved the struggle to translate the medical dialect of "diagnosis" and "prognosis" into the legal language of "rules" and "justifications."

Euthanasia as Suicide: From Sanctifying Life to Governing Death

The question underlying the legalization of euthanasia was whether it could be distinguished from ordinary murder. The first legal attempt to justify the practice of euthanasia was based on the argument that euthanasia is a specific case of the more general problem of suicide. Supporters of euthanasia emphasized the patient's wish to die, and the physician was construed as merely assisting the patient in the fulfillment of his wish. Euthanasia, accordingly, would not be murder but a particular way of committing suicide. The legitimacy of the first would then depend on that of the latter. While Williams's original proposal did not mention suicide, one of the very early reviews of the essay by Dr. Tollemache praised the proposal by describing it as an attempt to "legalize suicide by proxy." Moreover, Tollemache believed that Williams's proposal could have been stronger if he had advocated the more general "legalizability of suicide."[9] Therefore, the move to legalize euthanasia was tied up from its very inception with the legality of suicide.

Similarly, a leading legal scholar and a prominent member of one of the medical-legal societies defended euthanasia and suicide in the same breath:

> I believe that there are cases in which suicide is morally justifiable, and that there are also cases in which the ending of human life, by physicians, is not only morally right, but an act of humanity. I refer to cases of absolutely known incurable, fatal and agonizing disease or condition, where death is certain, and necessarily attended by excruciating pain; where it is the wish of the victim that a deadly drug should be administered to end his life and terminate his irremediable suffering.[10]

The linking of euthanasia to suicide was especially important, since the legal status of suicide underwent gradual change throughout the nineteenth century.[11] Suicide, which was considered a crime for many centuries, was slowly losing its criminal character. Thus suicide seemed to be a particularly appealing venue for grounding the legality of euthanasia. The decriminalization of suicide suggested that not every taking of human life would be considered murder.

C. J. Bond, a committed supporter of euthanasia, recognized the relevance of this change in the legal and social approach to suicide to the struggle of euthanasia. Discussing this change, he says,

> I mention these facts now because they have an important bearing on our present movement to place Voluntary Euthanasia on a sound legal basis. In fact without this change in public opinion any such movement would have been impracticable today.[12]

Juxtaposing euthanasia to suicide was more than a scholastic exercise. It raised a fundamental question regarding the grounds of the legal objection to euthanasia. The prohibition on euthanasia could no longer be stated in the simple terms of the sanctity of life, because that principle no longer governed the legal status of suicide. Even if euthanasia and suicide were not precisely the same, on what basis could the law continue to object to euthanasia while removing its ban from suicide? To understand the new grounds for the legal objection to euthanasia, we must undertake a deeper examination of the historical transformation of suicide.

Suicide was a crime under common law up to the nineteenth century. It was treated like any other crime and was punishable even when successfully performed. Bracton, one of the earlier common-law scholars who wrote in the thirteenth century, mentions two such punishments.[13] First, there was the financial sanction of forfeiture to the king of possessions held by the person who had committed suicide. In applying fiscal sanctions to suicide, the law treated suicide like many other crimes against the crown. However, a second punishment applied uniquely to the case of suicide. This punishment was to mutilate the body by driving a stake through it and then burying it at a crossroad. These sanctions were practiced throughout the eighteenth century and were still on the books during the first part of the nineteenth century.

Initially, Bracton seems to have drawn distinctions between different forms of suicide, depending on their motivation. While ordinary suicide, and especially suicide done with the purpose of escaping trial, was punished by the confiscation of all property, Bracton distinguishes the case in which "a man slays himself in weariness of life or because he is unwilling to endure further bodily pain." In the latter case "he may have a successor. But his movable goods are confiscated. He does not lose his inheritance only his movable goods."[14] The punishment in such cases was limited to personal property, whereas real property did go to the heirs.

However, this distinction was dropped in later centuries, and the more limited punishment was applied to all cases of sane suicide. As a rule, which persisted throughout the centuries, all suicides were treated equally. The only significant exception to this rule was the case of suicide driven by insanity. The suicide of the insane was not considered a crime, and for all practical purposes it was treated as a natural death. The law in the early American colonies was not different from that practiced in Britain, and here too suicide was considered a severely punishable crime up to the eighteenth century.

The original prohibition against suicide was grounded on the presupposition that suicide was an act of self-murder. The same logic that prohibited the taking of another's life applied to the taking of one's own. Suicide was known as the act of *felo-de-se*, a felony against oneself. "Just as a man may commit felony in slaying another," Bracton explained, "so he may in slaying himself." William Blackstone, in his *Commentaries on the Laws of England*, considered the offense an act against both God and crown—both a spiritual and a temporal offense. "Like God in the spiritual realm," wrote Blackstone, "the king in the temporal one, is sovereign, and man may not abandon his post and rush away unordered."[15]

Life belonged not to the individual subjects but to the king and to God. From the point of view of sovereignty, there is no difference between suicide and murder; in both cases, the sovereign's power over life is challenged. To name this care for life "the sanctity of life" is quite misleading. The law did not protect human life *qua* life; on the contrary, life was quite dispensable. This may explain the apparent paradox that legal historians have detected in English law: namely, that during the very period when it priced human life at the cheapest rate—by punishing theft with the gallows—it ranked self-murder among the highest crimes and punished it with about the same indignities as treason. Far from being an anomaly, this legal treatment manifests clearly that the concern with suicide was not about preserving all human life but only about maintaining the prerogative of the sovereign over life and death.

Gradually, however, the punishments inflicted were moderated. In 1701, Pennsylvania became the first to depart clearly from the common-law tradition by abolishing forfeiture as punishment for suicide. This position spread throughout most of the colonies by the end of the century.[16] Suicide, however, was still a crime in most states at the end of the eighteenth century. Blackstone admits that the laws of suicide may be too extreme, but still mentions them as valid law. On the other hand, Zephaniah Swift, who later became the chief justice of Connecticut, was much more critical. Speaking of the more modern approach to suicide, he wrote:

> There can be no act more contemptible, than to attempt to punish an offender for a crime, by exercising a mean act of revenge upon his lifeless clay, that is insensible of the punishment. There can be no greater cruelty, than the inflicting a punishment, as the forfeiture of goods, which must fall solely on the innocent offspring of the offender.[17]

And yet, Swift admitted that suicide was a crime:

> Indeed, this crime is so abhorrent to the feelings of mankind, and that strong love of life which is implanted in the human heart, that it cannot be so frequently committed, as to become dangerous to society.[18]

In the course of the nineteenth century, ignominious burial was also abolished. But although suicide was no longer punishable, for a while it was still considered a crime. However, this anomalous condition did not persist for long, and soon thereafter the crime as well as the punishment was entirely dropped out of the law books.[19]

That the law no longer understood suicide to be a crime did not mean that suicide became socially legitimate.[20] To the contrary, as the criminality of suicide was subsiding, the deviant nature of the act persisted. While it was no longer prohibited under the law, it became suspect in the eyes of the human sciences. For example, suicide was often considered an act of insanity, and those who attempted suicide were treated as insane and were often locked up in asylums to cure them of their destructive impulses.[21] Consequently, the legal status of suicide reemerged as a problem. Did the law merely decriminalize suicide, that is, remove the negative prohibition on suicide? Or did the law positively protect the right to perform suicide? Very tellingly, the question of the positive legitimacy of suicide was now tied to the question of whether suicide could ever be a rational act.

In 1895, an article appropriately titled "The Right to Commit Suicide" argued:

> Suicide is frequently a consequence of a species of insanity, particularly melancholia, but it is not necessarily a positive proof of a diseased mind. It is, therefore, unjust in many cases to declare the suicide a

lunatic, and while it may greatly benefit the relatives of the unfortunate as far as provisions through life insurance policies are concerned, to insist on this view and bless the law for it, it is certainly not proper for the thinker to admit it.[22]

The right to commit suicide became dependent on the rationality of suicide. The prevailing view was that not all suicides should be seen as illegitimate, only those that stemmed from irrational motivations. This new approach to the problem of suicide was, in an important way, diametrically opposed to the older legal tradition expressed by Blackstone. The latter, discussing the conditions for suicide to be a crime, wrote:

> The party must be of years of discretion and in his senses, else it is no crime. But this excuse ought not to be strained to that length to which our coroner's juries are apt to carry it, viz.: that the very act of suicide is an evidence of insanity; as if every man who acts contrary to reason, had no reason at all; for the same argument would prove every other criminal *non compos*, as well as the self-murderer. The law very rationally judges, that every melancholy or hypochondriac fit does not deprive a man of the capacity of discovering right from wrong, which is necessary to form a legal excuse. And therefore, if a real lunatic kills himself in a lucid interval he is a *felo de se* as much as another man.[23]

While for G. Boehm, a legal scholar of the nineteenth century, suicide is socially legitimate only if it is rational, for Blackstone, almost to the contrary, it is illegal and illegitimate only if it is rational. This historical reversal makes sense only if we understand the different kinds of problems that suicide posed.

Under the old legal regime, suicide that was committed while the person was of sound mind was viewed as a threat to sovereignty both temporal and divine, since it was performed in defiance of the crown. The suicide of the insane, on the other hand, could be treated with forgiveness.[24] However, with the decline of sovereignty—not only as a political form but, more important, as a way of perceiving the legal order and threats to it—suicide posed a new challenge to the social order. But this time the challenge was not to sovereignty but rather to the rational organization of society. It was therefore irrational suicide that now posed the greater threat.[25]

The shift in the conceptualization of suicide from a challenge to the sovereign's right over death to a problem of rational and scientific governance of life has been explored by one of the most insightful thinkers of modern times, Michel Foucault:

It is not surprising that suicide—once a crime, since it was a way to usurp the power of death which the sovereign alone, whether the one here below or the Lord above, had the right to exercise—became, in the course of the nineteenth century, one of the first conducts to enter into the sphere of sociological analysis. . . . This determination to die, strange and yet so persistent and constant in its manifestations, and consequently so difficult to explain as being due to particular circumstances or individual accidents, was one of the first astonishments of a society in which political power has assigned itself the task of administering life.[26]

The new concern with suicide had little to do with its offense against sovereignty, and much more to do with its offense against the rational order of society. The new legal and social question that the practice posed was not so much how to punish rational suicide but how to prevent irrational suicide. Suicide that could be rationally explained was less threatening and therefore more easily acceptable than suicide that had no rational or possible explanation. The more rational the suicide, the more likely for it to be socially and legally acceptable. The possibility of euthanasia becoming legal depended, therefore, on proving its rational grounds.

Euthanasia as Assisted Suicide: Preventing Abuse

Euthanasia could not be considered as a simple case of murder. The patient was not killed or preyed upon: he wished to die, and therefore it was more plausible to think of euthanasia as suicide. While in this respect euthanasia was closer to suicide than murder, in other respects it was not. The most important difference from a legal standpoint was that euthanasia was not self-administered but rather involved the intervention of another party, a physician. Opponents of euthanasia emphasized this distinction, allowing the *Journal of the American Medical Association* to defend the practice of suicide but strongly oppose the practice of euthanasia, as follows:

We may excuse the person who commits suicide to avoid inevitable torture or dishonor, but we can not justify in any way the physician who deliberately cuts short his patient's existence under any conditions whatever.[27]

The involvement of a second party in the performance of euthanasia allowed euthanasia to be thought of as akin to the practice of assisted suicide.[28] In both cases a second party is involved in performing the act, and the legal question regards this involvement. The question, then, was how would the decriminalization of suicide affect the practice of assisted suicide and, consequently, the practice of euthanasia? Not surprisingly, with the gradual decriminalization of suicide, the unlawfulness of assisting in the suicide was brought into question.[29] Following the formal logic of common-law reasoning, it was thought that decriminalizing suicide as the principal offense would lead to the decriminalization of the dependent crime of assisted suicide. Yet, while the law loosened its grip on the problem of suicide, it insisted on maintaining the criminal status of assisted suicide.

To maintain assisted suicide as a crime, a special intervention from the legislature became necessary. And indeed, in many states such laws were passed. Therefore, side by side with the disappearance of laws prohibiting the practice of suicide, new laws emerged prohibiting the practice of assisted suicide. This raises the obvious question: on what grounds would assisted suicide be prohibited when suicide itself was no longer a crime? Why did the law wish to guard the person committing suicide from the person who would assist in fulfilling that wish? The answer cannot simply be that the law wanted to prevent such a death, for suicide itself was not prohibited. What, then, was the law attempting to prevent? In other words, what was the danger of assisted suicide (or euthanasia, for that matter) if suicide itself was not a crime?

One possible fear, and perhaps the most essential one, was that the involvement of another person in the performance of the suicide would lead to possible abuse.[30] It would allow dying patients to be coerced into a death they did not truly wish to undergo. The involvement of another person in the action would allow for a coerced death that would merely have the appearance of suicide. This would clearly undermine the only possible justification for suicide, which was that it was coming out of someone's rational wish to die, by that person alone. And indeed, this was precisely one of the challenges that opponents of euthanasia raised.

This fear of abuse was demonstrated by the following case, which was introduced to the public debate by opponents of euthanasia:

An old man, very wealthy, is suffering from an acute attack of peritonitis. He has an unlawful child to whom he thinks to bequeath his estate. He also has a nephew who is nursing him, and who is aware of that fact. This nephew is very anxious to possess himself of this old man's estate. Something must be done to prevent the old man from carrying out his intentions. The attending physician is a poor man. The nephew offers him a thousand dollars to apply euthanasia. The physician yields to the temptation.[31]

The fear of abuse was particularly worrisome given the condition of the patient. "It would be unpleasantly easy for a wife who wanted to get rid of her husband, to put an end to the unfortunate person's existence, and to set up the theory that she had acted only by the express desire of the invalid." After all, "Dead men tell no tales."[32]

According to this account, the role of the law in prohibiting euthanasia was not to protect the sanctity of life—nor even to preserve the life of dying patients as such—but rather to prevent abuse. As one of the opponents of legalizing euthanasia explained, "Human beings are weak; temptations are great. Should law be silenced on this point? Some physicians might, under the pretense of doing a merciful act, really commit a deed of felony."[33] The problem of euthanasia became a problem of regulating the practice in a way that would prevent abuses. Opponents of euthanasia believed that the law could not prevent such abuse, and therefore such form of assisted suicide should not be legalized, while proponents of euthanasia, as will appear, believed that the law had the power to regulate the practice.

The decriminalization of suicide, on the one hand, and the reenactment of assisting suicide as criminal, on the other, points to a shift in the law's response to a self-wished death. In the move from common law to a regulatory regime, the role of law was reimagined. Law's mission was no longer simply to prevent such a death but to regulate it, that is, to determine how suicide attempts should be treated and under what precise conditions suicide can be tolerated. Once the goal of the law became regulation more than protection, suicide lost its criminal character. There were other, nonlegal and more efficient ways to regulate and prevent suicide. On the other hand, since the law's new role was concern with preventing abuses, assisting suicide was prohibited as an independent crime.

It is now clear that the legal status of euthanasia involved more than the simple prohibition on the taking of life. In the case of self-wished death, this principle was changing, and emphasis was increasingly put on regulating such desires rather than on preventing the act itself. The encounter of law with euthanasia bore the marks of this change. But this did not mean that euthanasia became lawful, only that the grounds for its unlawfulness had changed.

It was no longer possible to object to euthanasia on the traditional basis of taking human life—that is, as an offense against the sovereign, this-worldly or other. But neither was it possible to simply justify euthanasia as an act of suicide. There were two reasons for this. First, euthanasia was not suicide—it involved the help of another person, the physician, which made euthanasia closer to murder than to suicide. Second, even if euthanasia were understood as a form of suicide, it would still be open to social, if not legal, objections to its practice. The fear of irrational and unregulated suicides posed a great threat to the social and legal order. The attempt, therefore, to justify euthanasia by contrasting it with murder and drawing out its similarities to suicide or even assisted suicide, in the last instance, failed. How then could euthanasia be justified?

Thus, the prohibition on euthanasia was not simply the traditional legal prohibition of taking life but rather stemmed from the fear of an unregulated medical practice. Similarly, the legal intervention devised to solve the challenge called for more than a mere removal of the legal barrier. The new legislation had to become part of the medical practice and redesign it from within. The remainder of this chapter deals with the attempt to legalize euthanasia and emphasizes the positive role that law played in legitimizing the practice. The legalization of euthanasia depended on the possibility of overcoming the objections and threats posed by the institutionalization of suicide, on the one hand, and by assisted suicide, on the other: namely, the fear that patients would not truly wish to die, either because they were not in their right senses or because they were coerced into it by other parties.

Euthanasia as Medical Treatment: The Regulation of Technique

In the final instance, the similarities between euthanasia and assisted suicide worked against euthanasia advocates. The same fear of abuse that prompted laws against assisted suicide would prevent euthanasia from becoming lawful. But there also were differences between euthanasia and assisted suicide, and advocates of euthanasia believed they could employ these differences to their advantage. What proponents of euthanasia chose to emphasize was the medical context out of which euthanasia emerged. After all, proponents of the practice argued, euthanasia did not emerge primarily from a personal desire to bring one's life to an end, nor from the desire of relatives or physicians to murder the dying patient, but rather from a more calculated and institutional decision following the logic of medical practice. Euthanasia was not only (or necessarily) a form of self-determined death but also (or rather) a form of medical treatment. Euthanasia, according to this account, was much more about the emergence of a new medical procedure regulating the dying process than about assisted suicide. The force of the argument was that euthanasia was a rational form of suicide or, even more radically, that euthanasia was not suicide at all but rather a medical treatment that should not be seen as a taking of life.

S. R. Wells, an advocate of euthanasia, addressed this point succinctly when he explained: "[W]hat is advocated here is not suicide in the ordinary sense of the term, but self-destruction as a result of outside advice." Then, comparing medical euthanasia to Sir Thomas More's discussion of euthanasia in his *Utopia*, Wells concluded that modern advocates of euthanasia simply wish to replace More's priests and magistrates with the medical doctor. Summing up his ideal of euthanasia as a medical-bureaucratic service, Wells concluded, "the responsible choice ultimately rests with the medical attendant, who, if the practice became recognized, would in this respect become the officer of the State."[34]

In a similar fashion, C. J. Bond argued that euthanasia should be viewed as a medical act and should not be seen as murder. The doctor performing euthanasia, argued Bond, should not be labeled a "public executioner":

> The doctor should be compared rather with the anaesthetist. The anaesthetist specializes in the art of preventing pain by inducing insensitivity to pain. In like manner, a doctor who assists his patient to end his sufferings by euthanasia acts as an anaesthetist, the difference being that the relief he gives is permanent and not merely temporary.[35]

We can understand the logic underlying the attempt to reexamine the legal status of euthanasia, even if proponents of euthanasia did not formulate their thoughts precisely in this way. The legal hurdles that euthanasia was facing, which we explored earlier in this chapter, had to do with trying to understand euthanasia in legal terms—a way of thinking that was foreign to the nature of the practice itself. Euthanasia was not murder. Neither was it an act of suicide, or even a case of assisted suicide. All these attempts to characterize euthanasia were bound to fail, because they were legal abstractions of what euthanasia truly was—a medical practice. To legalize euthanasia, proponents of euthanasia would have to incorporate into the law the medical logic that gave rise to the practice. Law, in other words, would have to defer to the authority of medicine.

This is not to say that euthanasia supporters did not take seriously law's role in the institutionalization of euthanasia. However, it did suggest a shift of balance to the extent that law would adapt to the logic of medical technique, rather than the other way around. In their eyes, law would no longer be at the position of determining whether euthanasia was right or wrong; its role would now be limited to the regulation of the medical practice. Advocates visualized law as part of the institutionalization of euthanasia, no longer in its traditional capacity of determining moral right from wrong but rather in its new capacity as regulating medical practice. Such a regulation became necessary because of the dangers of abuse (to which the opponents of euthanasia were adamantly pointing). Even proponents of euthanasia did not deny the possibility of abuse but argued instead that the legal regulation of euthanasia would guard against such abuses. Law, in their eyes, was becoming the guardian of medical technique.

But why was it necessary to legally regulate euthanasia? Why was there a need to regulate this medical procedure more than any other procedure? Could not professional medical ethics perform the role of positive law?

Clearly, there was something about euthanasia that was unsettling from the medical point of view and that prevented the medical profession from regulating the practice on its own. The problem was not merely that human life was at stake in the practice of euthanasia and that the taking of human life could not be left to medical decision. This was only part of the problem. Nor was the problem that the medical profession was not responsible enough to make decisions regarding euthanasia. The true problem was that the medical profession had no tools with which to make such a decision on its own. The logic of medical technique could not in itself determine under what precise circumstances euthanasia should be given. The internal logic of the practice of euthanasia left the question as to the conditions of its applications unsettled.

This problem was acknowledged by both supporters and opponents of euthanasia. On the supporters' side, Dr. Tollemache admitted:

Either we are bound, in all possible ways, to stretch to the utmost the elastic thread of life, or we are not. If we are so bound, nearly all of us are guilty of great wickedness. But, if there are any limits to this duty, human reason must be the judge of those limits, and human welfare must be their test. In other words, the question of euthanasia should not be theologically prejudged, but should be discussed on purely social grounds.[36]

Medical technique is portrayed by Tollemache as having an almost unlimited capacity to prolong life. True, such a portrayal would be an exaggeration of the true powers of technique at the time, but the growing capacity of technique to prolong life independent of the well-being of the patient became a reality. Once science had the power to artificially prolong life, there was no longer any justification to speak of the "natural course of a disease" or "natural death" as guiding medical decision.

The time of death became in part subject to human will, and was no longer exclusively a question of human fate. And since it was clear that at times attempting to prolong life would only create more suffering, the question was how to decide when medical therapy should conclude and euthanasia begin. This question could not be determined from within the logic of medical technique, because it was in fact a question regarding the limits of medical technique. Thus law, through its agents, legal experts, and legal codes, was called in to make the decision medicine, through its agents, medical experts and medical ethics, could not make on its own.

Some contemporaries argued with Tollemache and insisted on drawing a distinction between withdrawal of medical treatment and actively hastening death:

> To give medical men such a power would be of very doubtful benefit. . . . A distinction may, however, profitably be drawn between directly hastening death and desisting from the effort to prolong life when this can only mean protraction of agony. In such cases the doctor may, without blame, act in the spirit of Kent's entreaty for poor dying Lear:
>
> > Oh, let him pass! He hates him
> > That would upon the rack of this tough world
> > Stretch him out longer."[37]

But the question is not how convincing Tollemache's argument was, but rather the logic underlying it. There was a danger in allowing medical treatment to prolong life beyond reasonable measure, and it was the role of reason and law to draw the line where medicine itself could not. Law therefore entered the picture as the mechanism, which was responsible for limiting the power of medical technique.

Opponents of euthanasia pointed to the same problem even more sharply, drawing opposite conclusions. Precisely because there was no way to draw a clear line between the acceptable practice of euthanasia and its opposite, they believed that euthanasia should not be legalized. This danger of abuse, referred to today as the "slippery-slope argument," was presented at the time as the "wedge argument."

The fear of abuse here was no longer the fear of abuse discussed earlier, stemming from the corruption of the individual will, that is, the fear that relatives of the dying patient would not be able to overcome monetary and other temptations. Rather it was a fear that the practice itself, not its practitioner, was liable to being abused. This fear of abuse, which pervades the euthanasia literature, was captured in the remark, "Should the portals to the application of euthanasia be open, there is hard telling at what stage they would close."[38]

A similar concern was stated by a committee appointed by the South Carolina Medical Association to report on the subject of euthanasia in its various aspects. In this report, Dr. J.F.M. Geddings stated that while, morally, "humanity might be entitled to the same mercy accorded the brute creation, and have its death artificially hastened to relieve it from an agony which could only end in dissolution," yet, "should the door be opened to such practice, it would lead to manifold horrible abuses."[39]

Thus, euthanasia was attacked primarily on the grounds of the danger of nonconsensual euthanasia. The argument was that the same rule would be applied to people suffering from paralysis and unable to talk:[40]

[O]nce allow that such things may be done with due precautions, and the precautions will soon be neglected as troublesome formalities. Why bother the doctor and the parson, why ask the sick man's consent, when the case is so clear?[41]

In a similar vein, Dr. Wells, speaking before the Medico-Legal Society of London, asked his listeners to consider the "terrible dangers of abuse." And to illustrate the danger, he brought up the following hypothetical situation:

Plague, for instance, invades a country; it is thought justifiable to destroy the hopeless case. Where should we stop? Why not destroy all the infected? Surely they are a great danger to the community. . . . Why not treat men as we do pigs when an epidemic of swine fever breaks out? Is not destruction of the infected animals found to be the most effective way of stamping out the disease? Surely in times of panic we should hear sentiments such as these expressed, and how could we answer them if we had once given away the central principle?[42]

The most important point about most objections to the practice of euthanasia is that its opponents were not arguing that euthanasia was in itself wrong but emphasized the unintended negative consequence that legalizing euthanasia might have. That the main objection to euthanasia was the fear of abuse, stated as a fear of a slippery slope, is quite revealing. It suggests, for one thing, that euthanasia in itself was not objectionable. Furthermore, for both opponents and proponents of euthanasia, the purpose of the law was to prevent abuses, not to determine whether the practice itself was legally acceptable.

Treating euthanasia in such a way meant that the law was no longer imagined as claiming the power to determine "on its own terms" the legality of euthanasia and had to defer to the reasoning of the medical profession and public opinion. This important shift represents the law giving in to the logic of technique. The new role of the law in the regulation of technique was reflected in the first euthanasia bills that emphasized the need to prevent abuse.

The First Euthanasia Bill

In the early years of the twentieth century, the debates on the legal status of euthanasia progressed into actual attempts to legalize the practice. Proponents of legislation sought a legal change that would not only allow the practice to take place but also regulate it, that would not only remove the prohibition against euthanasia but also make clear under what circumstances it may take place. The power of the law was imagined as constitutive and formative, not only preventive and nay-saying.[43] How the law transformed to face this challenge is the question before us now.

Before we enter into the discussion of legalization, it is important that we not take for granted the very possibility of legal intervention. True, there was nothing new about the power of legislative codes to overrule existing law. But in the nineteenth and twentieth centuries, the balance of power between judge-made common law and statutory law reversed. Whereas judge-made common law had been the primary source of law, legislation overcame it as the main source of law during this period.[44]

The first attempt to legalize the medical hastening of death was launched in the Ohio legislature in the winter of 1906.[45] This first bill, like the first euthanasia proposal, was drafted by a layperson, Anne S. Hall of Cincinnati, whose call for legalized euthanasia was motivated by the experience of her mother's death. Hall regretted the fact that chloroform could not be used to ease the final suffering of her cancer-ridden mother. The importance of this formative experience notwithstanding, Hall's proposal only put into legal words notions that were already prevalent in America's public discourse. The bill received a great deal of publicity thanks to the support of the famous Dr. Charles Norton, a former Harvard professor and a man of letters. Dr. Norton was best known for his highly praised translation of Dante's *Divine Comedy*.

The bill was introduced into the Ohio legislature on January 23, on behalf of Anne S. Hall. The bill was titled "Concerning administration of drugs, etc., to mortally injured or diseased person." This apparently was the first euthanasia bill ever introduced to a legislature in an English-speaking country. The bill stated:

> [W]hen a person of legal age and sound mind is fatally hurt, or so ill that recovery is impossible, or is suffering great physical pain without hope of relief, his physician, if not a relative or interested in the person's estate, may ask him or her, in the presence of three witnesses, if he or she wants to be killed. If the answer is affirmative three other physicians are to be called in, and if they agree that the case is hopeless, they are to proceed to do the job in a neat and convenient way. . . . [46]

This bill placed the euthanasia initiative on the physician. The physician is allowed to offer the patient death as a medical treatment, and the patient may choose to accept or decline it. While the consent of the patient is required, the language of the bill reveals that the legitimacy of the practice stemmed primarily from its medical logic rather than from patient autonomy.

Another interesting feature of the 1906 bill is that it offered medical euthanasia to three different categories of patients: (1) a person who is fatally hurt (for example, through an accident); (2) a patient who is irrecoverably ill (from a disease); and (3) any person suffering from pain without hope of recovery. What all three groups share is the notion of an irreversible, fatal state of suffering. The two dimensions of hopelessness and painfulness discussed in Williams's earlier proposal are repeated here as conditions sine qua non.

When the bill was introduced before the legislature, an opponent of the bill, a Mr. Hill, moved that the bill be rejected. However, his motion was defeated by seventy-nine votes to nineteen, and the bill was read for the first time. The following day, the bill was referred to the legislature's committee on medical jurisprudence. Yet when the bill was finally voted on, it failed by a vote of twenty-three to seventy-nine.[47]

No doubt there were many reasons why the bill failed, not least important of which was the objection founded on fear of abuse. Several days later, reflecting this concern, the *New York Times* published a letter to the editor titled "Euthanasia in Practice." The letter began with the following lines: "At a recent meeting of our club the Ohio Euthanasia bill was unanimously approved. Next day Smithers, our Secretary, providentially, it would seem, was run over by an automobile and was fatally hurt. . . ." The letter, a brilliant parody of the euthanasia bill, continued by telling how a physician and three bystanders who gathered around Smithers offered him euthanasia while he was still lying on the ground. After Smithers consents, three physicians were summoned: Dr. Dodd (the allopath), Dr. Gusher (the osteopath), and Dr. Winks (the accomplished veterinarian). The bill's requirements seeming to be fulfilled, these physicians would have administered euthanasia on the spot if not for the question as to who would pay for it. The letter concluded by reproaching the physicians for not respecting the law and for ignoring the fact that Smithers's estate would be liable for the physicians' fees.[48]

Indeed, one of the strongest, repeated criticisms of the 1906 bill was that it was open to exploitation, that the medical procedure it was offering did not have the proper mechanisms to safeguard it from abuse. While the bill did require the participation of witnesses and several doctors, it left at least two factors too widely open: the urgency of performing euthanasia and the identity of the physicians involved. All bills that followed this 1906 proposal would have to take into account these specific concerns and, more generally, the fear of abuse. In defense of their proposals, euthanasia advocates continuously argued that "precautions and safeguards could be multiplied *ad libitum*."

The true challenge of the supporters of euthanasia was to draft a bill that would not be open to any risk of abuse. The role of the law was to offer full regulation of the medical procedure. If such a certainty could be established, nothing could stop the success of the euthanasia proposal. Or so at least its supporters believed.

The Bills of the 1930s

In the following years, there was very little discussion of euthanasia and its legalization. With few exceptions, which will be discussed later, the euthanasia debate went into a long hibernation. The next attempt to legalize euthanasia took place more than two decades later, in the 1930s. But the wish to create a bill that would be abuse-proof was still on the minds of euthanasia supporters. A bill with this intent was eventually drafted by an English physician, C. Killick Millard; and though it was made in England, its effects were soon noticed in the United States. The details of the bill are offered here at length to convey the frame of mind underlying the new euthanasia process and the logic underlying its legalization.

Millard's original bill was prefaced by the following statement:

> The object of this Bill is to provide for the granting of Permits which will render it legal for persons who are certified to be suffering from incurable, fatal, and painful disease to receive Euthanasia, if they so desire, and thus to shorten the severe physical suffering entailed by certain forms of disease.[49]

Euthanasia was still defined in this bill as a painless death brought about by artificial means in anticipation of death from disease. And the bill was designed to prevent any form of abuse and to guarantee that euthanasia would only be offered to patients who are hopelessly dying and express an explicit wish that their death be hastened.

The first part of the proposed bill laid out with great detail the complex procedure required for achieving the "euthanasia permit." The first requirement of this procedure was a personal statement from the patient expressing awareness of a fatal condition and desire to accelerate death by euthanasia. Second, the patient had to testify that he had informed his close relatives of his wish to die and that his affairs were in order. Third, this statement had to be attested to by a magistrate or commissioner of oaths. Fourth, the bill required that two medical certificates be added to this statement, acknowledging the patient's hopeless condition and the lack of any chance of recovery. Unwilling to rely solely on written documents, the proposed bill made the administration of euthanasia conditional on a personal interview before the "euthanasia referee," a state official designated by the bill. The referee was to interview the applicant and satisfy himself that the latter understood the meaning of euthanasia and truly wished to die. The fifth stage of the process was a meeting of the patient and his family with the referee.

The sixth stage necessary for attaining the euthanasia permit was an appearance before the court. The referee was to personally come before the court and present the application, as well as answer any questions the court might wish to put. The referee was also responsible for notifying the family in advance of the date and time when the application would come before the court. Therefore, the court hearing was also an opportunity for the relatives to come forward and present any objections they might have about the decision.

If the court was satisfied, it would issue the necessary permits: one to the applicant to receive euthanasia and one to the medical practitioner (named in the application) whom the applicant desired should administer it. The permit would be valid for a period of three months, after which it would lapse. However, it could be renewed if a fresh application was made.

After setting out the requirements for obtaining the permit, the bill then designed the proper procedure for administering euthanasia. According to the bill, euthanasia could not be performed by any medical doctor. Rather, the bill designated an "official euthanisor" who would be appointed in every area by the minister of health. To prevent any abuse in the process of administering euthanasia, the bill required the presence of an official witness. The latter had to belong to "a certain class," such as justice of the peace, medical practitioner, minister of religion, or solicitor. In his presence, euthanasia could finally be administered.

Like any official matter, the process was complete only after being well documented. The bill established the proper procedure of documentation. After euthanasia had been effected, the euthanisor would immediately issue the certificate, which had to be countersigned by the official witness. A report would then to be sent to the euthanasia referee.

Millard's proposal was, no doubt, the most elaborate of the euthanasia proposals, and for this reason it served as a model for many euthanasia bills in the years to come. The bill accurately represents the kind of concerns that supporters of euthanasia were facing and the response that these supporters were ready to offer. The bill expresses clearly the role of the law in the legalization of euthanasia. It was much more than the need to remove a legal barrier. The law had a formative role.

In particular, it is striking that the patient himself does not present his case before the law, nor does he appoint an agent to do so. Rather, the official referee, on behalf of the state, presents the case before the court. More generally, the presence not only of the doctor but also of state officials—the referee, the euthanisor, the witness—demonstrates the new bureaucratic order that governed death. Even in later proposals, the fact that there is no explicit demand for these officials is only because of the underlying assumption that two or three physicians are responsible enough to serve as state officials as well as medical practitioners.

We cannot help but notice the overtly bureaucratic character of the administration of death. The all-too-familiar mechanisms of bureaucracy are set in motion: the long and detailed procedure, the multiple forms, hearings, permits, and reports, not to mention the involvement of almost a dozen officials involved in these procedures. This is euthanasia as bureaucracy, death as administrative justice.

CHAPTER THREE

Conclusion

Early in the struggle for institutionalization, euthanasia supporters believed that the law was the greatest difficulty facing them. The law, they rightfully assumed, would not tolerate the taking of human life. From a legal standpoint, euthanasia was nothing but murder. The problem of legalizing euthanasia was to bridge the gap between the medical understanding of the practice and its legal status. At first, the two were at odds. Even assuming that physicians were ready to embrace the practice, the law was not.

The solution to this disparity involved more than changing the content of the law; it entailed more than the passing of a bill that would decree euthanasia as legal. For euthanasia to become lawful, a fundamental change in the law and its relation to the medical practice of euthanasia had to take place. While the common law maintained an unwavering stand on the question of euthanasia, the newly emerging legal regime withheld judgment and limited its discretion to setting the conditions under which the practice could take place. From being an obstacle standing in the way of euthanasia, law became a necessary component in its practice. Law as regulation could determine under what conditions euthanasia should be practiced and could guard the practice of euthanasia from possible abuses.

The move to legalize euthanasia was an integral part of the development of euthanasia as a technique. Euthanasia as a manifestation of medical technique required the intervention of law to regulate it. Law, newly perceived as regulation, no longer posed a challenge to the practice of euthanasia; on the contrary, it became a necessary condition of its application. The practice of euthanasia without legal regulation was seen as the greatest threat, so much so that the regulation of euthanasia became more important than the justice of the practice itself. As we shall see in the following chapter, the Nazi euthanasia project was condemned not only because euthanasia was practiced involuntarily but, even more important, because it was practiced without legal regulation.

Euthanasia as Public Policy: The Euthanasia Society of America

Introduction

IN THE PREVIOUS CHAPTERS, we saw how dying was delivered from the hands of the priest to those of the physician and how euthanasia, as the modern art of dying, changed first from a religious ethic into a medical duty and then, with the early attempts at legalization, into state law. This chapter follows the story of euthanasia into the second half of the twentieth century, as it takes yet another turn.

Nothing could manifest this next development more than the establishment of the Euthanasia Society of America (ESA) in 1938;[1] and no one could better capture this transformation than its founder, Dr. Charles Potter. Speaking of the moral barriers standing in the way of institutionalizing euthanasia, Potter explained:

> [P]ublic opinion . . . is the only morality, as sociologists well know, even if clergymen do not. The law may warn; medical ethics may frown; and the church may threaten with the fires of hell, but public opinion is stronger than all three. If you doubt that fact, you have but to look at the parallel case of birth control, which indeed the Roman Catholic authorities have coupled with mercy-killing already.[2]

Euthanasia was no longer first and foremost a religious, medical, or legal problem. Potter's words imply the rise of euthanasia as a *social* concern. The most obvious manifestation of this change was the growing importance of public opinion for the euthanasia struggle. The founding of the Euthanasia Society of America was meant to address this change.[3]

While the ESA was still committed to the legalization of euthanasia, passing euthanasia bills was no longer its single goal. Unlike the previous sporadic attempts to legalize euthanasia, the ESA launched a comprehensive war on several fronts. During its first years, in addition to introducing euthanasia bills, the ESA sought the support of thousands of members, publicized pro-euthanasia petitions, actively fought the opposition to euthanasia, and began educating society on the benefits of the practice. The law did not disappear from the struggle, but rather it was restructured to fit as part of a broad array of organizational tactics.

But the transformation of euthanasia entailed more than just a change in organizational tactics. It manifested a more radical shift in the understanding of euthanasia and its goals. Both the problem of dying and its solution—euthanasia, which had initially been understood as confined to medical concerns—were now understood more broadly as social concerns. Dying became one among a broad array of public health issues, such as birth rates and mental health. Similarly, euthanasia became one among several new practices regulating the biological processes of birth and death, such as birth control, abortion, and sterilization.

Even more important, euthanasia no longer meant merely hastening the death of patients who were already dying. Rather, by the early twentieth century, euthanasia was advocated as a solution to a broader range of cases, which included the "mentally retarded" and the "physically handicapped." For both its supporters and its opponents, euthanasia was no longer confined to the dying patient.

The underlying argument of this chapter is that these two changes—namely, the new sense of euthanasia as a solution to a variety of human sufferings, and the new role of the law within the struggle to institutionalize involuntary euthanasia—are interrelated. It is only on the basis of the "socialization" of the problem of dying that law could assume a new role as the mechanism necessary for governing the production of death. This transition should be understood in light of the broader transition of dying from art to technique and raises the more specific question of the role that law played in this transition.

Therefore, this chapter is divided into two parts. The first part will discuss the emergence of euthanasia as a solution to the "social" problem of dying, while the second part will address the role of the law in implementing this solution.

The "Socialization" of Euthanasia

Founders and Foundations

On January 16, 1938, the ESA was incorporated in New York City under the temporary name the National Society for the Legalization of Euthanasia. With its establishment, the efforts to legalize euthanasia entered a new phase. The society set as its goal to "create public demand for the legalization of voluntary euthanasia, and to secure the enactment of state laws permitting voluntary euthanasia with procedure as simple as is consistent with security against abuse in the state of New York."[4]

The founder of the society, Dr. Charles Potter, played a leading role in the society through its early decades. Potter was a doctor of literature, not of medicine, and served for many years as a clergyman until his radical views led him to leave the church.[5] He was the intellectual guide of the movement and was not only its founder and first president but, after yielding his term as president, followed the society for a quarter of a century and returned as its president from 1959 to 1962. His background, as well as that of the other leading figures of the ESA, reveals a great deal about the motivations and aspirations of the new movement.

Potter explained his commitment to institutionalizing euthanasia on the basis of personal experience: "My experience as a clergyman for many years has forced me to recognize the necessity for laws permitting euthanasia. In certain cases and under proper restrictions. I have seen many middle-aged and elderly persons, mostly women, dying in prolonged agony from such diseases as cancer. They have begged me to bring them secretly some quick-acting poison pills to put them out of their misery."[6]

What made Potter's involvement with the society unique was neither his personal commitment to the project nor his prominence as a public intellectual. Rather, Potter and other members of the ESA differed from previous advocates of euthanasia in viewing euthanasia as part of a broader struggle for social betterment.

Potter had long been involved in promoting social causes and was especially known for his opposition to the limitations imposed on public policy by arcane religious dogma. Euthanasia was only one among a list of social causes he fought for, which included abolishing capital punishment, "equal treatment" for women, outlawing war, improving working conditions, and promoting public health. As one scholar attempted to generalize about these efforts, "All reflected his belief that human beings could use their knowledge to control events and better their lives, and contradicted the fatalism of many traditional religious and secular thinkers."[7]

Many of the other ESA directors were also involved in a variety of struggles for social change. Perhaps two of the most important issues to consider are birth control and eugenics. Through ESA members' involvement with these goals, we can learn more about the new way in which dying was perceived as a problem, and euthanasia as its solution.

Birth Control and Death Control

Several of the leaders of the new euthanasia movement were veterans of the struggle for birth control. Dr. Clarence Cook Little, one of the leading members of the Society and later the head of the ESA, was the president of the American Birth Control League during these earlier years. Similarly, Eleanor Dwight Jones, who served as president of the Birth Control League from 1929 to 1935, joined the ESA in 1937 as its secretary and later became its executive vice president.[8] Perhaps most notably, Margaret Sanger, the head of the birth-control movement and the founder of the league (and its president from 1921 to 1928), joined the ranks of the ESA and became one of its most prestigious supporters.[9]

The relation of birth control to euthanasia was not merely that many of the euthanasia advocates were involved in both struggles. There was a more concrete relation between the two. As we shall see, the struggle for euthanasia was the immediate successor of the struggle for birth control.

In the years preceding the founding of the ESA, Potter was involved in founding an organization called the First Humanist Society. The humanist society was committed to promoting different social goals, and it especially focused on forming a structured response to religious fundamentalism, which spread during the first decades of the century. Clarifying the relation between the ESA and the First Humanist Society, Potter explained:

> The new organization is not a part of the First Humanist Society of New York but is a definite outgrowth of the policy of the Humanist Society, which fosters and assists all projects of human betterment. We have for years been active in the birth control movement and, since that fight is largely won, we feel free to transfer some of our efforts to the euthanasia enterprise.[10]

The fight for birth control, in which Potter and many others of the ESA leaders were involved, was a struggle to make birth-control means publicly available.[11] Specifically it was a struggle against the prohibitions on distribution of information concerning birth-control methods that prevented many from learning about the important potentials of the practice. The focus of the struggle was the Comstock Act, a federal statute passed by the U.S. Congress in 1873 as an "Act of the Suppression of Trade in, and Circulation of, Obscene Literature and Articles of Immoral Use."[12] The act criminalized publication, distribution, and possession of information about or devices or medications for "unlawful" abortion or contraception.

The struggle for birth control began in the United States in the 1910s and was led by Margaret Sanger.[13] In 1912, Sanger gave up nursing to devote herself to the cause. Soon thereafter, she was indicted for mailing materials advocating birth control, but the charges were dropped in 1916. Later that year, she opened the first birth-control clinic in the United States, in Brooklyn. She was arrested and charged with maintaining a "public nuisance," and in 1917 she served thirty days in the Queens penitentiary. Her sentencing and subsequent episodes of legal harassment helped to crystallize public opinion in favor of the birth-control movement. Sanger's legal appeals prompted the federal courts first to grant physicians the right to give advice about birth-control methods and then, in 1936, to reinterpret the Comstock Act of 1873 in such a way as to permit physicians to import and prescribe contraceptives.[14]

In 1936, a New York court, in a case known as *United States* v. *One Package of Japanese Pessaries*, ruled that contraceptives could be sent through the post if they were to be intelligently employed by conscientious physicians for the purpose of saving life or promoting the well-being of their patients.[15] In its decision, the court handed a fatal blow to the Comstock Act and allowed Potter to declare in 1937 that the battle for birth control had been "largely won." Many of the members of the birth-control movement, sharing Potter's sense of victory, were searching for a new cause. For a large number of birth-control veterans, euthanasia became that cause. And they brought to it their confidence in the possibility of legal and social change. They believed that they could overcome legal and religious prejudice and that even the medical profession could not stand in the way of euthanasia. One ESA activist proclaimed, "As for the organized medical profession, it is hopeless—now! But it was forced to recognize birth control; and it will be forced, in time, to give its sanction to euthanasia."[16]

One question is, What allowed for such a smooth transition from birth control to euthanasia, that is, from a fight for distributing information about contraceptives to a struggle for hastening the death of hopelessly ill, dying patients? How was the struggle for euthanasia understood during the 1930s so that its affinity with birth control became self-evident?

One obvious connection between these struggles is that euthanasia was an attempt to control death, just as contraceptives and abortion were attempts to control birth.[17] Both movements sought to allow more control over biological processes at the extreme ends of life. Some even suggested a slogan under which the ESA could run: "Legalize Death Control."[18] The underlying grounds of this affinity—namely, the need for such control—needs further examination. The question now is, What similar problems did birth and death pose to which their control was a possible solution?

Potter hinted at one possible answer: "The same humanitarian impulse which animates the workers for birth control, namely, that children may be properly born, extends to the end of life as well, so that we desire that human beings in great suffering may have an easy death." The humanitarian concern was clearly a strong motivation underlying both struggles. Sanger, like Potter and many other supporters of both causes, was motivated by heart-wrenching personal experience in facing both ends of life. Sanger encountered miserable conditions in her work among the poor as a nurse and was inspired to take up her crusade when she attended a woman who was dying from a criminally induced abortion. Similarly, Potter had seen the misery and suffering involved in the prolonged process of dying.[19]

But the humanitarian concern with individual suffering was only one side of the birth-control/death-control equation. The other side of this equation was a growing concern with birth rates and, similarly, with death as a "social problem." Birth was no longer considered the problem of the mother and baby alone; it became a problem of the social body. The burdens of child care were now social burdens that society as a whole would have to carry. In a similar way, dying was no longer merely a problem for the suffering patient but became a "social problem." The humanitarian sensibility did not emerge solely from a concern with pain and suffering. It was a specific kind of suffering that had to be controlled, a suffering that was experienced at the same time in the individual and in the social body.

Sanger and other supporters of birth control were concerned with the effects of undesired children on the social fiber. The goal of the birth-control movement was not merely to save individual women and families from the burden of undesired children. There was something in addition to this humanitarian concern, even if not totally unrelated to it. It was a growing concern with the connection between birth rates and social welfare. It sought more than the well-being of individual families; and it understood even this well-being as part of a broader phenomenon with broader implications. The struggle for birth control was as much a struggle to prevent poverty and crime as it was to secure the well-being of individual families.

In other words, the struggle for birth control raised two issues that were seen as complementary.[20] On the one hand, the struggle was about women's control over their life, and the family's ability to prevent unwanted birth.

On the other hand, there was the social concern with birth, and the economic burden that uncontrolled births placed on the lower class. These motivations may seem contradictory to a contemporary liberal reader, to the extent that we have come to see individual freedom in opposition to social needs.[21] But this was not the case for advocates of social change in the 1930s—neither in the birth-control movement nor, as we shall soon see, in the euthanasia society.

The struggle for contraceptives was only one manifestation of the rise of birth as a social problem. One other more radical but very telling expression of the same concern was manifested by the eugenic movement, which became highly popular during the early decades of the twentieth century.[22] The role of eugenics in the euthanasia movement was as significant as in birth control, and together eugenics and birth control were the two most common commitments that leaders of the euthanasia movement shared.[23]

Eugenics and the Social Problem of "Defectives"

The eugenic movement in the United States was thriving in the early decades of the twentieth century.[24] In its pure form, as discussed by scientists, eugenics was the attempt to improve the genetic stock of the population. Originating in England in the late nineteenth century, eugenics was defined as "the movement to improve the inborn qualities of the human species both physically and mentally by manipulating the mechanisms of social control in such a way as to encourage the breeding of genetically superior individuals [positive eugenics] and discourage the breeding of genetically inferior individuals [negative eugenics]."[25]

But the eugenic movement was understood in the popular culture in much broader terms, which may help explain its remarkable influence on public policy.[26] Broadly understood, the eugenics movement professed faith in the methods of modern science to produce efficient technical solutions for a whole array of sociobiological problems.[27] Thus, inspired by eugenic ideas, new national associations were founded to fight tuberculosis, cancer, mental illness, occupational injuries, and many other sociomedical problems.[28]

Eugenic ideals were most notably behind the sterilization movement in the United States. Sterilization is especially interesting because of its affinity with euthanasia. Unlike birth control, where the law was merely an impediment that had to be removed, in sterilization—as in euthanasia—the law played an active role in drawing the specific standards under which the practice could take place.

Supporters of eugenics advocated sterilization as a solution to procreation among the socially defective. Other programs of negative eugenics that were applied at the time included marriage restrictions, sexual segregation, and, in the United States especially, immigration restrictions. Interestingly, eugenicists generally refused to consider abortion to halt the birth of "defectives."[29]

Eugenics legislation had a remarkable success in the United States.[30] In 1911, six states already had sterilization laws on the books. Most of these laws provided for the voluntary or compulsory sterilization of certain classes of people thought to be insane, mentally retarded, or epileptic; some applied equally to habitual criminals and sexual deviants. In most cases the purpose was clearly eugenics, though some laws tacitly permitted sterilization for economic rather than genetic reasons.

By 1931, sterilization laws had been enacted by twenty-seven states in the United States, and by the mid-1920s some twenty thousand sterilizations had been legally performed in the United States. This number almost doubled by 1941.[31]

To understand the relation between sterilization and euthanasia, we must ask ourselves again: What logic underlay both sterilization and euthanasia? And again, the answer cannot be simply the desire to control biological processes, for that would only raise the question, Control to what end?

To better understand the purpose of sterilization, we take an example from the Sterilization Act of Virginia, approved on March 20, 1924. The act states that the health of the patient and the welfare of society may be promoted in certain cases by the sterilization of "mental defectives," under careful safeguard. Sterilization may take place by vasectomy or salpingectomy.[32]

The constitutionality of the act was challenged in the Supreme Court of the United States. The Court, in upholding the act, accepted the following justification given by the state of Virginia:

The Commonwealth is supporting in various institutions many defective persons who, if now discharged, would become a menace, but, if incapable of procreating, might be discharged with safety and become self-supporting with benefit to themselves and to society, and that experience has shown that heredity plays an important part in the transmission of insanity and imbecility. The statute enacts that, whenever the superintendent of certain institutions, shall be of opinion that it is for the best interests of the patients and of society that an inmate under his care should be sexually sterilized, he may have the operation performed upon any patient afflicted with hereditary forms of insanity, imbecility, etc., on complying with the very careful provisions by which the act protects the patients from possible abuse.[33]

Like birth control, sterilization was justified on both humanitarian and social grounds, a justification repeated in the case of euthanasia as well. There were, however, a few differences between sterilization and birth control both in practice and in justification. The first difference was that the "target" groups of birth control and sterilization were different. In birth control, the emphasis was mostly directed at the poor, while in the case of sterilization it was directed at "defectives." The second difference was that while birth control was voluntary, sterilization was forced. The third difference, as mentioned above, was that while the struggle for legalizing contraception mostly involved the removal of the legal barrier, the law took an active role in regulating the practice of sterilization. We shall soon see how euthanasia proposals oscillated between these two options. Some of the euthanasia advocates were pushing to model euthanasia on the basis of enforced sterilization, whereas other advocates within the movement favored the birth control model.

If birth control and sterilization could not offer the ultimate solution to "the problem of defectives" in society, it was because this problem was not perceived strictly as a eugenic problem. The fear was not only that "defectives" were threatening the genetic pool but also simply that they existed at all. To solve this problem, neither sterilization nor contraceptives would be enough; a more radical solution would have to be offered. This is the context in which euthanasia emerged as a solution to "the problem of defectives" in society.

From Eugenics to Euthanasia

While most leading eugenicists rejected euthanasia as a solution to the problem of the unfit,[34] many euthanasia supporters did base their arguments on eugenic and quasi-eugenic reasoning. Among the eugenicists involved in the Euthanasia Society were: Henry H. Goddard, a member of the advisory committee and professor of psychology at Ohio State;[35] Forster Kennedy, a professor of neurology at Cornell Medical College, later to become the president of the society; and Arthur A. Estabrook, an admirer of Nazi sterilization policies.

Oscar Riddle, another president of the Euthanasia Society and a veteran researcher at the Carnegie Station of Experimental Evolution, devoted most of his career to searching for ways in which science could control human heredity. He was a prominent eugenicist, who in 1936 called for the "selection and control either of those permitted to live or of those permitted to reproduce."[36] Finally, there was Wyllistine Goodsell, a professor of education at Columbia, who served on the executive committee of the American Eugenics Society. Other eugenicists who were asked to join declined because they were too busy with other work or were unsure they were willing to commit themselves to the project.[37]

The eugenicists were especially concerned with the social problem posed by the mentally retarded. The need for a solution was reinforced by statistical data regarding variations in the rate of the mentally retarded within the United States. Thus, in 1935 the *New York Sun* informed its readers that

> Figures just published by Frank K. Shuttleworth of Yale University confirm those published last year by Lorimer and Osborn, indicating a slow but steady decline in the intellectual level of the United States. Uniformly, the feebleminded produce more children than do the college graduates.[38]

Though eugenic reasoning was popular among euthanasia supporters, some members of the ESA supported euthanasia on different grounds. Laypeople such as Ann Mitchell were attracted to the euthanasia ideals on the basis of more personal concerns. "Mitchell first became interested in euthanasia when, as a university student many years before, she visited several mental institutions. She later became a patient in such an institution, an experience which strengthened her belief in euthanasia for inmates who were beyond hope. Mitchell, a wealthy New Yorker, contacted Potter, and offered to finance an organization dedicated to legalizing euthanasia."[39]

The connection between eugenics and euthanasia is far from obvious. Unlike birth control, it did not merely prevent the birth of undesired population but also terminated such life after it was born. Nevertheless, euthanasia was closely tied to birth control in that both sought to use medical means to minimize social suffering by regulating undesired life. It is, therefore, no accident that the initial discussion of euthanasia as a eugenics solution was raised in the context of deformed babies. The problem of monstrously deformed children presented a growing concern to eugenics supporters, and euthanasia became one possible solution to this problem. The idea of offering euthanasia to newborn babies was first proposed several years before the euthanasia society was established.[40] It became a matter of public discussion and debate during the 1910s, when the case of Dr. Harry J. Haiselden and the Bollinger baby stirred America.[41]

Anna Bollinger gave birth on November 12, 1915, to an infant who suffered from multiple physical anomalies, "including absence of a neck and one ear, deformities of the shoulders and chest, very slow reaction of the pupils to light, and an imperforate anus."[42] After performing further medical examinations, Haiselden—the surgeon who headed the hospital staff—concluded that "surgery could correct the intestinal defects and thus save the infant's life but that gross physical and mental abnormalities would remain, and he urged the parents not to request an operation. The Bollingers agreed, and five days later the baby died."[43] Haiselden repeatedly refused to treat newborns who, in his judgment, suffered from irreversible physical dysfunctions that would make their life and the lives of their surrounding family unbearable and a burden to society at large.

Haiselden not only refused to treat such babies but, at least in one case, took positive measures to end a life of a newborn. He admitted giving the baby a narcotic drug in order to ease the baby's pain and, he implied, to speed the impending death. The two-year-old child, Paul Hodzima, was a microcephalic who was reportedly choking from a constricted windpipe.[44]

Haiselden did not try to hide his actions; to the contrary, he wished to publicize them in order to promote a public discussion of the topic. Haiselden was not alone. A substantial number of prominent early-twentieth-century Americans favored letting deformed infants die.[45] With Haiselden, "the problem of defectives" moved from a question of how to prevent birth to the question of how to shorten (or not prolong) life. Haiselden did not explicitly advocate killing such babies, but others before him and after him made note of this possibility.[46] It is interesting that although Haiselden's acts were in many ways aligned with the ESA's concerns, leaders of the ESA such as Potter did not necessarily support such acts.[47]

One could suggest that the practice of euthanasia on newborns was the missing link between eugenics and euthanasia. What remained a constant in the progression from birth control, to sterilization, to infanticide was not only the will to control birth but, more specifically, to remove from existence certain forms of incurable social suffering. The case of euthanasia for the dying, which was the main interest of the Euthanasia Society, falls squarely within this set of mind.

To summarize: The problem of the dying patient was no longer seen in isolation from other social concerns. Euthanasia became the panacea for some of the essential ailments of society. The problem of death control was closely linked to the problem of birth control, and the regulation of life and death were part of a larger project of social betterment. An examination of ESA members points clearly to a new worldview through which the problem of dying was now understood. There was an odd mix of university professors (mostly from zoology and sociology; some from economics, biology, and psychology), several physicians, and a handful of clergymen (Protestant and Jewish—none was Catholic). What is most striking about this list is that, as one historian has pointed out, "only a few directors had not previously been involved in a wide variety of social and intellectual activities."[48]

The case of the dying, like that of the mentally retarded and the physically handicapped, involved a very specific kind of suffering. It was a suffering that was located in the social body as much as in the individual's body and was experienced as a problem for family and friends, the taxpayer, and the state. It was no longer the pain of the individual in itself that justified euthanasia but rather the way in which it reflected a new kind of social suffering.

Dying as a Social Problem

If we limited ourselves to the strictly scientific sense of eugenics, it would be hard to understand how the problem of dying became a eugenic concern. Hastening the death of dying patients could by no means improve the genetic pool of the population. Dying patients posed no threat to heredity, and the problem of a good death could not be construed as a problem of good genes. We need to realize that if eugenicists were nevertheless interested in euthanasia, it was due to the broader sense of eugenics at the time as offering solutions to new forms of social suffering.

To see how the problem of dying changed from individual suffering into social suffering, we need to return to how the problem of pain in dying was understood in the late nineteenth century. As we have seen, the most popular argument among doctors regarding the pain of dying was its nonexistence. The medical profession argued that the body of the dying patient only seemed to be in pain, but in truth dying was seldom painful at all.

As the pain of the dying patient became a mirage, as seen through the medical view, a new concern with suffering at the deathbed emerged. It was not the suffering of the dying patient but rather that of the surrounding family, physician, and friends. "The dying struggle," one late-nineteenth-century physician explained, "is painless to the unconscious patient, but it is awfully painful and harrowing to all who stand at the bedside and witness it."[49]

The concern with the pain of the dying was evidently more complex than merely empathizing with the pain of another sentient human being. While the dying patient was seldom suffering from pain at all, it was the bystander who was surprisingly not only concerned but actually suffering from pain.

Similarly, Dr. E. P. Thwing reported his own experience facing the death of a sixty-six-year-old widow stricken with apoplexy and hemiplegia. "Automatic movements," he wrote, "like pulling of the clothes, lifting the hand to the head and other signs of restlessness, continued until near her end. . . . The reality of suffering I could not admit, but the appearance of its actions purely reflexed was painful to me."[50]

It is almost as if a law of the preservation of pain was applied, and as less suffering was attributed to the dying patient, more pain was felt by the surrounding family and friends. The pain of the bystander, though originating in the condition of the dying patient, no longer depended on the experience of pain suffered by the dying patient. The medical imperative to relieve the pain of the dying patient was therefore not so much a result of the intolerable pain suffered by the dying patient but perhaps as much a solution to the pain suffered by the family and friends. One physician reported a case in which, at the request of the parents, he "administered ether to a child suffocating in membranous croup, and produced euthanasia, not less to the relief of the parents than to that of the patient."[51]

The frustration of not being able to cure the disease was overcome by the medical capacity to remove the pain of dying patients as well as that of those around them:

> To sit by as a passive spectator under such circumstances, believing that nothing can be done, or attempting to relieve by stimulants which rather aggravate the sufferings by increasing action without giving power, is a painful position for those practicing the healing art; but the power of alleviating not only this last distress of the dying but also of the relatives around, is as encouraging.[52]

Relieving the suffering of the relatives surrounding the deathbed became as important as relieving the possible pain of the dying, and at times the only relevant concern. The pain of the relatives, friends, and bystanders, not to mention the physician, was slowly becoming as much a justification for the practice of euthanasia as the pain of the dying patients themselves.

> We must consider the friends who, besides the immediate suffering of nursing the sick man, often permanently impair their constitutions and nervous systems, and who, moreover are thus exposed to a sort

of moral suicide; I mean they curtail their own powers of usefulness far more than a dose of laudanum would curtail those of their dying friends.[53]

Tollemache is hinting here at a possible distinction between the suffering of dying patients and that of the surrounding family and friends. The suffering of the latter is not simply seeing the pain of the dying patient but a combination of being exposed to that pain along with the duty to take care of the dying. It is this particular combination of suffering and dependence that marks the new concern with dying patients.

The same mixture of concern with suffering that we find very close to the deathbed echoes the more general public concern with dying patients. Euthanasia, originally a solution to the suffering of dying patients, was now offered as a solution to social suffering.

On these grounds, euthanasia advocates could distinguish between euthanasia and suicide. While euthanasia for the terminally ill could relieve the burdens on society, ordinary suicide only increased these burdens:

> It may be well to point out the wide line of demarcation which separates euthanasia from what is ordinarily called suicide. Euthanasia, like suicide, is a voluntarily chosen death but there is a radical difference between the motives which prompt the similar act. Those who commit suicide thereby render themselves useless to society of the future; they deprive society of their service, and selfishly evade the duties which ought to fall to their share; therefore, the social feeling rightly condemns suicide as a crime against society.[54]

The rise of this form of "social suffering" superseded, at times, the private pain of the dying patient to the extent that the dying patient himself is portrayed as motivated by the wish to relieve the suffering of others more than his own physical pain. Potter, the founder of the ESA, asserts this point very clearly:

> Those opponents of euthanasia who claim that a sufferer is only a coward if he or she wishes to end his life, forget that most such sufferers are much more concerned about the anguish they are causing their dear ones than they are about their own pain.[55]

And similarly:

> Suppose your patient is suffering from an incurable throat disease. You know that even an operation is impossible. He is suffering acutely and months of agony are inevitable before his death. Toward the end

112

it will be a "hideous race between strangulation and starvation." You and his dear ones suffer with him as you watch his slow, agonizing decline, and he suffers doubly because he knows he is causing his family to suffer.[56]

We can now begin to understand on what grounds euthanasia was conceived as one among several practices of controlling life and death. Euthanasia, eugenics, and birth control were all attempts to alleviate by medical means suffering that was conceived simultaneously as social and personal. It is on the basis of this affinity that euthanasia eventually could become a solution not only to the problem of dying but also to that of the "mentally defective" and the monstrous newborns.

Pain and hopelessness, the underlying drives behind the early euthanasia proposals, were still at work in the early decades of the twentieth century.[57] The sense of these conditions, however, was significantly transformed, leading to euthanasia proposals that included not only the dying but other "hopeless" and "painful" conditions as well. Pain, as we have seen, was reinterpreted to include social suffering as well as physical pain. In a similar manner, hopelessness gained a slightly new meaning. It no longer addressed the terminal condition of the dying patient but rather the social condition of the unfit person, who became a burden to himself as well as to society. Hopelessness was expanded to engulf the whole existence of the unfit person, and it was no longer limited to the final stage of life. Euthanasia, which originated as a solution to the problem of the dying patient (literally, an easy death), was expanded to solve the new social problem of pain and hopelessness.

The Legalizing of Euthanasia

The British Euthanasia Society

Having shown the transformation of euthanasia from a confined medical problem into a broader social concern, we are now ready to explore the legal implications of this change. We shall see how the law, which in the common-law tradition served as an independent barrier to the practice of euthanasia, was now subordinated to a regulatory regime accountable only to public opinion. The specific role that the ESA designated to the law was not merely its decriminalization but its regulation. This fact becomes clear when the ESA's attempts to legalize euthanasia are compared with those already taking place in England.

When Charles Potter founded the first Euthanasia Society of America in 1937, he had a model to follow. A similar society had been founded three years earlier in England, called the British Society for Legalisation of Voluntary Euthanasia. During its first years, the ESA saw its British counterpart as a source of inspiration and advice. The first project the ESA took upon itself was to pass a bill similar to the one the British society formulated and introduced in the House of Lords in 1936.

The British society, founded in 1935, had a promising start. It won immediate recognition due to the high profile of its supporters, among them some of England's most eminent men, including Dr. Julian Huxley, the Earl of Listowel, and Lord Denman, the former governor-general of Australia. This group of respectable gentlemen was later joined by George Bernard Shaw. Other public figures who were active members of the society included Dr. Havelock Ellis and Professor George Trevelyan. Most notably, the society was headed by one of England's most respected medical men, the operating surgeon Lord Moynihan, who was the first president of the British Society and its advocate in the House of Lords.

One of the more active members of the society, later to become its president, was the same Dr. Millard whose euthanasia bill was discussed at length in the previous chapter and now served as the basis for the first attempt to legalize euthanasia in England. Within a few months the original bill, with slight changes, was introduced before the legislature. The revised bill added the requirement that the patient be at least twenty-one years old. It did not lay out as detailed a procedure but rather authorized the ministry of health to design some of the procedure. What remained unquestionable was the limited scope of the bill. Euthanasia was restricted to dying patients who consented to the practice. Millard had already made this point clear, but it was important enough for Lord Moynihan to repeat it in the society's inaugural meeting. In this meeting, held only a few months before his death, Lord Moynihan clarified:

> It has already been asked, and the question will doubtless be repeated, whether cases other than these are to be considered. At present "No." There are doubtless cases of mongolian idiocy, or of mental defects of one kind or another that may possibly come for discussion. Now, however, we are directing our attention to no other cases than those I have mentioned.[58]

The bill to legalize euthanasia was presented before the House of Lords on November 4, 1936. Lord Moynihan, who had planned to introduce the bill, had passed away earlier that year. His death had devastating effects on the reception of the bill, for it was now introduced by a member of less distinction and with no medical credentials. Following the usual custom, the first reading was agreed to without debate, and on December 2, the debate on the second reading took place.

The bill was eventually defeated, although more than a quarter of the House members supported it, in a thirty-five to fourteen vote. The failure to pass the bill did not discourage the British Euthanasia Society, which maintained its efforts to legalize euthanasia in the coming decades. Similar attempts to introduce a euthanasia bill were defeated in 1950 and in 1969.[59]

The British Euthanasia Society rejected the possibility of legalizing non-voluntary euthanasia from the outset and, in the years to follow, never returned to seriously contemplate this idea. Though the British society greatly influenced its American counterpart, it treated the question of nonvoluntary euthanasia quite differently on its side of the Atlantic. In exploring American attempts to legalize euthanasia, we should note that the possibility that euthanasia was fundamentally illegal, and that changing the law would counter not only moral principles but also fundamental principles of criminal law, never emerged as a problem for the euthanasia advocates, not even in their discussions of nonvoluntary euthanasia. In America, nonvoluntary euthanasia, as with nonvoluntary sterilization, was in the final analysis a question of public opinion and public policy.

Legalizing Euthanasia: The Nebraska Case

In America, even before the founding of the ESA, the possibility of legalizing nonvoluntary euthanasia won greater support than in England. In 1937, shortly before the ESA was founded, a bill was introduced in Nebraska that recommended the administration of euthanasia to a broader range of patients. This unusual bill was promoted by Inez C. Philbrick, a physician and former member of the University of Nebraska faculty.[60] Philbrick was already known for her involvement in other social causes: she believed in birth control and in sterilization of "degenerates" and "criminal defectives." Philbrick also presided over two important institutions: the Nebraska Medical Women's Association and the Medical Women's Club of Lincoln. A newspaper described her efforts as the struggle of "an elderly woman physician" "lined up against organized medicine in a fight to sanction euthanasia."[61]

In preparing her legislative proposal, Philbrick enlisted the aid of State Senator John H. Comstock, an attorney from Nebraska.[62] On February 5,

1937, Comstock introduced bill number 135 into Nebraska's unicameral legislature.[63] The bill, which passed a first reading, was referred after the second reading to the committee on public health and miscellaneous. The bill was similar to other bills regulating euthanasia, which required that the patients in question be suffering from an incurable and fatal disease and that pain be liable to be protracted. The bill also required that patients be in their right mind but added an exception that did not appear in other bills of its kind. It is this exception that made it significant.

The bill permitted the administration of euthanasia to adults who were mentally incompetent, if the next of kin made the application. Similarly, a parent (or guardian, if neither parent was alive) of a minor suffering from the same conditions could fill out an application on the minor's behalf.[64] The bill was limited to address only dying patients and did not include other hopeless cases. Nevertheless, it raised the possibility of nonvoluntary euthanasia.

The underlying logic of such legislation was that euthanasia was a medical treatment. Patients who were not capable of making medical choices for themselves could be assisted by close relatives and legal guardians. The general logic of ordinary medical treatment was applied to the case of euthanasia.

The bill was strongly opposed by the Nebraska State Medical Association, on grounds similar to previous oppositions to euthanasia. The association challenged the power of medicine to determine with precision the hopelessness of dying:

> Inasmuch as science is not yet sufficiently advanced to be sure that death must ensue in such cases we do not approve the bill especially since, in the last few years, advances have been made which have saved lives in cases where death would once have been certain. The use of insulin in sugar diabetes and liver extract for pernicious anemia are illustrations.[65]

Although the bill failed, Philbrick continued her involvement in the struggle to legalize euthanasia. Reflecting on its failure, she noted that an ideal bill would be more inclusive and would not be limited to dying patients suffering from incurable diseases. Such a bill would include mandatory euthanasia in the case of "idiots," "monstrosities," "the insane," and the "criminal insane."[66] The scope of euthanasia remained an open question for the ESA members to discuss.

Legalizing Euthanasia: The Euthanasia Society of America

As did their British predecessors, ESA leaders raised the possibility that euthanasia would be offered not only to dying patients but also to other incurables. But unlike the British society, the ESA did not remove this possibility from its agenda. It is this difference between the two societies and the role given to law in this context that is of interest to us.

Soon after founding the society, Potter made himself quite clear on the matter:

> Not only incurables suffering pain should be euthanized, but also incurable imbeciles. Few people realize the extent to which incurable insanity has spread. There are one-half a million people in our insane asylums, most of whom are incurable. It is well-known by doctors and nurses in these institutions that patients discharged usually return, sooner or later, and die in the asylum.[67]

Potter had an opportunity to further explain: "New York State alone spends thirty million dollars annually for the up-keep of its insane asylums, [thus] it is obvious that this is becoming a practical question." And, he continued, "this isn't merely a matter of high taxes. It is a matter of eugenics and the future of the race. Dr. Oscar Riddle has recently pointed out that 2.5 % of all unions of sperm and egg are bound to go bad."[68]

Significantly, when the ESA was first founded, it bore the name of the National Society for the Legalization of Euthanasia. Its original name, while resembling that of the British society, quite markedly featured euthanasia, rather than voluntary euthanasia. This variation does not seem to be coincidental; it very likely reflected the wish to expand euthanasia to nonvoluntary cases and specifically to mentally retarded patients. Similarly, the ESA's mission defined euthanasia as "the lawful termination of human life by painless means for the purpose of avoiding unnecessary suffering and under adequate safeguards."[69] This seems to be a deliberately broad definition of euthanasia to include more than only the dying patient.

What was peculiar about the suggestions to offer euthanasia to a broader host of cases was, as we have seen in the cases of birth control, the integration of humanitarian and social concerns. Thus, Potter could say in the same breath that "[c]ongenital idiots, the hopelessly insane, and the incurable sick whose every breath is a torture, should be put to death, these incurables are a worry to relatives and a big expense to the State."[70]

For Potter the application of euthanasia to a broader category of sufferings was fairly unquestionable, at least initially. The ESA as a society, however, was much more cautious. During its first meeting on March 30, 1938, the executive committee discussed whether the ESA should support euthanasia for incurable idiots. The discussion ended with the decision that while the ultimate aim of the society did include such cases, it would be well not to raise the issue in the first bill to be introduced. The committee decided that its first goal would be limited to securing the legislation of voluntary euthanasia.

Most members seemed to agree with the decision, yet they differed in their reasoning. Rabbi Goldstein of the Free Synagogue of New York, who also was a professor of sociology at the Jewish Institute of Religion, explained that the first step should be to legalize what doctors were already doing illegally, that is, shortening the period of suffering.[71] Dr. Wolbarst, following the same logic, said that what should determine the decision was the tendency of the medical profession, of whom 74 to 75 percent were in favor of euthanasia.[72] On the other hand, a Mrs. Jones (the identity of the speaker is not fully certain) argued that many physicians were interested in euthanasia for the incurably insane and "mentally defective."

In a letter dated June 16, 1940, Dr. Little, the president of the ESA at the time, wrote to the dean of a very prestigious American medical school:

> As a physician, you may feel that the bill should be broadened to give relief to classes which it does not now include, such as imbeciles and congenital monstrosities. These have not been included for reasons of legislative expediency. To secure enactment, the bill as originally presented must be simple and open to as few objections as possible. Once it is enacted, its scope can be broadened by amendment.[73]

The ESA offered an alternative reason for the limited scope of the bill in an official letter to an inquiring member, Dr. Edward L. Hayes (who despite the title was not a physician), dated June 21, 1939:

> The reason they ["mental defectives" and "monstrous births"] are not included in our proposed legislation is a purely practical one and based on the fact that in order to get any legislation whatsoever upon the statute books we must simplify it as much as possible and choose as our entering wedge that class of sufferer against which the opponents of the bill cannot level the charge that we are depriving people of life against their will.[74]

Unable to decide what strategy would be best in the long run, the ESA decided to consult the British society on the matter. The British society seemed to be firm in its denial of euthanasia to any but consenting dying patients, and the Americans wished to understand why. Millard's response was very clear:

> I am sorry that I am not in favour, at least not at this stage, with advocating euthanasia for the feeble minded or insane. One difficulty is that there is no sharp dividing line between low-grade mentally deficients, who are no better than animals, and [high-grade] M.D.s who are only a little less intelligent than many who are not certified. To apply euthanasia except where the sufferer desired it would mean in practice applying it where the sufferer (and very many do not suffer physically or mentally) strongly objected. It would seem to many like murder, and I feel sure that to put any one to death against his will, just because we thought they would be better out of the way, or just to save expense, would in practice greatly shock public opinion that, even if such a law were ever passed, which I think is most unlikely, it would very soon be repealed.[75]

Millard, however, was willing to make an exception. "Of course, the position is very different as regards hopelessly imbecile infants, but there again, if you tried to carry it out without the parent's consent you would be asking for trouble. . . . I feel sure we shall be wise to concentrate first upon voluntary euthanasia."[76]

Some in the American society went as far as to argue that euthanasia for the mentally retarded and the physically handicapped was much more important than euthanasia for the terminally ill. Such a position was held by Foster Kennedy, the ESA president from 1939 to 1940. Kennedy resigned from the society after it became clear that most of its members were willing, at least for the time being, to limit the euthanasia struggle to dying patients. Years later, reflecting on his decision, Kennedy wrote:

> I came gradually to see that this voluntary exercise of power in mercy, by physicians, did not begin to touch the heart of the problem. And the heart of the problem is one that is seldom heard of, because it is little known. The shortening of a life that is truly running out is not the most important consideration in the matter. What is truly important is permitting a life that is young, which is geared perhaps for six or seven decades of existence, to continue when that life is at once defective, without value and tortured.[77]

Kennedy was clearly committed to the eugenic program and believed that the ESA should adopt that program to its fullest extent. But there were other opinions in the society that drew a clear distinction between eugenics and euthanasia. Dr. Samuel J. Holmes, a professor of zoology at the University of California, Berkeley, declared that the only purpose of the new euthanasia society was to relieve needless human suffering. He insisted that it had no fantastic ideas concerning the betterment of the human race biologically through the elimination of the hopelessly diseased. Dr. Holmes's opinion is particularly interesting, because he himself was a eugenicist. Nevertheless, he did not think that euthanasia was a viable eugenic solution. For him the motivation for euthanasia appeared to be simply humanitarian. But even Dr. Holmes considered the possibility that in cases where the patients' "minds have gone, the parents or a guardian or next to kin would make the decision."[78]

One of the most striking cases of the attempt to legalize nonvoluntary euthanasia for retarded patients took place in Oregon during the early 1940s. Dr. Goldenweiser, a professor of sociology at Reed College in Portland, advocated death for hopelessly feeble-minded children.[79] He argued in the press that the law should permit the chloroforming of idiots and that such actions "are needed from a humanitarian standpoint." His proposal was seconded by Dr. S. B. Laughlin of Willamette University, who argued that "one has only to visit the Oregon State Feeble-minded Home and look at those children lying in bed, unable to lift their heads from their pillows, to agree with me that they should be chloroformed.[80]

The publication created a public furor, not least because of its impact on its potential "beneficiaries." The day following the publication, five patients fled from a mental home in Oregon. The medical supervisor of the home, Dr. Roy Byrd, explained that the inmates got excited over a sociologist's discussion of mercy deaths for hopeless "mental defectives" and fled from their ward. The head psychologist at the home, L. D. Idleman, reported that patients were repeatedly asking when they were to be chloroformed.[81]

The question about whether euthanasia should be applied to the insane reemerged again and again through the following years. Thus, in March 24, 1941, at a board meeting of the society, a Mrs. More asked the members of the board what their attitude would be on the inclusion in the euthanasia bill of "recognizable monsters and grossly defective infants," with one or both parents' consent. She believed that such a change would enlist the support of many younger people and might also enlist greater legislative support owing to its social and economic implications. The board rejected the change on the practical grounds that a version of a bill was already present before the legislature but decided that, if opinion warranted, another bill would be drawn.[82]

What is most striking about the ESA's internal debate is not that a small group of individuals believed that mentally retarded patients should be killed. The debate showed a much broader and more troubling phenomenon. At no point along the way, as far as the documents can tell, was the question raised whether the killing of the mentally retarded was justified independently of its social benefits. Most concretely, the question whether the law itself posed a challenge to such a practice, one that could not be overcome by legislation, was never seriously debated. The only obstacle that seemed to stand in the way of legalizing nonvoluntary euthanasia was public opinion.

To the members of the ESA, there was no point in attempting to pass a bill that would legalize nonvoluntary euthanasia because such a bill could not yet gain public support. Thus, not one of several bills that were drafted under the auspices of the ESA mentioned the option of administering euthanasia to the mentally and physically handicapped or to deformed babies.

The standard ESA bill stated that a person of sound mind at least twenty-one years of age who suffered from a painful and incurable disease could petition any court of record or judge thereof (except appellate courts) for euthanasia. The court was to appoint a committee of three persons, at least one of whom was a physician, to determine the merits of the request. If two or more of the committee members agreed that merciful death was warranted, and if the court approved, then the patient's life could be terminated. Death would be administered by a physician, or any other person under a physician's direction, in the presence of two witnesses.

WWII and the Nazi Euthanasia Program

While these efforts to pass bills legalizing euthanasia were ongoing, euthanasia was being practiced on a massive scale in Nazi Germany. Knowledge of the Nazi euthanasia project arrived in the United States long before the war had ended. As early as 1941, American newspapers were reporting that the Nazi government had put to death "85,000 blind, incurably ill or aged Germans."[83] One might expect that knowledge of the Nazi atrocities would have brought an end to any attempt in the United States that might even remotely resemble such actions. One might expect that euthanasia supporters in the United States would finally give up the hope of offering euthanasia to "defectives" and focus on the hastening of the death of terminally ill patients. But this was not the case. The ESA did not change its course of action, or its name, until the late 1960s.[84]

The war did have some effect on the society's activities. In 1943, it decided to postpone all attempts to promote euthanasia bills until the war ended. The reason for this decision had little to do with the fear that the ESA euthanasia proposals might be compared with the Nazis' attempt to clear the Reich from all forms of "unworthy life." It was more a reaction to the fact that since the nation had more important concerns to deal with, the ESA had difficulty in securing financial and moral support during this period.[85]

Yet immediately after the war, the ESA was ready to gather its troops and again launch the battle to legalize euthanasia. As a postwar letter sent to the members of the society asking for financial contributions to the endeavor explained:

> Through the war we have been quietly but steadily building up support for the legalization of voluntary euthanasia, to make merciful release available for incurable sufferers. . . . The time has come to start systematic preparation for a legislative campaign next winter. But we haven't enough money. . . .[86]

And indeed, the society flourished during the years after the war. There were clear signs of growing interest in the question of euthanasia. In 1946, forty-three new members joined the society, making a total of 305 members, and in addition 158 members were registered to the special Physician Committee for Legalization of Voluntary Euthanasia in New York, which now numbered 965.[87]

With the fall of the Nazi regime, new evidence of the Nazi atrocities was obtained. The Nuremberg trials revealed more details of the nature of the Nazi "euthanasia" plan.[88] The bad name the Nazis had given to euthanasia clearly affected the ESA. The society could not ignore the obvious comparison that would surely be made between the kind of euthanasia they were advocating and the kind practiced by the Nazis.

Pressure was starting to build up, especially from the Catholic Church, which hurried to identify the ESA proposal with Nazi Germany. Alerting the American people to the dangers entailed in such proposal, a widely spread pamphlet by the Catholic Church warned:

> What about the fate of minority groups in this country if the complete program (of euthanasia) should be legalized? One need but look to Germany for the answer. The Nazi doctors who carried out Hitler's euthanasia program have recently been brought to trial on the charge of murder by the United States Army courts in the very courtroom which the Nazi leaders themselves were condemned to death.[89]

More than any other aspect of the ESA activity in those years, the way in which the society attempted to defend itself from such comparisons may be the most revealing. The simple way by which the ESA could distinguish its euthanasia struggle from that of the Nazis was to emphasize that the society was only advocating euthanasia for terminally ill patients, on the basis of humanitarian concerns. This would have been an excellent opportunity for the ESA to resolve once and for all its dilemma regarding euthanasia for the unfit and to focus on the administration of euthanasia on humanitarian grounds alone.

That, however, was not the choice the ESA made—at least not for the first decade after the war. The ESA continued to toy with the possibility that nonvoluntary euthanasia could be offered to the unfit in the United States. Although throughout the years the society maintained its traditional approach that, as a practical matter, it should focus on euthanasia for the hopelessly sick, there was a growing sense that, given a more general change of opinions, the society should also be prepared for advocating a more comprehensive bill that would include other cases of hopelessly suffering humans. Thus, in 1943 the new president of the ESA appointed a committee, which included Dr. Potter, to draft a bill legalizing euthanasia for "idiots, imbeciles and congenital monstrosities."[90]

Nevertheless, the society was very critical of the Nazi euthanasia and was at times sincerely shocked by attempts to confuse its proposal with the Nazi atrocities. A letter sent by the ESA to the editor of the *New Republic*, referring to the Nazi atrocities, clarified, "The Euthanasia Society of America [is] shocked at this inhonorable slaying of innocent, by which the national [German] government seeks [to rid] itself of the economic burden of the physically unfit."[91] There is no reason to doubt that the ESA truly believed that a clear and distinct line separated its euthanasia agenda from that of the Nazis.

A similar concern was expressed in an annual meeting of the ESA in 1943:

Misunderstandings of our aim still exists. Some people think we're in favor of the government secretly killing off defectives, as in Nazi Germany; others believe that even now, before the law is amended, the Society can somehow arrange to have euthanasia administered, as we receive piteous appeals from hopeless sufferers. So during the past year we have taken every opportunity to explain that we are opposed to illegal, surreptitious, compulsory "mercy killings," that what we are working for is to legalize medically supervised euthanasia for incurable sufferers who ask for it.[92]

The problem with Nazi euthanasia, according to the ESA, was not so much its nonvoluntary character as its arbitrariness manifested by its "illegal, surreptitious," and "compulsory" character. In a single word, the problem of the Nazi euthanasia was its *unlawfulness*, while the moral superiority of the ESA proposal was its lawfulness.

The law was seen as a means of controlling the dangers of an unfettered application of euthanasia. The Nazi euthanasia allowed medical technology to run amok, while euthanasia, according to the ESA, would be restrained by the law. The law was therefore praised for its capacity to implement public policy and medical technique, and not for its independent moral judgment, independent from both public opinion and technical concern.

There were other ways in which supporters of the ESA distinguished its euthanasia proposal from that of the Nazis. In an interesting letter to a daily paper, Inez Philbrick expressed her outrage at any attempt to compare the goals of the euthanasia movement with that of the Nazis. Philbrick moved quickly from condemning the Nazis on moral grounds to condemning them for the unscientific basis of their struggle. The problem with the Nazi euthanasia program was not in the practice itself but rather in the fact that it did not comply with legal and scientific standards.

> It is acme of unreason to attribute to the sole authority responsible for these killings, that sadist madman now run amok in Europe, or to his henchmen, possession of an iota of the sentiment of mercy. . . . Nor is eugenics the basis of these actions. Only releasing vast sums of the making of munitions and the maintenance of an army of devastation, pillage and slaughter, can explain the wish to rid Germany from "unproductive lives."[93]

Not all members of the ESA accepted its postwar position, and these dissenters rejected the society's attempt to distinguish itself from the Nazi practice of euthanasia. Thomas A. C. Rennie, a medical doctor of psychiatry from New York Hospital, resigned from the society and explained his decision:

> The right to terminate the life of another seems to me fundamentally incompatible with Christian ethics. In war we permit and glorify the experience. . . . I believe that the "humanitarian" aspects of euthanasia are likely to be rationalizations for the act which in the last analysis is an act of aggression and hostility. In retrospect we can see that the Nazi terrorism came after the phase of medical elimination of the

unfit and disabled. Who in our society has the right to determine what is unfit? I think the Nazi experiment was only the first symptom of a mass pathological phenomenon, which ultimately led to the unleashing of such dreadful hostilities as to be characterized as the shame of the world. Mankind in our troubled times carries within itself the potentialities for unbelievable destructiveness.[94]

In response to growing criticism both from within and from without, the ESA was seriously considering changing its name to include the word "Voluntary" in it. Such a change, the society's bulletin explained, would "ease the minds of incurable sufferers who, even though in excruciating pain, prefer to linger to the end."[95] But the change did not take place, and as late as 1954, the bulletin saw no problem in publishing the following article, under the title "Euthanasia Provided for Animals":

The animal shelter for the Society of the Prevention of Cruelty to Animals, which was dedicated last May, is equipped with a "euthanasia air chamber" in which animals can be put to sleep humanely. How long will it be before hospitals for humans make any provision for putting them mercifully to sleep?[96]

Conclusion

The rise of euthanasia as public policy had several manifestations. First, promoters of the euthanasia cause viewed euthanasia as part of a bigger endeavor to improve society by medical and technological means. Second, euthanasia was offered as a solution to a growing variety of social problems. Dying became only one among several forms of social suffering; it was no longer the suffering of the individual who was dying that could justify the practice. Third, public opinion became the last instance for determining the legitimacy of euthanasia.

These changes had a direct effect on the role of law in the struggle to institutionalize the practice. The law was no longer an independent source of determining the legitimacy of euthanasia. First, legality became dependent on securing public opinion and support. Second, the role of law was no longer to judge whether the practice of euthanasia was just but only to secure the regulation of technique. Thus, the role of law became merely one component in the rule of technique.

Lethal Dosing: Technique beyond the Law

Introduction

IN 1936, a bill was introduced before the British House of Lords, the purpose of which was to legalize medical euthanasia under certain conditions and limitations.[1] The bill failed to pass a second reading, though it won the support of more than a fourth of the House members. The Catholic members of the House, whose unwavering position against euthanasia was predictable, strongly objected to the bill. The scales were tilted, however, not by religious objection but by a speech delivered by Lord Dawson, one of England's eminent physicians.[2] Lord Dawson presented before the House of Lords medical and social considerations opposing the legalization of euthanasia. His argument was surprising. Dawson did not argue that the practice of euthanasia violated medical, moral or legal norms. His main argument was, rather, that there was no need for the law. Physicians, he believed, were ever more willing to alleviate the pain of the dying, even when it involved the shortening of life. The development of these new medical practices would serve as an alternative solution to euthanasia. These practices, which heretofore had not been popular, were now spreading among the medical profession and reaching the laity as well. In time, Dawson predicted, there would be no need to discuss the legalization of euthanasia: The pain of terminally ill patients would be alleviated even at the price of hastening the time of death. According to Dawson, the development of medical and technological practices would serve as an alternative route, deeming legislation needless.

Dawson saw ahead of his time. In his 1936 speech, he foresaw the emergence of a new medical practice that could be named "lethal dosing." In it, physicians would provide terminally ill patients with the necessary dosage to alleviate their pain, knowing that such action would hasten their death.

Over the course of the century, this medical practice that took off in the early decades of the twentieth century gradually turned into a widely accepted medical practice.[3] Today, lethal dosing is not only regularly practiced in hospitals and hospices but is openly recognized and recommended by the medical profession and, more recently, by state law. In 1988, for example, the American Medical Association adopted the position that "the administration of a drug necessary to ease the pain of a patient who is terminally ill and suffering excruciating pain may be appropriate medical treatment even though the effect of the drug may shorten life."[4] In a similar way, Justice O'Connor of the United States Supreme Court recently commented:

> There is no need to address the question whether suffering patients have a constitutionally cognizable interest in obtaining relief from the suffering that they may experience in the last days of their lives. There is no dispute that dying patients in Washington and New York can obtain palliative care, even when doing so would hasten their death.[5]

Justice O'Connor, fulfilling Dawson's prophecy, accepts as self-evident that lethal dosing has become an integral part of the medical treatment of the hopelessly ill and suffering patient, and on these grounds dismisses the need to determine the legal status of physician-assisted death.

While lethal dosing is a well-known and documented medical practice, it is not clear how often it is used, or even how often the use of such a measure is called for.[6]

What is clear is that physicians believe that the practice of lethal dosing is ethically permissible. A national survey showed that in the case of patients in severe pain who had no hope of recovery and who asked to have the pain eased, knowing it might shorten their life, 82 percent of physicians said it would be ethically permissible to administer drugs to relieve the pain even at the risk of shortening life.[7]

There is a striking difference between the legal and medical approach to lethal dosing and euthanasia. While lethal dosing is routinely practiced without raising any legal, moral, or medical controversy, the practice of euthanasia, even when intended to put an end to the suffering of the dying patient, is against the law and medical ethics.

Before us lie two actions prompted by similar motivations and identical consequences, with a dramatically different legal status. What matters is that the fundamental difference between these two practices is not merely that one is legitimate while the other is not. What makes the practice of lethal dosing unique is that it was institutionalized without undergoing any legal, moral, or public scrutiny. On this ground, the practice of lethal dosing differs not only from the unlawful practice of euthanasia but also from other medical practices that have been legalized, such as withdrawal of life-support machinery or physician-assisted suicide by medical prescription (which is legal in Oregon). Unlike lethal dosing, these practices were in-stitutionalized only after a long legal and public struggle. Lethal dosing, on the other hand, gradually became legal without any dispute. Lord Dawson was therefore right when he predicted the manner in which this medical practice would spread among doctors in a "silent, cautious and irresistible manner."

To be sure, the question before us is not whether lethal dosing is or ought to be a crime in the United States but rather why the question of its legality has not been seriously considered in the process of its institution-alization. In other words, the question before us is not about the legality or illegality of lethal dosing but rather about its "sublegality." This term is used here in an analogous way to the reference psychology makes to "sub-liminal stimuli," which are not detected by the sensory system. In a simi-lar way, one might suggest that the medical practice of lethal dosing is not detected by the sensory organs of the legal system.

The unquestioned legitimacy of lethal dosing is even more surprising considering that it is relatively new. The practice of administering lethal doses of pain-relief medication was unequivocally banned during the first half of the twentieth century by law, medicine, and religion. Raising the question of lethal dosing in 1901, two legal scholars made the following assessment:

> Should a case occur where it would be imperative to administer the maximum dose of a remedy, with the intention of assuaging pain and suffering, and should the attending physician anticipate that such quantity is apt to produce simultaneously cessation for the vital func-tions, and thus anticipating, should he still run the risk and administer that dose, what would be his liability? The law in such cases implies malice. He would therefore, be guilty of homicide.[8]

In a similar vein, in 1912 a famous physician complained about the con-tinuous opposition of physicians not only to medical euthanasia but also to lethal dosing. While some physicians, he observed, are slowly consenting,

> many of them hesitate and, like misers, measure out drop by drop the clemency and peace which they grudge and which they ought to lav-ish, dreading lest they should weaken the last resistance, that is to say, the most useless and painful quivering of life that does not wish to give place to the coming quiet.[9]

These observations notwithstanding, it is hard to imagine that lethal dosing was not practiced in secret by physicians throughout history. Yet it is only in the course of the twentieth century that we can find public recognition for the need of the practice, and its centrality in the treatment of dying patients. The first public approval was voiced in the early twentieth century, but the significant change took place in the late 1950s and early 1960s. We will return to this change in what follows.

The question raised in this chapter is, What is it that distinguishes lethal dosing from euthanasia, which allowed the former but not the latter to pass unnoticed under the scanning radar of medical ethics and criminal law? How is it that a practice that was condemned by religion, medicine, and law for a long period of time could become openly and widely practiced without raising any objections? More generally, what does the practice of lethal dosing reveal regarding the modern art of dying, and what does it disclose about the power of law to regulate lethal dosing as a form of technique, albeit a different one from that of medical euthanasia?

This chapter explores different hypotheses by which the institutionalization of lethal dosing can be explained. The first part considers the most common moral justification of the practice, known as "the doctrine of double effect." Discussion of this doctrine sheds some initial light on the practice of lethal dosing but ultimately fails to explain its peculiar status. The second part of this chapter discusses in detail the legal treatment of lethal dosing and makes it possible to gain more insight about the nature of the practice. In the last instance, however, the sublegal status of lethal dosing cannot be explained on the basis of either morality or law, but rather lies in particular aspects of medical technique. This radical way in which medical technique is at work in lethal dosing may explain its sublegal status, as well as the difference between euthanasia and lethal dosing.

What is ultimately at stake in this inquiry is the way in which technique transforms the nature of dying in the modern age. The growing use of lethal dosing to secure a painless death replaces the need for euthanasia and brings the technical control of dying to its ultimate conclusion. That the law is not even involved in the process of institutionalizing lethal dosing is further proof of the uninterrupted reign of technique. With lethal dosing, the transformation of dying from an art to a technique reaches its completion.

Religious and Moral Justification

The simplest way to justify the practice of lethal dosing is by bringing about a balance between competing values. In the case of lethal dosing, the dilemma confronting the physician can be resolved, it would seem, by a value judgment. On the one hand stands the value of the sanctity of life. Life as such is worth preserving, and no one has permission to end another's life without justification. On the other hand stands the humanist need to alleviate the pointless suffering of a dying patient whose days are numbered. A decision to justify the practice of lethal dosing could be based on the preference of one value over another, under specific circumstances.

While theoretically such a justification would be plausible, lethal dosing has not been justified in this manner. In fact, during the first decades of the twentieth century there was hardly any public discussion of the matter at all. Lethal dosing simply crept into common practice under the protection of quiet, common assumptions about the treatment of the dying. It is only *after* lethal dosing became a routine practice that the question of its legitimacy became central to ethicists. But even today, most discussions tend to focus on how to justify lethal dosing, rather than on whether to do so.

Moreover, the balancing of values cannot be the grounds for the institutionalization of the practice, because this very same logic can justify medical euthanasia as well. If the patient is indeed suffering from pain that can justifiably be alleviated at the price of shortening life, why would one way of shortening life be preferred over another?

Accepting this logic, the English scholar Glanville Williams has denied any significant moral or legal difference between lethal dosing and euthanasia.[10] Addressing the common attempt to distinguish between these practices, Williams explained that it is only for "psychological" reasons that we tend to prefer the practice of lethal dosing to that of euthanasia.[11]

One could agree with Williams that it is hard to find a moral or legal difference between the practice of euthanasia and lethal dosing yet still remain unsatisfied by his attempt to eliminate the distinction between these practices as "psychological." The challenge before us is precisely to distinguish between these practices. Even if we can find no moral or legal distinction, the fact that physicians clearly distinguish between lethal dosing and euthanasia cannot be denied. One is a common medical practice, while the other is not. What is the basis for drawing such a distinction?

The exception to the prevailing silence over lethal dosing, during the mid-twentieth century, came from a surprising source. The Catholic Church, an otherwise zealous defender of the sanctity of life, openly discussed and even defended the legitimacy of lethal dosing.[12] In 1957, Pope Pius XII's endorsement of lethal dosing not only approved the practice but also established the grounds for its justification. The 1957 encyclical was written in response to questions presented to the pope by a group of anesthesiologists. Central among their questions was whether narcotics may be used at the approach of death, even if their use might shorten life. Pope Pius XII responded:

> If no other means exist, and if, in the given circumstances, this does not prevent the carrying out of other religious and moral duties: Yes. In this case, of course, death is in no way intended or sought, even if the risk of it is reasonably taken; the intention is simply to relieve pain effectively, using for this purpose painkillers available to medicine.[13]

The justification that the pope implicitly relied on is known as the doctrine of double effect. The doctrine was imported from medieval Christian morality and has its roots in the thinking of Thomas Aquinas.[14] It became widely accepted among medical ethicists and slowly penetrated into the medical profession at large. This justification has become so popular that even strictly medical articles refer to the doctrine as a justification of lethal dosing, and physicians often refer to lethal dosing itself as the practice of double effect.

What is the doctrine of double effect? Can it explain the sublegal status of lethal dosing? And if not, how did lethal dosing become legitimate and openly practiced?

The common rendering of the double-effect doctrine is that when an action has two effects, one good and the other bad, that action may be justified as long as the following four conditions apply:

> (1) the act itself, prescinding from the evil caused, is good or at least indifferent; (2) the good effect of the act is what the agent intends[15] directly, only permitting the evil effect; (3) the good effect must not come about by means of the evil effect; and (4) there must be some proportionately grave reason for permitting the evil effect to occur.[16]

The doctrine applies to the case of lethal dosing, because the physician's intention is to relieve pain (good effect) and because, although he foresees the hastening of death as a bad effect of this action, he does not intend it.[17] In particular, the hastening of death is not the *means* for achieving pain relief but merely an unintended *consequence*. The fact that the physician uses only the necessary dosage of narcotics to relieve pain and does not overdose the patient with the intention of causing death shows that the pain-relief medication is administered only for the purpose of alleviating pain. The doctrine, on the other hand, does not apply to the practice of euthanasia, where the explicit intention is to hasten death.[18]

At first, applying the doctrine of double effect to the case of lethal dosing may seem both appropriate and compelling. Any objection to its applicability may appear, at best, as a minor contribution to the field of medical ethics and, at worst, as a tedious exercise in medieval scholasticism. However, the question before us is not whether the doctrine can be applied to the practice of lethal dosing but rather whether its application can explain the institutionalization of the practice, particularly its sublegal status, as a modern-day medical practice.

Underlying the logic of the doctrine of double effect is a problem that pertains to Christian morality and makes little sense in the context of modern medical practices. One of the fundamental principles of Thomist morality is that actions are judged as good or evil in themselves, regardless of their consequences. Accordingly, performing an act that is evil in itself cannot be justified by its good consequences. Evil, in other words, can never serve as a means for achieving a good end. This approach is known as moral absolutism, because of the absolute value it gives to the action itself, rather than judging it relative to the results it achieves.[19]

The principle of absolute prohibitions creates a strict moral system in which evil deeds should not be performed even for the sake of good effects. The doctrine of double effect is designed to overcome the problem of absolute prohibitions by drawing a distinction between intended and foreseen consequences. This doctrine maintains that the evil effect is no longer absolutely prohibited and will not taint the action as long as it is not intended, even if it is foreseen.[20]

However, the double-effect doctrine makes little sense in the context of modern medical practices. For one thing, the problem of absolute prohibitions arises neither in medical practice nor, more generally, in the moral and legal principles governing medical action. The modern way of making moral and ethical decisions is based on seeking a balance between different values. A value judgment is required in order to decide whether the good is more to be desired than the evil is to be avoided. The value of the action is commonly weighed according to the result it achieves. In particular, the question whether the evil effect is a means for achieving a good result or an independent effect of the action is irrelevant in determining the morality of an action.

Not only is the problematic of absolute values alien to the modern secular context but the solution provided to this problematic—namely, drawing a distinction between foreseen and intended consequences—is also highly questionable. It is hard to understand why a physician would be less responsible for a consequence he foresaw than for one he intended. It is precisely the physician's medical knowledge that suggests he would be accountable for any result of his medical practice that was known in advance.[21]

To understand how implausible the doctrine of double effect is to the modern mind, one need only recall other attempts to apply the doctrine—attempts that were highly criticized within the same medical and ethical circles that were now endorsing the double-effect doctrine. In the case of abortion, the Catholic Church drew a distinction between killing the fetus in order to save the mother's life and performing an operation such as the removal of an impregnated Fallopian tube intended to save the mother's life and unintentionally (though foreseeably) killing the fetus. In the case of abortion, the medical profession (with the exception of Catholic ethicists) did not adopt the doctrine of double effect—not because it was misapplied but because of it clearly departed from the modern moral and legal thinking.[22]

The doctrine of double effect, in short, cannot be divorced from the religious context in which it was formulated. This is not because the doctrine makes reference to divine will or because it is based on scripture, rather it is because the doctrine is based on grounds that are alien to the modern practice of medicine as well as to the legal supervision of law.

To argue that the double-effect doctrine cannot justify the contemporary practice of lethal dosing is not to propose that lethal dosing should be prohibited or that any attempt to distinguish between lethal dosing and physician-assisted suicide is bound to fail. To the contrary, precisely because a clear distinction is made within medical practice, legal analysis, and public awareness between lethal dosing (which is taken for granted) and physician-assisted suicide (which is strongly disputed), the question arises as to the grounds on which this distinction lies.

Although the doctrine of double effect cannot explain the sublegal status of lethal dosing, it is important to bear in mind the way in which it attempts to solve the *moral* problem of lethal dosing. Rather than merely balancing between values and arguing that the good consequence outweighs the bad consequence, the doctrine of double effect establishes an essential difference between the two. The intended consequence (or the goal) is what determines the moral character of the action, while the unintended consequence (or the side effect) plays a secondary role. Although the double-effect doctrine itself has a limited capacity to explain the sublegality of lethal dosing, it takes us one step further in solving this riddle. For what the doctrine does above all is blur the causal relation between the treatment of the patient and the death of the patient, making the decision to treat morally and legally unproblematic. And it is precisely this blurring that is crucial for understanding how lethal dosing became a routine medical practice.

The doctrine of double effect does not solve the problem of the sublegal status of lethal dosing, even though it takes us one step further in our journey. We thus need to return to our opening question: How is it that lethal dosing is so commonly and uncontrovertibly practiced? The answer to this question can be found in the technical logic governing the conduct of lethal dosing. However, before we discuss the technical nature of lethal dosing and its implications, a brief discussion of its legal status is warranted.

Legal Justification

From a legal point of view, the practice of lethal dosing is, prima facie, murder. Shortening the life of a person, even of a dying patient who has very little time to live, is not different from killing. Moreover, the distinction between foreseen and intended consequences, which often serves to justify lethal dosing, makes no legal difference.[23] Indeed, the common-law tradition and the American model penal code do not distinguish between intended and foreseen homicide, since both manifest the degree of culpability, or mens rea, that is required for a murder charge.[24] This prima facie criminality of lethal dosing leads us to wonder about the relative ease with which lethal dosing has escaped prosecution. It is also on the basis of this prima facie criminality that the law's few attempts to confront the question of lethal dosing should be understood. While these scattered encounters may suggest that the problem of lethal dosing has been treated by the law, in fact they prove precisely the opposite: they show how the law uncritically gave it sanction long after lethal dosing became a mundane medical practice.

As is well known, neither the common law nor the Model Penal Code are a final authority on matters of law. State legislators have the authority to enforce their sovereign will as long as it does not violate constitutional principles. Indeed, one may find several legislative acts that specifically permit the practice of lethal dosing. Michigan law, for example, permits the use of medication as long as it is designed "to relieve pain or discomfort and not to cause death, even if the medication or procedure may hasten or increase the risk of death."[25]

These legislative acts were enacted long after lethal dosing became widely and openly practiced and, even then, only in response to the challenge posed not by lethal dosing itself but by physician-assisted suicide. This is particularly true of the Michigan law, whose aim was to stop the active killings of patients by Dr. Kevorkian, a highly visible public figure at the time who has since been convicted of murder. In these legislative acts, the discussion of lethal dosing is only incidental, and is meant to clarify the distinction between physician-assisted suicide (which these acts declared as criminal) and the practice of lethal dosing (which remains unquestionably legal). These legislative acts take the legitimacy of lethal dosing for granted and, in affirming it, merely reflect existing medical practices.

It is telling that the question, "How is it that lethal dosing is permitted, while physician-assisted suicide is prohibited?" was never publicly or legally raised, not even by zealous opponents of physician-assisted suicide.[26] The reverse question, however, did become a central constitutional concern. In the case of *Vacco v. Quill*,[27] the task before the Supreme Court was to determine whether the state legislature had a legitimate basis for prohibiting physician-assisted suicide while legalizing lethal dosing. In a very brief passage addressing this question, the court concluded that the two practices *could* legitimately be distinguished. The court drew a distinction between lethal dosing as a case in which a doctor provides aggressive palliative care that "may hasten a patient's death, but the physician's purpose and intent is, or may be, only to ease his patient's pain," and of physician-assisted suicide as a case in which the doctor, "must, necessarily and indubitably, intend primarily that the patient be made dead."[28]

This decision is quite perplexing, for it seems to accept the same dubious distinction as the double-effect doctrine.[29] It also seems to contradict, or at least ignore, the rejection of precisely this distinction within criminal law. In any event, it gives no independent justification for the practice of lethal dosing and only says that physician-assisted suicide may be prohibited even if lethal dosing is not.

Perhaps the constitutional discourse on the question of physician-assisted suicide is not the best place to search for the legal response to the problem of lethal dosing. Perhaps it would be better to turn to a clear case in which lethal dosing was brought before the courts. There are very few cases in which charges were brought against physicians for practicing lethal dosing. In *Kansas v. Narmore*, one of the few cases reported in the district court, an osteopathic physician was convicted of attempted murder of a terminally ill patient as well as of the second-degree murder of another patient. In an uncommon move, the court of appeal decided to reverse the jury's verdict and found the physician not guilty on both charges.[30]

The grounds for the acquittal are quite revealing. The court found that the jury's decision was highly unreasonable and that, on the basis of the evidence, it should not have found the defendant guilty. The court reasoned that there was ample evidence that administering pain medication to dying patients—even with the clear knowledge that the effect of the drug could hasten death—was a regularly practiced and widely accepted medical treatment. In other words, the court deferred to the judgment of the medical profession in determining the appropriateness of the practice.

The explicit reasoning given by the Kansas court is the same that works implicitly in all cases that do not find their way to the judicial system. The question of legality is decided by medical practice. The law dutifully obeys and even welcomes the rule of technique.

The case of *Kansas v. Narmore* takes us one step further in understanding the sublegal status of lethal dosing. This status is closely related to the routine acceptance of the practice among the medical profession. But this answer, alone, will not suffice, for two questions remain unanswered.

First, it is unclear why the court was willing to accept so easily and uncritically the standard set by the medical profession. While it is not unusual for the courts to base legal decisions on professional standards, such a deferment cannot be taken for granted, especially not when the involvement of the law in all the other medical practices of hastening death is so prevalent. Second, it is unclear why the medical profession itself accepted the practice of lethal dosing as legitimate. How can such a position be explained in light of the clear stand that the medical profession has taken in regards to euthanasia?

There is a single answer to both questions that—although it requires further clarification—can be summed up in the following observation. The practice of lethal dosing has been challenged neither by the medical profession nor by the law because the physician is not seen as responsible for the consequences of his action. The death of the patient does not need to be justified because, as far as the medical profession is concerned—and as far as the law, which accepts the medical point of view, is concerned—the physician did not cause the death of the patient. This startling observation is captured in the following report given by a physician who was personally involved with the practice of lethal dosing.

> I frequently use MS [morphine sulfate] to keep patients asleep at the end. I give them more than they need to control pain. I feel perfectly comfortable with it. . . . I turned up the morphine drip. . . . She was in [emotional] agony. I kept turning it up, just in case, even after she was unconscious. She died later that day. I don't think I killed her.[31]

The reminder of this chapter is dedicated to exploring this possibility. How could the practice of lethal dosing foreseeably cause the death of the patient without implicating the physician who administered the lethal dose? The answer lies in the radical way in which the use of medical technique became involved in producing this painless death.

To understand better the nature of the practice, we need a closer examination of its historical origins. An important change took place in the treatment of the dying, which can be summed up as a transformation in the treatment of the dying from *pain relief* to *pain management*. This transformation is a manifestation of the expanding rule of technique in the treatment of the pain of dying patients and will shed light on the emerging institutionalization of lethal dosing during the early 1960s.

Lethal Dosing as Technique

The practice of lethal dosing emerged as a response to a crisis in the medical treatment of dying patients. The development of medical knowledge, technologies, and institutions for solving the problem of pain in the latter part of the twentieth century marked a new era in pain management.[32] Sophisticated medical procedures, such as surgeries and local pain blockage, have been tried with varying degrees of success, to a large extent minimizing the suffering of pain. While modern medicine is able to control most of the symptoms in the course of the disease, in the last stages of terminal illness, such as cancer, the ordinary use of analgesics cannot always relieve suffering. Symptoms that cannot be controlled despite aggressive efforts are identified as refractory. Such symptoms include (in addition to severe pain), shortness of breath, agitated delirium, and persistent vomiting.[33] The practice of lethal dosing is meant to solve such problems of severe and uncontrolled suffering incurred by dying patients. In such cases, high doses of narcotics are necessary to alleviate the suffering.

There are many forms of lethal dosing. Perhaps the most common today is that of terminal sedation by the use of a morphine drip.[34] The morphine drip, which was invented in the early 1980s, involves a continuous intravenous (CI) infusion, in which a constant level of morphine is maintained in the patient's blood circulation. Dying patients are commonly hooked up with a morphine drip in the last phase of their life. Given the fragile condition of the dying patient, the administration of such doses may lead to death. This is especially true in the case of patients who are already suffering from breathing difficulties, since one effect of sedation is the repression of respiration.

Some patients die within a short hour from the beginning of the treatment. Others fall into a state of coma, which may persist for days and even weeks. Often, the practice of terminal sedation is accompanied by the withdrawal of nutrition and hydration. In these cases, the patient is bound to die either from the narcotics themselves or from dehydration.

The practice of terminal sedation and the use of the morphine drip belong in an obvious way to the realm of medical technique. They involve the use of highly sophisticated instrumentation grounded by an advanced scientific knowledge. Yet the legitimacy of lethal dosing does not lie in the technological instrument itself. The mere use of any particular instrument in the hastening of death could never render such killing legitimate. Rather, it is the *logic of technique* that precedes any technological innovation and underlies its practice that we are interested in. We therefore seek to examine the logic of technique, not in terms of any particular method of relieving pain, but rather in terms of the rise of a technical regime under which the relief of pain has been transformed into a problem of technique.

The most important transformation in the administration of drugs to dying patients took place in the 1960s and was closely related to rise of the hospice and the hospice mentality in treating the dying. Cicely M. Saunders, the founder of the hospice movement, criticized the existing routine of administering pain-relief medication as inappropriate for the care of dying patients.

Before the hospice revolution, the prevalent treatment of pain was based on the idea that pain-relief medication should be given only upon the patient's request and should be strictly limited, both in dosage and in frequency. Even when the patient was in agonizing pain, morphine would not be given more often than every six hours and even then only after repeated requests from the patient. This procedure was known as PRN (*pro re nata*, literally meaning "for the thing born")—that is, only to meet an emergency. There was a great fear that given a higher frequency of dosage, the patient might die of an overdose. Alternatively, a higher frequency might cause tolerance or addiction to the drug.

The new solution to the problem of pain in dying that was offered by the founders of the hospice movement was at once trivial and revolutionary. Instead of waiting until the effect of the pain medication subsided, a constant dosage of pain relief was provided so that patients should not have to ask for relief of pain, nor should they suffer from severe pain before analgesics were granted. This solution was trivial to the extent that it merely suggested that pain relief medication would be given more frequently and in higher dosage. And it was revolutionary to the extent that it transformed the treatment of pain from pain relief to pain management, and from the personal relation between patient and physician to the impersonal relation between patient, physician, and machine.

To speak of technique governing human action is not to draw a distinction between human action and machine but rather to show how human action itself became subordinated to a technical regime. These transformations constitute a further radicalization of the technical logic governing the treatment of pain.

In the traditional treatment of the dying patient, the relief of pain was not the sole obligation of the medical profession. The physician had to balance between two duties: prolonging life and relieving pain. The same need to balance was still operative in the new regime of treatment as long as there was still hope of cure. But when the reality of death became clear, there was no longer any point in prolonging life. The duty to relieve pain not only trumped the prolonging of life but deemed the latter irrelevant. There was no longer a need to balance between competing values because, from the moment the medical profession could no longer prolong life, its struggle was directed to the control of pain. Medical technique sacrificed the goals it could be interested in achieving for those that it could secure with certainty.

In this context, medical technique is not merely a neutral means that the physician may choose to apply. The very fact that the physician could relieve the pain of the dying patient became the driving force to do so. Refraining from treating the pain of the patient was likely to be considered a violation of medical norms.

Furthermore, the problem of pain was no longer how to relieve the suffering for the patient once it occurred but rather how to avoid suffering altogether. Pain went from being an internal symptom of disease to a syndrome that was understood apart from the disease and could be overcome independently from its cure.

One may claim that the purpose of medical treatment was no longer to alleviate pain. Ordinarily, alleviating pain is a solution to the experience of pain. The practice of advanced palliative care, however, became one of treating the pain before it was even experienced; and a transformation took place from treating the patient as a whole to managing the patient's pain.

Finally, and as a consequence of the above, the relation between the care provider and the patient changed. The conflict between the patient and the physician or nurse that arose from the constant negotiation over the quantity and frequency of pain medication was resolved: the patient was no longer required to ask for pain relief, and the physician was no longer expected to be attentive to the patient's voice. The previously more personal, if contentious, relation between health provider and patient was replaced by an impersonal relation between a pain-relief producer and a pain-relief consumer.

All these transformations took place in the 1960s, long before the invention of the morphine drip. It is only on their basis, however, that the morphine drip became possible. In essence, the morphine drip is a more advanced deployment of these earlier transformations. The morphine drip, as a means for producing terminal sedation, is a solution limited to the dying patient. The dosage level of the morphine drip is adjusted so that sedation is effectively achieved. The dying patient who is hooked up to the morphine drip is therefore freed not only from pain but also from any other human experience. And finally, the relation between patient and physician, already reduced to a minimum, is replaced by a new relation between pain and machine.

Having explored some of the underlying logic of technique governing the practice of lethal sedation, we are now in the position to reexamine the place of this practice in relation to the realm of ethics and law.

The Sublegality of Lethal Dosing

How, then, does the technical practice of lethal dosing (and in particular, that of the morphine drip) relieve the physician from the responsibility of hastening the death of a patient? Lethal dosing escapes legal regulation because of the manner in which technique transforms the basic components of human action—namely, actor, intention, and causation. Not only are these the principal building blocks of human action, but also they lie at the foundations of moral responsibility and criminal law.[35] In the performance of lethal dosing, it is no longer clear who, precisely, the actor was, what the intention in mind was, and whether the effect was the consequence of any particular action.

The impersonal relation between the patient and the physician, which is now mediated not only by the medical machine but also by the growing number of medical personnel, blurs the identity of the actor. The fact that, in lethal dosing, death is usually not the immediate consequence of any one medical action but rather a result of the cumulative effects of lethal-dosing treatment calls into question the causal relation between lethal dosing and death. A similar effect is induced by the delay between the administration of the dose and its lethal consequence. Finally, attempting to determine whether the physician's intention was to kill the patient or to relieve pain is not a distinction that makes much sense in the day-to-day practice of medicine. The ordinary use of intent to determine culpability is not the proper means for judging the physician's actions. The only intent of the physician in this sense is to carry on his job and benefit the patient to the extent possible.[36]

The doctrine of double effect sought to release physicians from their responsibility because they lack the subjective intent to cause death. Now, however, it becomes clear that the subjective intent of physicians is not central to the practice of lethal dosing any more than their subjective state of mind is relevant in performing an operation. Physicians are merely partaking in the medical practice, the only purpose of which is to relieve the pain of the dying patient. As long as they follow these accepted norms, which are based on the logic of technical operation, their subjective intentions become irrelevant.

No less important, however, in understanding how technique transforms human action and moral responsibility is the power of command that modern technique has over physicians. The management of pain is not merely an option that physicians can choose to fulfill but rather an imperative they face in the treatment of dying. The administration of pain relief is based neither on the patient's request for pain medication nor on the medical judgment that such medication is necessary at a given time. Rather, the timetable is replaced by the continuous drip, which now sets the pace for human action.

All these characteristics are not arbitrary consequences of lethal dosing, of course. They arise out of the logic of technique underlying the practice. Technique is not merely the human application of advanced instrumentation; it is also the governing of human action by the logic of technique. In other words, for the medical profession, lethal dosing is a duty grounded not in morality but in "technicity."

These observations may also explain how physician-assisted suicide is distinguishable from lethal dosing. The distinction between the two is not that one includes an intention to kill while the other entails a mere foresight of this result. Rather, lethal dosing is legitimate because it belongs to the ordinary practice of pain-relief treatment. The same morphine dose, or morphine pump, that is used to treat dying patients is used in the treatment of regular patients without risking their lives. Physician-assisted suicide, on the other hand, introduces new means, which do not belong to the ordinary treatment of pain. Moreover, physician-assisted suicide is more personal and immediate in its effect. One may then translate the imperative set by the double-effect doctrine, "Do not intend to kill, intend to relieve pain" into the language of technique: "Do not digress from technical procedure."

The legitimacy of lethal dosing arises, therefore, from the way in which it is continuous with the day-to-day management of pain and is forced from this realm. Euthanasia, which—as we have seen—also emerges out of the day-to-day treatment of the dying, nevertheless is also a break from that treatment. It is for this reason that legal intervention is called for in the case of euthanasia and completely unnecessary in that of lethal dosing.

Conclusion: Ethics, Technique, and Human Action

The doctrine of double effect should not be dismissed offhand as a justification for lethal dosing. It is not merely a mistake that has brought what some would wish to characterize as a dark-age doctrine into the light of day. Rather than asking whether the technomedical practice of lethal dosing should be understood in light of the doctrine of double effect, perhaps the question should be whether the doctrine of double effect can be understood in light of the technical and medical practice.

Indeed, the doctrine of double effect in contemporary ethics has often been applied to problems raised by the advancements of modern technique. This may suggest a broader link between problems raised by technique and the doctrine of double effect. The doctrine, for example, has been applied to the problem of strategic bombing, in which the aim to hit military targets is joined by the unintended though foreseen consequence of killing innocent civilians. This suggests that there may be some deeper connection between the doctrine and the use of technique.

What the doctrine of double effect attempts is to bring back human agency and moral responsibility to a realm from which the two have long been expelled. Why rely on a medieval doctrine for such a noble task? One possible answer is that the modern moral framework cannot offer reasonable solutions to these problems. And indeed, the dominant moral framework of balancing between competing values and interests (which finds its clearest application in utilitarianism but is also is used in rights discourse to balance between competing rights) cannot be applied to the realm of technique. The latter poses the relief of pain as its absolute end.

The doctrine of double effect, on the other hand, is more suited to capture the logic of technique. Like technique, it does not primarily strive to balance between good and evil. Rather, its logic is based on a distinction between foreseen and intended effects. This distinction bears a structural resemblance to the distinction between the ends set by technique and other ends (or consequences) that technique is indifferent to. To push the analogy further, we may say that the doctrine of double effect shares with the logic of technique a moral blindness to consequences that do not directly belong to its mode of operation.

Finally, whether this affinity suggests that the attempt to reintroduce human agency and moral responsibility into the realm of technique can be successful or whether any such attempt is naive at best and hypocritical at worst is a question that at present we shall leave open. What seems to be clear is that while the doctrine of double effect may have little power to transform the reality it is judging, it can reveal a great deal about it.

Mercy Killing: The Limits of Technique

THE HISTORY of euthanasia, presented in the previous chapters, began with the decline of the *ars moriendi* tradition in the early nineteenth century. The passing of the traditional art of dying was accompanied by the rise of medical euthanasia as a new way to die. Shortly thereafter, euthanasia moved beyond the medical sphere into the realm of positive law and social policy. Finally, during the mid-twentieth century, the technical mastery over dying furthered its reign with the emerging practice of lethal dosing. With lethal dosing, euthanasia disappeared as a problem and death became a mere side effect of the medical effort to relieve pain.

The story of euthanasia would not be complete, however, if viewed only within this line of development, that is, the medicalization, legalization, and bureaucratization of euthanasia. While there is no doubt that the latter developments have become central to the way we die, we must also note alternative forms of euthanasia that have existed alongside and in tension with the attempts to regulate death.

This chapter presents a different practice of euthanasia, performed by a layperson rather than by a doctor. I shall refer to such cases as *mercy killings* proper, to distinguish them from the practice of medicalized and legalized euthanasia discussed in earlier chapters. Mercy killing, as opposed to euthanasia, involves neither the white-robed physician nor the black-robed lawyer. What further distinguishes mercy killing from legalized euthanasia is its ambiguous legal status. Though mercy killers act in clear violation of state law, they often receive surprisingly lenient punishments.

> "Mercy killings," a New York magazine reported in 1939, "now occur in the United States at the rate of about one a week. Mercy killers are those who take the lives of some member of the family afflicted with insanity or some incurable malady. They are seldom convicted. The longest sentence given a mercy killer was three months in prison."[1]

The magazine report overstated the leniency in punishment, but the overall picture it portrayed was generally accurate. In more than seventy documented cases of mercy killing from the 1920s to the 1960s, nearly half did not even arrive in the courts.[2] Of the thirty-three cases in which court results are available, two-thirds of the defendants were acquitted, and in less than a handful was the defendant convicted of murder. With few important exceptions, juries sentenced mercy killers to very short prison terms, at times fully exempting the defendant from punishment. As one scholar noted, "Whatever the legal basis on which [such cases] were acquitted, the public will always look upon them as mercy killers."[3] Most mercy killers were indeed acquitted, since juries and judges have refused to call the act murder.[4] For many on both sides of the euthanasia debate, however, the ambiguous legal treatment of mercy killings posed a serious problem. Common sense demanded a clear decision: either such killings were justifiable, and therefore they should be formally legalized, or else mercy killings are unjust and should be punished accordingly. Charles Potter, the founding figure of the Euthanasia Society of America, conveyed this sense of uneasiness:

> I recognize fully the fact that there are a number of individuals who should be mercifully put out of their misery—certain types of idiots and imbeciles, and hopeless sufferers in the last incurable stages of painful diseases such as cancer. But the act of mercy should not be performed by private citizens as it is increasingly done today. Nor should it be done secretly by physicians. The law itself should speedily be brought into accord with public opinion. Euthanasia should be legalized and supervised."[5]

ESA members further criticized the "impossible situation" in which mercy killings were being unlawfully performed, while the courts were reluctant to punish those who took the law into their hands. "Potter charged that the spread of this 'secret euthanasia' was 'threatening our morality and undermining our laws.' "[6] He believed that there should not be a law on the books that is consistently violated with no proper recourse. The gap between codified law and law in action must be minimized, and for this to happen, either the law or the practice must change.

In a similar vein, the following argument for legalized euthnasia appeared in a New York daily paper: "The proposed bill . . . would permit the hopelessly ill person himself to petition a court for painless death without waiting for the slow process of nature. It would afford escape for the sufferer without stigma or embarrassing publicity for anyone involved."[7]

For the ESA, mercy killing was a symptom of the problem and by no means its solution. The fact that family members were driven to kill their loved ones to save them from suffering was proof of how necessary it was to legalize euthanasia and have it performed only by authorized physicians. Potter argued that lenient judgments proved that the public was ready to accept euthanasia as a solution to the hopeless suffering of individuals. From the standpoint of proponents of regulation, mercy killing appeared as an aberration, an excess, which had to be brought back into the well-defined parameters of the legal order.

But is it not possible that mercy killing was (and still is) not merely a precipitate and underregulated form of euthanasia? Rather than conceiving mercy killing as a threat to the legal order, perhaps we should try and understand it on its own terms and ask what it is about mercy killing that gives rise to an ambivalent legal and moral response. From this perspective, mercy killing would not merely be a violation of the law, but rather an exception that does not fall under state law. Rather than prejudging mercy killing in light of the standards of regulation, we would do better to reexamine the desire to regulate euthanasia in light of mercy killing. Mercy killing would thus appear as a challenge to the very attempt to systematize euthanasia through medicalization and legal regulation. This murderous act of mercy, neither medicalized nor legalized, may lie beyond the reach of bureaucratic regulation, adhering to no written law and constituting a law of its own.

What, then, is the unwritten law to which mercy killing adheres? And what can mercy killing as an exception tell us about the attempt to establish the medical treatment of dying as a rule?

Case History

The year 1923 was an eventful one for the Greenfield family, which was expecting its first child. The great joy occasioned by the birth of a son turned into sadness with the growing realization that he was not developing normally. The baby was only a few weeks old when the parade of doctors began, "ranging from the neighborhood doctor to the specialist to the super-specialist."[8] Jerome, the experts informed the parents, was suffering from Laurence-Biedl syndrome, a condition of gradual mental degeneration. Indeed, at the age of ten the child could not talk, only babble. Despite his mental retardation, he was well-developed physically and had the body and presumably the passions of a near-adult. At the age of sixteen Jerome was six feet tall and weighed more than 170 pounds, but had the mental age of a two-year-old.[9] Frequently, he suffered violent and painful fits that almost drove his parents out of their minds with anguish.[10] Jerome was not fit to attend public school, from which he was eventually barred due to his "social and intellectual unfitness."[11] On two occasions the Greenfields placed the child in an institution, but each time he was taken out at his mother's insistence because he lost weight and was not cared for in what she considered a proper manner. His loving parents decided to bring him back home. "I loved him more than a mother loves a normal child," explained Anna Greenfield. "I felt that if I looked after him myself a miracle might happen and he might show some improvement."[12]

Jerome spent his early adolescence living with his parents in a small apartment in the Bronx. Louis Greenfield was a once-prosperous forty-five-year-old milliner and World War I veteran, who lost his fortune after the war and could no longer afford the costs of a private institution or outside help. The responsibilities involved in raising Jerome rested solely on his wife and himself.

As the boy grew older his condition worsened—Jerome became dangerous to the people around him. One doctor, an authority on impaired children, warned the Greenfields that they should have the boy sterilized because he posed a threat to his mother. Several attacks of paralysis increased the burden on his parents. The boy's suffering caused both his parents to deteriorate mentally and physically. "I began to pray," said his mother, "sometimes on my knees—always in my heart, that God would take him away."[13] For months Louis Greenfield was haunted by the need to bring to an end the suffering of his son, his wife, and himself.

January 12, 1939, was a cold winter's day in the Bronx. Louis Greenfield rose early after a sleepless night. At 9 A.M. he asked Anna to go to their millinery shop and assist his partner, Edward Rothenstein. Sometime between 10 and 11 A.M. Jerome suffered a particularly severe attack, and his father put the 170-pound youth to bed, fully clothed. When the boy fell asleep, Louis took the bottle of chloroform he had purchased in advance and emptied the contents onto two freshly laundered handkerchiefs. He placed the soaking fabrics over the boy's mouth and nose, leaving them there for fifteen minutes. For an hour afterward, he did nothing except pace through his apartment.

At 12:30 P.M. Louis Greenfield summoned the doorman of the house, told him what he had done, and asked him to notify the superintendent. When the latter appeared, he told him to call the police. During the police interrogation Greenfield insisted that his wife knew nothing of his intention to kill the boy.

The killing had been premeditated months in advance. According to

Greenfield's confession to the police, he traveled the preceding November 15, to Trenton, New Jersey, where he purchased three ounces of chloroform for fifty cents in a drug store. He had had to travel to New Jersey after his first attempt to purchase chloroform in the Bronx failed, because the druggist refused to sell it.

After hearing District Attorney Samuel J. Foley and seven witnesses, the Bronx grand jury indicted Louis Greenfield on a charge of first-degree manslaughter for killing his son. The grand jury deliberated more than an hour before handing down the least severe of three indictments it might have returned—the other two being first- and second-degree murder.

The defendant was released on bail that was fixed at $3,000. The trial before Judge Lester W. Patterson in Bronx County Court opened on May 9, 1939. In his opening speech, the prosecutor remarked, "Even I, the prosecutor, have to approach this case with sympathy for the defendant." However, he went on to declare that the father had broken the laws of God and man and should not be exempt from punishment.[14]

Greenfield was represented by Samuel J. Leibowitz, one of the nation's top criminal lawyers who later became one of New York's most distinguished judges. Leibowitz argued for acquittal on the basis of Greenfield's temporary "defective reasoning" brought on by years of agonizing over his son's condition. Leibowitz called to the witness stand a stream of psychiatrists and educational experts, who described Jerome as "unfit" and a "menace" to himself and others. The strain on the family was thoroughly described by Anna Greenfield and several of the couple's friends. But the most crucial testimony came from Louis Greenfield himself.

The milliner answered the questions posed by his counsel in a firm, measured voice. But he broke down when Leibowitz asked, "You loved this boy, didn't you?" Greenfield dropped his head, covered his face with his handkerchief and sobbed for a full minute before answering, "I loved him more than anything in the world." After Greenfield regained control of himself, the attorney asked, more in the tone of a prosecutor than a defender, "Well, you killed him, didn't you?" Greenfield acknowledged, "Yes." Why?" asked the lawyer. "Because I loved him; it was the will of God."

Greenfield then went on to describe how irrepressible "voices" that came to him during his sleepless nights and commanded him to "stop his suffering," and that such was "the will of God." Greenfield told the court that these voices forced him to slay his sixteen-year-old-son as an act of "mercy." Asked why he had chosen chloroform to kill his son, Greenfield replied, "The unknown voice in my dreams told me it was the easiest way. . . . It said that Jerry would just go to sleep forever." Finally Leibowitz posed the question that would determine the legal outcome of the trial, "You knew it was against the law, didn't you?" "I knew it was against the law of man," replied the defendant, "I didn't want to do it, but God urged me to stop his suffering. The law of God is mightier than the law of man."

In his concluding remarks, the state prosecutor, a Mr. Tilzer, urged the jury again and again to return a verdict of guilty and leave the question of mercy up to Judge Patterson. On each occasion he was reprimanded by the judge upon the vehement objections of Leibowitz. In his charge to the jury Judge Patterson, who quoted at length from a recent decision of the court of appeals concerning "defect of reason," said: "If you find the defendant was suffering from an insane delusion—if you find that God appeared to him and urged him to commit this act, then you must acquit him." Leibowitz requested the court to charge the jury that "if for any reason the defendant was suffering from defect of reason—any cause whatsoever, it need not have been insanity, any cause—so as not to know the nature and quality of his act, then he must be acquitted." Judge Patterson so charged the jury.

After four hours of deliberation, which according to one commentator, could have been shortened to four minutes, the jury returned with a verdict of not guilty.[15] An enthusiastic outburst took place among the fifty spectators in the courtroom. "I'm thankful to justice," sobbed the father after he heard the jury's verdict. "Justice has been vindicated, but I can't be happy, for after all, I loved Jerry more than anyone in the world."

Several newspapers responded favorably to the jury's decision. An editorial in a California paper considered, "That, somehow seems to be the universal rule: fathers and mothers lavish affections upon a child that is physically or mentally unfit. . . . But great, indeed must be the love of a parent who can decide upon and actually carry out such a deed. . . . [W]e take it, the jurors must have been completely satisfied as to his sincerity and truthfulness." Nevertheless, the editorial went on to recommend, "It would be much better to leave the decision of life or death to a commission of reputable physicians, as was proposed in the British House of Commons a few years ago."[16]

Louis Greenfield killed his son. The father planned the killing months in advance, and performed the act in cold blood. According to the general principles of criminal law he should have been charged with first-degree murder and sentenced to life imprisonment, perhaps even to death. The possible justifications for his action should have made no legal difference. An intentional and premeditated killing of another human being is murder, notwithstanding the benevolent motives underlying it. Thus, the fact that the boy's life became a prolonged torment, and that his condition impaired the emotional and physical well-being of his parents, should not have made any legal difference. Nor could Greenfield's lawyer argue self-defense, since the boy did not pose an immediate threat to the life of his parents, and even if he did, such a threat could have been prevented by less severe means.

Therefore, despite the unequivocal standards of criminal law, Greenfield was not indicted for murder, but only for the lesser offense of first-degree manslaughter. The charge of first-degree manslaughter is a puzzling one, for it implies a lack of intent to kill. The less severe charge runs counter to the undisputed facts of the case and can only be explained by the grand jury's conscious decision to go beyond the law. This decision is also reflected in the final verdict of the trial jury to acquit the father even from the lesser charge of manslaughter.

The killing of Jerome Greenfield was characterized by the press, the public, and even some jurists as a case of "mercy killing." The case reflects a patent discrepancy between the severity that the law requires in treating mercy killings and the de facto exemption from criminal responsibility it granted this particular culprit.

Though each mercy killing encompasses a drama of its own, a similar pattern emerges in many other cases. Several years after Greenfield killed his son, Carol Paight, a twenty-one-year-old college student, shot to death her ailing father in his hospital bed. Sergeant Paight was a seemingly healthy man and an active policeman in his early fifties. A few days prior to the incident he began to complain of severe pains in the abdomen. He was admitted to Stamford Hospital for an operation. After the operation, Dr. William E. Smith reported to the sergeant's wife and their daughter, Carol, that Sergeant Paight was riddled with cancer. He told them that the condition was inoperable and he estimated the patient had between six weeks to two months to live. Carol began to cry and screamed, "Don't tell daddy," and kept screaming as her mother led her out of the hospital.

After learning of Sergeant Paight's condition, the mother and daughter drove home. There, Carol searched for her father's service revolver and once she found it, drove to a wooded area where she took a practice shot. She then returned to the hospital and fatally wounded him.

The case was decided in the court of public opinion even before the official trial began. "Community leaders and other residents expressed deep sympathy for twenty-one-year-old Carol Paight," said Mayor George T. Barrett of Stamford, striking a note of sympathy that was echoed by other Stamford residents. The mayor emphasized the unusual emotional forces that Carol was undergoing, suggesting that her body may have performed acts that had no connection with her moral intent or inclination. He also pointed out that this was no ordinary crime and that Carol was no ordinary criminal. Implicitly alluding to the possibility that no charges would be brought against Carol, the mayor concluded, "Extreme leniency should be shown, and great latitude should be allowed to the District Attorney in the exercise of that leniency. . . . It is my honest belief and firm conviction that the case of Carol Paight deserves extreme sympathy and leniency."

Despite massive public support, Carol Paight was indicted for the death of her father and charged with second-degree murder. She pleaded not guilty to the charge, which carried a mandatory sentence of life imprisonment.

The trial lasted only two weeks. There were no disputes about the actual facts of the crime, and the jury's verdict was anxiously awaited by Carol's family and friends. The jury found Carol not guilty on the grounds of temporary insanity.

The similar pattern of circumstances, motivations, methods, public reaction, and legal outcome which appeared in the *Greenfield* and *Paight* cases characterizes many other documented cases of coups de grace. On the one hand, it was hard to think of mercy killing as ordinary murder, which is what the law stipulated. On the other hand, very few people were willing to seriously consider legalizing the killing of a hopelessly ill, retarded, or disabled person by his family members. The Reverend Lloyd F. Worley, who conducted Sergeant Paight's funeral, spoke of this ambivalence: "I believe in . . . the general principle of mercy, but not that any individual should have the right to decide whether another individual should live or die. I sympathize with the family, and I should plead for mercy, but would not justify the act."

How should we understand the ambivalent, perhaps even contradictory, response to mercy killing exhibited by the courts as well as by both advocates and opponents of legalized euthanasia? On the one hand, we encounter full comprehension of the deed and feelings of empathy toward the doer; on the other hand, we see a reluctance to support the act and an uneasiness vis-à-vis its practitioner. Mercy killing appears to operate in an ambiguous zone between violence and sainthood, between life not worth living and life as sacred, between calculation and madness, between justice and mercy. The practice of mercy killing appears as a mirror image of legalized euthanasia. Mercy killing brings into question precisely what the medicalization, legalization, and bureaucratization of euthanasia has strived to achieve, namely, the certainty of law in the regulation of death. What is it about mercy killing that inspires this exceptional legal and moral response?

The Gift of Death

The key for deciphering the phenomenon of mercy killing lies not in the extraordinary suffering that the act is meant to relieve but rather in the ordinary relationship of care between perpetrator and sufferer: the relationship of kin. It would be hard to imagine an act of mercy killing outside of the kinship framework. If Sergeant Paight had not been shot dead by his distraught daughter but rather by a well-intentioned stranger, or even by a friend, the jury would most likely have convicted that person of murder. But there is no need for speculation. All documented cases of mercy killings have been committed within a kinship relation (with perhaps one exception, in which the killer was a very close family friend). This generalization is only valid, of course, with the qualification that killings performed by physicians or medical staff by definition fall under the different category of medical euthanasia and not mercy killing proper. Yet, it is not so simple to understand why. There is, of course, an obvious explanation: a close relative is likely to be aware of the person's suffering and have both motivation and opportunity to perform the act. But practical considerations alone cannot explain the extraordinary legal status of mercy killing. Kinship, as we shall see, goes deeper to the heart of mercy killing, for it stands as a law on its own, at times superseding the positive legal prohibition on murder.

Several years prior to the *Greenfield* case, Andrew Beers, aged seventy-seven, killed his young daughter. He feared that with his approaching death there would be no one left to take care of Frances, a "mentally defective" twenty-four-year-old. With the passing of his wife only a year earlier, he could not stand the thought that after his own death Frances would fall into the less kindly hands of an institution for the insane. On July 12, 1930, in an act he himself later described as a "mercy killing," Beers poisoned his daughter and, when that attempt failed, used a wrench and an ice pick to crush her skull. "She was a sick baby. She was born that way," he explained to the reporters. "And we always gave her more attention than the other children because she needed more. She could not help herself, she was always my little girl."[17] Beers, unlike Greenfield, was never tried. A court-appointed committee of two doctors declared him insane.

What did it take for Andrew Beers to kill his daughter? As strong as his love for Frances must have been, it was not this feeling alone that drove him to action. His murderous act was not performed in the heat of passion but was guided, as often is the case with mercy killing, by forethought and advance planning. As her father and sole provider he was committed to Frances's well-being. Thus, in killing his daughter, Beers did not merely act on his emotions but was also guided by an ethical duty of care. Mercy killing, in this sense, is not merely a passionate violation of the law but constitutes a moral duty of its own. It is precisely this conflict between two normative orders, the family and the state, that marks the difference between mercy killing and medical euthanasia. It is for this reason that attempts could be made to bring medical euthanasia under state law, whereas no such attempt could be made with respect to mercy killing.

Mercy killing follows a law of its own, a law whose source lies in family relations. But it is not kinship as such that motivated Andrew Beers. Not just any close relative would perform such a dreadful act. It was Beers's unique and untransferable role as Frances's sole provider that led him to kill her. It goes beyond the fact that Frances had to be cared for and that Beers fulfilled her needs in a way anyone else could have. His obligation was unique, stated in the first-person singular, an inalienable commitment. And this led Beers to rule out the option of leaving Frances in the care of a mental institution. We may thus characterize mercy killing as an act of destruction arising out of a familial obligation to care. This extraordinary taking of life follows a paradoxical justification: "Only I truly cared for her, therefore I had to kill her."

The shift from caring into killing also appeared in the case of a twenty-seven-year-old mother who walked into the Newburgh, New York, Police Headquarters with a dead child in her arms, and explained: "I could not feed him. I could not see him hungry. So I walked into a creek until the waters were over his head." The mother was first sentenced to death and sent to the infamous Sing Sing "death house," but upon appeal the punishment was limited to a short jail term.

How does the duty to care transform into a death wish? Mercy killing can be perceived as the final step in a long series of acts of care. It is only after the duty to care for life becomes frustrated that ending life emerges as a possibility, perhaps even as a duty. Andrew Beers and his wife always gave Frances "more" than they gave to their other children. It is only out of the frustration of his duty to do more that Beers felt the need, the duty, no doubt even the privilege to take the life of his daughter. His act of mercy killing can be seen as the final act of giving bestowed on his child.

It is an act undoubtedly more questionable but not less demanding than the giving of life—the poisonous gift of death.

As the above cases demonstrate, the most common relationship in mercy killings is that between parent and child. At times, however, the deed is committed by a sibling or loving partner. Here, too, the governing principle remains the same. The killing is not performed by just any close relative but is confined to the unquestionable caretaker. For that person, mercy killing appears as an inescapable task, just as the caring itself had been. Thus, when two sisters killed their mentally retarded brother, whom they had nursed day and night for twenty years, they justified their action by claiming that they did so not only out of love for their brother but also to fulfill a promise to their mother to care for their dependent sibling. Although they were tried for murder, as in so many cases of mercy killing, the sisters ultimately received a lenient sentence, and were released within a short period from the Broadmoor Institution for the Criminally Insane.

Mercy killing is motivated by an inalienable duty to care. As a one-sided duty, mercy killing does not depend on the expressed death wish of the suffering person. Unlike attempts to legalize euthanasia, the logic of mercy killing does not require consent. In this sense, too, mercy killing follows the logic of a gift,[18] which remains a gift whether or not requested or even expected. Legalized euthanasia attempts to turn the gift of death into a contract. Under legalized euthanasia the spontaneity of the gift assumes the predictability and calculability of a legal transaction. This is not to suggest that mercy killings are never preceded by a death wish. Rather, the point is to understand that a request for mercy killing by the victim is not a precondition for the act's unique legal status. As the following 1920 case of *People v. Roberts* demonstrates, the lenient treatment afforded to mercy killing does not at all depend on the voluntary nature of the act.[19]

Kati Roberts was only thirty years old when she was diagnosed with multiple sclerosis. Within one year her condition deteriorated badly, and she wished to end her life. Her husband, fulfilling her last wish, mixed some Paris green in a glass of water; after drinking it, Kati died quickly. Here, too, caring comes to an end in a final act of destruction, though unlike many other cases of mercy killing, Frank C. Roberts's primary motivation seems to have been the repeated requests of his dying wife. Yet in this case, rather than receiving a lenient punishment, Roberts was found guilty of murder in the first degree and sentenced by the court to life imprisonment and hard labor.

The harsh sentence that Roberts received can partially be explained by the fact that he pleaded guilty in court. This does not, however, explain why he was originally indicted with murder rather than with manslaughter. In any event, the lack of correlation between the leniency of punishment and the voluntariness of the deed is notable in many other cases of mercy killing. This has led one observer to complain: "The wheels of justice do not grind evenly. In the same year in which Paight and Braunsdorf [20] were so acquitted Harold Mohr in Pennsylvania was convicted for voluntary manslaughter for the killing of his blind, cancer stricken brother . . . [E]ven though, in contrast to the other cases, there was in the Mohr case evidence that the accused had acted upon his brother's urgent and repeated requests."[21]

The complaint, however, is misguided. It is based on the false assumption that mercy killings are more justifiable when preceded by an explicit request to be killed. But the merciful taking of life is not an ordinary legal transaction, and consent is not one of its premises. Even if one does not go as far as suggesting that a request may have a countereffect on the verdict, one thing seems clear: the question of whether the killing was performed at the request of the deceased is irrelevant. This proclaimed act of mercy originates first and foremost in the duty to relieve the unbearable suffering of a close relative and not out of respect for autonomy and self-determination. Indeed, "to the press, the public, and many euthanasiasts, the killing of one who does not or cannot speak is no less a 'mercy killing' than the killing of one who asks for death. Indeed, the overwhelming majority of known or alleged 'mercy killings' have occurred without the consent of the victim."[22]

A sincere commitment to care underlies most reported cases of mercy killing. But the desire to relieve the suffering of a close family member is not the only motivation underlying the practice. Mercy killing is not merely a benevolent act of grace. What makes it a complex phenomenon is precisely the way in which care for another is accompanied by care for oneself, and the altruism of the merciful deed is joined by the self-interest of relieving oneself from the burden of care. Louis Greenfield killed his son, not only to relieve the boy's suffering, but also to save his wife and himself from the impossible life they had come to live. A similar motivation led Daniel W. Cahill, a former mayor of Watertown, New York, to strangle his wife who had been ill with a nervous disorder for nearly eight years. In a public statement justifying his action he did not hesitate to point out his self-interest in her death, allowing the newspapers to report: "her illness had worn him out because of the care he had to give her and from lack of sleep."[23] This less favorable aspect of mercy killing is not accidental but is inherent to the practice and further sets it apart from medical euthanasia. For a physician to ethically perform euthanasia, he must assure himself and others that the killing is purely for the sake of the suffering patient, and that the physician has nothing personally or institutionally to gain, otherwise his act will be morally tainted.

With mercy killing, however, it is impossible to separate motives in this way. The special relation of care is at once the source for both altruistic and egotistic motivations. Self-interest does not taint the moral character of the deed but, on the contrary, gives the act its unique moral aspect. Mercy killing is at once a performance of the duty to care and the annihilation of that duty. Thus, a further paradox of mercy killing comes to light in a more precise reformulation of its justification: "Out of care for her suffering, I killed her to relieve myself of my own suffering." One judge justified his lenient verdict in a 1954 case in which John Petyo strangled his sick wife. Judge Edward A. McGrath explained: "There are times when a human being cannot take it any longer. Petyo was a devoted husband. Few men are as kind to their wives."[24] Here we have an example of a judge expressing the paradoxical nature of mercy killing by suggesting that few men are as kind to their wives as to strangle them when they can't take it any longer.

Another important aspect of the phenomenon is the relatively large number of mercy killers who follow up their deed by committing suicide. Of the seventy cases examined, nearly a quarter attempted suicide, nine of which succeeded. What could be the reason behind this urge for self-destruction? Perhaps, as in the case of a Mr. Kent who murdered his wife, it was the emptiness left by the loss of a loved one. "It hurt me see my wife suffer—so I killed her. I never did anything to harm my wife, before this happened—never. Now she won't have any more asthma attacks. . . . I got a pillow and held it over her face. When I lifted it off she was quiet. She wasn't gasping or wheezing any more. She was very still." Kent told the police that he tried to kill himself. "I wanted us to be together like we always were. But I couldn't do it. I got panicky when I couldn't get my breath and pulled the bag off my head."[25]

Perhaps it is not loneliness but guilt that leads to self-destruction. Whatever the reason, the mercy killing of a loved one is a life-shattering experience. And whether it leads to suicide or to insanity, life does not continue as before. Again, a clear distinction may be drawn here between mercy killing and medical euthanasia. The latter seeks to turn euthanasia into a mundane affair, one that will become another duty of the physician to his patient and will leave as little effect on his life as possible.

Although not all mercy killers seek their own death, they all share in common a total commitment to their action and do not recoil from the potentially grave legal consequences. In mercy killing, unlike legalized euthanasia, there is always the possibility of punishment even if, de facto, most mercy killers are rarely punished severely. The mercy killer may hope he will not be punished for his deeds, but there is no guarantee, and the consequences are so extreme that it is hard to imagine that a cold, rational weighing of pros and cons takes place before the act is performed. In this sense, all cases of mercy killing are a form of self-sacrifice, even when they do not end in suicide. This, of course, does not suggest that there are no hesitations, but these are not likely to be a result of a rational calculation and choice. The final formulation of the mercy-killing justification thus has the following form: "I killed the suffering person I had a duty to care for, in order to relieve myself of suffering, and thus brought upon myself unbearable suffering."

Mercy killing embodies a tragic collision between the goodwill of the perpetrator and the horrifying prospects of the deed, between the unwavering prohibition of the legal system and the merciful compassion of the bystander, and most significantly between two normative orders, that of the state and that of the family. It is almost as if underlying the well-ordered legal system of the modern state lies hidden a different moral order: the natural relations of the family counter to the human-imposed laws of the state. But it is not as if the natural relations of blood forcefully overpowers the authority of the state. On the contrary, it is precisely within the legal operations of the state that the alien laws of blood are recognized. And it is at the altar of the modern legal system, in the courtroom, that sanctuary is granted to the mercy killer.

Mercy Killing in Court

The most striking aspect of mercy killings, as we have seen, is the disparity between the severe sanction that exists on the books, and the lenient sentencing that takes place in practice. We are now in a better position to understand this discrepancy and explain why judges and juries overwhelmingly acquit mercy killers even as the law demands that they be found guilty of murder and punished accordingly.

Unlike ordinary criminal trials, there is usually little dispute concerning the facts in mercy killings. The perpetrator most often turns himself in to the police immediately after committing the deed, prior to any investigation or criminal trial. Lack of incriminating evidence is not, therefore, the reason for the high rate of acquittals.

It is very likely no coincidence that in the one notable case in which the killer did not confess his actions, the court found him guilty of murder, and sentenced him to death by electric chair. This was the case of John F. Noxon, a well-to-do lawyer from Pittsfield, Massachusetts, who was charged with killing his mentally deficient son. The prosecution charged Noxon with first-degree murder for killing his six-month-old Down-syndrome son by wrapping him in a lamp cord and electrocuting him. Noxon denied he killed his son and claimed that the child's death was an accident. He testified that he was about to repair a broken radio in his library when he realized he forgot his toolbox in another room. When he returned to the library after a brief absence he found the baby entangled in an extension wire lying on the floor. He said he had put the child in a metal tray on the floor because he feared the infant might fall from a chair where he had been left. The prosecution contended that an electrically charged wire had been purposely "clamped" to the baby's arm. Noxon was convicted of first-degree murder. His death sentence was commuted to life. Later, his sentence was further reduced to six years to life in order to make parole possible; this was granted shortly thereafter. The Massachusetts Supreme Court affirmed the trial court's decision and denied Noxon's appeal for a new trial based on technical grounds.[26]

As likely as the defendant is to confess the facts, he is equally likely to deny his guilt. It is rare for the accused to express any remorse for committing the deed. But neither will he speak out against the law, call for its amendment or imply any injustice. Most mercy killers do not wish to defy the law but nevertheless refuse to adhere to it. They act as if their murderous deed is not governed by ordinary criminal law but instead comes under a higher legal order. In the *Repouille* case in 1939, the defendant killed his "blind, deaf and deformed" thirteen-year-old child, calling this an act "of mercy." He later told the detectives: "If I had to do it again, I'd do it. . . . I know I did the right thing in ending my son's misery."[27]

As noted above, the absence of incriminating evidence is not the reason for the high rate of mercy-killing acquittals. And yet it is relatively rare for a jury to return a verdict of not guilty in ordinary murder cases when the defendant admits to the facts of the case. On what grounds, then, do juries and judges find the defendant not guilty?

The most common line of defense in mercy-killing trials is insanity. In some instances, the mercy killer is not even brought to trial because the state psychiatrist declares him or her mentally insane and thus legally incompetent. In such cases, the defendant is likely to be confined to a mental institution. In other cases, however, the defendant is declared competent enough to stand trial but is exempted from criminal responsibility on the basis of the more limited "temporary insanity" defense. Courts may find a defendant temporarily insane if his attorney can demonstrate that at the time of the crime, due to a disease of the mind, the defendant was unable to understand the nature of his actions or their wrongful moral character. The legal defense of temporary insanity does not require that the defendant show previous signs of a mental disease. This line of defense allows great flexibility for juries and judges to acquit.

For many observers, the insanity defense, whether temporary or prolonged, serves as a loophole offering an easy way out for juries who sympathize with the defendant and do not wish to convict.[28] But the legal defense of insanity suggests something beyond that, and we should consider it at more than face value. Declaring mercy killing as an insane act implies that the action escapes human intelligibility. But insanity here does not simply mean craziness in the popular or medical sense. The insanity of the mercy killer signifies more closely what the ancients meant when they spoke of *mania* and attributed manic powers not only to the madman but also to the prophet and poet. Rather than being unintelligible, the latter transcend ordinary intelligibility. In the same way, the mercy killer does not merely violate the law but transcends it by obeying a different legal order arising from a kinship relation or at times, as in the Greenfield case, following a command from God.

In this sense, the insanity defense is a way of saying something very simple but striking: "We, judges and jury, understand that the action performed by the accused was not committed in defiance of state law, but instead followed a law of its own, and therefore cannot be judged by the standards of ordinary criminal law." The act of mercy killing is not unintelligible but instead belongs to a different order of intelligibility, and it is this level of understanding that can be granted to the accused. As Ella M. Haug, who was acquitted after killing her loved one explained, "I'm so glad you could understand," she told the jurors. "That means more to me than freedom."[29]

There are good reasons for seeing at least some mercy killings as insane. A further aspect of mercy killing that distinguishes it from medical euthanasia are the extreme means used to bring about death. The sterile death produced in medical euthanasia by using chloroform or morphine is replaced in mercy killing with violent means. One need cite only a few instances, such as Andrew Beers, who killed his daughter with a wrench and an ice pick, or the case of Kathleen Mumford, who put her son in a gas oven after the doctor pronounced the child to be incurably retarded. Or the horrifying case of Robert H. Matlock, who admitted striking his mother with a jar, hammer, and bottle and stabbed her "15 or 20 times" above the head with a hunting knife.[30]

The defense of insanity is only one channel for passing a lenient judgment in mercy-killing cases. The strict application of legal rules has not been a common response to this act of mercy. The courts are more likely to match the mercy of the killing with the mercy of judgment. One of the most striking trials in this respect took place in the courtroom of Judge Clyde Webster in 1952. The defendant, William R. Jones, a factory worker, was charged with electrocuting his diabetes-ridden wife. Jones told how his wife was in constant pain after both her legs were amputated and begged him to "take me out of all this." Both Jones and his wife agreed to a suicide pact. They were to take turns sitting in a bathtub of water with electric wires wrapped around their bodies. Jones's wife, who went first, died almost instantly, but a relative arrived unexpectedly before he could fulfill his part of the bargain.

Jones, aged sixty-two, was convicted of second-degree murder and sentenced by the judge to serve a year and a day, "a minimum sentence." The sentence was passed during a tearful courtroom scene. Both judge and defendant wept freely as the case was reviewed before the sentence was passed. "I want to thank you, Judge, but I can't talk" said Jones, when it was all over. "I can't either, very well," said Webster as both men lifted handkerchiefs to their eyes to dab away tears. "I can't hold that you had a right to kill your wife," Webster told Jones. "All I can do is show you every consideration I can. With the sentence I hope you'll still have some happiness ahead."[31] Defense counsel said a request for parole would be made immediately, and the judge prepared an urgent appeal to the state parole board for leniency.[32]

Conclusion

By closely examining reported cases of mercy killing, we may better understand not only the phenomenon of mercy killing but also its counterpart, medical euthanasia. In many ways, mercy killing is precisely what legalized euthanasia is not. Rather than the well-ordered killing sought by advocates of legalized euthanasia, mercy killing takes place in clear violation of existing law. Instead of the professionally reasoned act of the medical doctor, we find the desperate measure taken by a family member. The assured and tranquil outcome of anesthesia and lethal dosing is replaced by the gory method of stabbing with an ice pick, drowning, or strangling with bare hands. The certainty of regulation is replaced by the uncertainty of mercy, and a well-regulated legal transaction is replaced by a tragic gift, as the taking of life becomes itself a life-shattering experience.

Modern society, whether as an opponent or proponent of euthanasia, has become increasingly attracted to the idea that treatment of the dying and, more specifically, the ending of life should be carefully regulated by state law and medical practice. Mercy killing, however, poses a challenge to this modern ethos. Not only is mercy killing unregulated, but the very thought of regulating the taking of life by a family member—that is, setting the necessary and sufficient conditions under which such killing would be permissible—is offensive to our moral conscience. Yet if it would make no sense to regulate mercy killing and codify in law the terms under which a father may kill his disabled child, or a daughter her terminally ill father, how can we make sense of the attempts to regulate medical euthanasia and determine under what conditions a physician may end the life of a patient?

Mercy killing not only challenges the attempt to legalize euthanasia, it also challenges the idea that prohibiting euthanasia could be regulated. The lesson from mercy killing, if there is a lesson to be learned from such an extraordinary human act, is that the notion of regulating the taking of life fails as much in the prohibition as in the affirmation. Despite a clear ban on the practice of mercy killing, when the act is performed it is rarely subject to legal sanction.

Through mercy killing, the troubling nature of the taking of life is brought to the fore, a concern that the medicalization of euthanasia has all but obliterated. In a world in which the power of technique is a global phenomenon, and the place of art has been diminished by the reign of technique, mercy killing is a violent reminder of the untamable character of taking life.

The subject of mercy killing is not presented here as a solution to the problem of euthanasia. On the contrary, it is offered as food for thought on the impossibility of finding solutions to this dilemma. It is appropriate to conclude with the words of the law itself on this act of coup de grace. In 1926, Elmer Blazer, a Colorado physician, was charged with killing his daughter by chloroform. She was legless, armless, deaf, mute, and retarded, and for thirty-two years her father had debated that condition. At the trial, the defense argued temporary insanity. The jury was deadlocked. When the district attorney realized that eleven jurors were in favor of acquittal, he decided to drop the charges. Dr. Blazer's attorney sought a new trial to obtain full acquittal. In striking this motion, Judge Johnson declared: "The court believes there was not a better solution than disagreement and dismissal of the jury. There are many riddles in this life that are never solved. This court is through with the Blazer case forever."[33]

Art and Technique, Death and Freedom

Our study of euthanasia in America began with colonial times, when the word still signified a pious death blessed by the grace of God. It continued with the medicalization of death in the nineteenth century, which was soon followed by attempts to legalize the hastening of death. The struggle to legalize euthanasia took a radical turn with the founding of the Euthanasia Society of America, when proposals to hasten death were applied to handicapped and mentally retarded patients. The final section of this study compared the legalization of euthanasia with two alternative means of actively hastening death; the sublegal act of lethal dosing and the supralegal act of mercy killing.

The history of euthanasia recounted in the preceding pages concludes in the 1960s, but the story of euthanasia does not end there. On the contrary, for many scholars the story *begins* in the 1960s, with the advancements in medical techniques and the rise of patient rights. As one scholar wrote, "Ever since the 1960s, when medical science became capable of prolonging the dying process beyond bounds that many patients would find acceptable, people have sought 'death with dignity,' or 'a natural death,' or 'a good death.' "[1]

Our study has attempted to correct the prevailing account of the history of euthanasia. To consider euthanasia as a late twentieth-century dilemma is both historically inaccurate and conceptually misleading. Euthanasia is not a response to the advance of medical technology nor to the ability of medicine to prolong life beyond acceptable bounds. As we have seen, euthanasia proposals first emerged in the late nineteenth century, long before medicine achieved its unprecedented ability to prolong human life. More important, associating euthanasia with advances in medical techniques overlooks the connections between euthanasia and deep cultural changes that made euthanasia possible. For euthanasia to emerge, no significant medical breakthrough was necessary but rather fundamental changes in the ways we wish for our lives to end; namely, the decline of the art of dying and the rise of technical mastery over death.

And yet, it would be a mistake to ignore some important developments that have taken place in the latter half of the twentieth century. While it is beyond the scope of this work to offer a detailed study of these changes, this epilogue will examine what is arguably the most important development of all: the Oregon law legalizing physician-assisted suicide. Thus, the task of this concluding section is to suggest rather than prove the relevance of the history of euthanasia for understanding some of the more recent developments in the field.

The most significant difference between contemporary euthanasia proposals and those made more than half a century ago is the growing emphasis on patient rights and autonomy. Clearly, the current wave of euthanasia debate and legislation emerged in a very different context than that of the 1930s. At that time, euthanasia was cast in the language of eugenics and social Darwinism and was offered as a solution to the burdens the dying patient imposed upon society. The context of the contemporary euthanasia dilemma is quite different. Current proposals are concerned with patients' rights to determine the time and manner of their death and with protecting patients' freedom from medical intervention and state coercion.

But how radical is this change? Opponents of euthanasia and some historians argue that the change is merely rhetorical. They argue that the requirement of consent and the language of autonomy are illusions that conceal the continuing desire of families, interest groups, and the state to alleviate the emotional and economic burdens imposed on them by the dying.[2]

My argument is different. While important changes have taken place in the discourse and practice of euthanasia, there has been confusion in understanding the significance of these changes. In light of the history of euthanasia, I suggest that considering euthanasia in terms of rights does not represent a break from the past but rather radicalizes existing historical trends. The rise of the "right to die" is not only a reaction in the name of patient autonomy against the growing invasion of medical technique but also and more forcefully a further triumph of the reign of technique over the way we die. Paradoxically, the struggle to further human freedom and autonomy at the end of life has augmented the reign of technique and has ultimately failed to comprehend the true nature of both technique and human freedom.

To see how and why this is the case, we must explore the ways in which the regulatory regime of rights has come to shape the current euthanasia debate and the way we die. I will refer to this new framing of euthanasia question as the rise of the "regulatory-rights regime."

The Discourse and Practice of Autonomy

Throughout most of the twentieth century, euthanasia remained an unrealized ideal, often debated in the public arena but never lawfully practiced. Only on the brink of the twenty-first century did euthanasia move from the realm of the possible to the realm of the actual.

On November 8, 1994, the citizens of the state of Oregon voted to enact the Death with Dignity Act, allowing physicians to actively assist patients in hastening their death. The Oregon act should be seen as the final product of a century of euthanasia debates and legislative drafts. In many ways it resembles the original 1870 euthanasia proposal, and even at the crucial points where the Oregon measure diverges from earlier proposals, it is only against the backdrop of its predecessors that its full significance can be appreciated.

Using the title "Death with Dignity," Oregon became the first, and today still the only, state to authorize a practice better known as physician-assisted suicide. According to the act:

> An adult who is capable, is a resident of Oregon, and has been determined by the attending physician and consulting physician to be suffering from a terminal disease, and who has voluntarily expressed his or her wish to die, may make a written request for medication for the purpose of ending his or her life in a humane and dignified manner. . . . Actions taken in accordance with [this Act] shall not, for any purpose, constitute suicide, assisted suicide, mercy killing or homicide under the law.[3]

The clear emphasis of the act, and of similar proposals of its kind,[4] is on patient consent and autonomy. Many of the safeguards prescribed by the act are intended to ensure that the patient, of his or her free volition, indeed wishes to die and is under no physical or emotional duress.

The most apparent distinction between the Oregon act and earlier euthanasia proposals is its explicit prohibition against medical euthanasia, limiting the medical intervention to assisting rather than causing death—that is, prescribing, but not administering, the lethal medication. The act clarifies its purpose as follows: "Nothing in [this Act] shall be construed to authorize a physician or any other person to end a patient's life by lethal injection, mercy killing or active euthanasia."

In addition, the act clearly intends to distinguish itself from previous attempts to legalize euthanasia which targeted a much broader population.

Thus it includes a restricting clause, which did not appear in earlier proposals, excluding certain groups of patients. The act declares that "[n]o person shall qualify under the provisions of [the Act] solely because of age or disability."[5] The importance of this statement can be easily understood in light of the abusive ways in which euthanasia was practiced in Nazi Germany but also, to no lesser a degree, by the more immediate history of the Euthanasia Society of America.

Finally, the Oregon act should be viewed as part of a larger endeavor during the last quarter of the twentieth century to secure through law the autonomy and rights of dying patients. This movement began with the famous 1976 case of Karen Ann Quinlan, when the Supreme Court of New Jersey recognized for the first time a constitutional right of patients to withdraw life-sustaining machinery, and culminated in the similar 1990 Nancy Cruzan case, in which a constitutional right to die with dignity was recognized by the United States Supreme Court. In the more recent case of *Glucksberg v. Vacco*, the Supreme Court has clarified that the constitutional right to die with dignity is limited to withholding and withdrawing life-sustaining machinery and does not include a right to physician-assisted suicide or euthanasia. Nevertheless, the court held that individual states may legalize the practice of physician-assisted suicide and euthanasia, so long as these laws have adequate safeguards preventing abuse and protecting the autonomy of the individual patient.

In light of these apparent distinctions, it may be tempting to draw a clear line separating the pre–World War II euthanasia proposals and those of the latter half of the century. Without denying these evident differences, I wish to emphasize the continuity in the history of euthanasia. I do so not for the sake of taking sides in the euthanasia debate but rather to offer a more complex view of both the history of euthanasia and of current events.

Autonomy Reexamined

To understand the real significance of the emerging rights regime and to overcome the overly simplified oppositions of *past and present* and *coercion and freedom*, we should examine the contemporary notion of autonomy in concrete rather than abstract terms. The basic argument I propose is that patients' rights and human autonomy have come under the sway of technical mastery. This is true not because autonomy is denied the dying patient but rather because autonomy is incorporated into the regulatory regime. As autonomy becomes part of regulation, it acquires two discernible characteristics: it becomes *bounded* and *constructed*.

The most telling aspect of autonomy under the regulatory regime is its bounded limits. The Oregon act and similar proposals of its kind do not legalize hastening death in general but rather limit its scope to dying patients alone. Not even excruciating pain can, by itself, justify the hastening of death. Only the combination of suffering and dying may do so. But if autonomy—that is, the patient's right to hasten death—was the true basis of the act, why would autonomy be limited to dying patients alone? The act should, therefore, be read primarily as a new way to regulate death and only secondarily as a means of protecting human autonomy.

The priority given to the framework of regulation manifests the affinity between current and earlier proposals to hasten death. By insisting on patient autonomy, the Oregon act does not break from the past but rather takes a further step in the modern attempt to regulate the time and manner of dying. From this perspective, autonomy is a more sophisticated way of regulating end-of-life decision making. It is more sophisticated because it does not use coercion to impose a regulatory regime on the dying but rather makes use of autonomy to enhance the power of regulation.[6]

This point becomes clearer when we examine the way in which autonomy is constructed within the rights regime. The Oregon act does not accept the will of the patient as a given. And although the act recognizes the patient's autonomy, and thus does not impose a specific desire on the patient, it outlines the precise process through which this desire shall be constructed.

Thus, a central component of the Oregon act—which has its roots deep in the nineteenth century—is the role played by the accompanying physician at the deathbed. As we have seen, the presence of this "master of ceremonies" should not be taken for granted.[7] While it is true that the physician has the required expertise to administer drugs, as well as the authority of the state to do so, practical considerations alone did not bring the physician to the deathbed.[8] The presence of the physician has a deeper cultural significance, manifesting the medicalization of death and, more specifically, the rise of the modern wish for this-worldly salvation precisely when all hope is lost.

Beyond the question of *who* will make the final decision—which sets patient autonomy against medical authority—lies the more important question of *what* kind of decision will be made. This latter question draws patient autonomy and medical authority together. The answer to the question, even if given by the patient, is formed within a medical context.

Thus, the patient may choose to reject life-prolonging treatment or even palliative care, but the law will require him or her to form this decision in light of the alternatives. The mechanism by which the law guarantees the medical structuring of the patient's decision is known as "informed consent."

Under this requirement, attending physicians must present to patients and discuss with them all existing alternative treatments. Informed consent should not be understood naively as offering all available information to patients, nor should it be understood as a subtle attempt to pressure patients to change their mind, although in many cases this may happen. Rather, informed consent is a means by which the patient's autonomy is structured within the regulatory regime of modern medicine.

Another way by which the Oregon act and similar euthanasia proposals structure the patient's decision is through an elaborate array of safeguards. In addition to an informed decision by the patient, these include: an oral and written request for lethal medication; two witnesses attesting to the fact that the patient signed the request voluntarily; a confirmed diagnosis by a second physician that the patient is indeed terminally ill; a referral of the patient to counseling if appropriate; a recommendation that the patient notify next of kin; and finally, an elaborate report mechanism documenting all of the above and indicating the steps taken to carry out the request. We have seen a similar list of safeguards, although perhaps less elaborate, in the ESA proposals.

Clearly these safeguards are designed to prevent abuse under the act and minimize the possibility that the patient is operating under illegitimate pressure. But there is another way to regard this list of safeguards; it creates a process through which the desires of the patient will be constructed and not simply discovered. In addition to the attending physician, the Oregon act introduces both the family and the therapist to the process of decision making. The principle of autonomy allows the patient to reject their involvement but does not allow the patient to ignore them.

Perhaps the most subtle and yet powerful way in which the patient's autonomy is constructed is by demanding that his request to die be repeated, once orally, and again in writing. We cannot help but be reminded of the Methodist deathbed and the way the surrounding visitors would question the dying patient on the condition of his soul. Hope for salvation would not sastisfy the bystanders. The question was repeated again and again until certainty would conquer any doubt. Here again, we come across a similar desire for certainty at the deathbed that is constructed through the modern *ars moriendi* laws.[9]

Conclusion

We have suggested from the outset that what is at stake in the turn from art to technique in the way of dying is human freedom. With the history of euthanasia in mind, it is now time to return to the ethical challenge it poses. The basic question is not whether euthanasia should be legalized. Starting off with this question overlooks the fact that euthanasia has become a reality even for those who oppose it. The rise of euthanasia as an option is an event that is in itself ethically significant, and our study has sought to explain why. Thus, we have been guided not by the fundamental question "What ought we to do?" but rather "Who have we become?"

This question requires us to look deeper into the relations between technique, freedom, and law. It is common to think of law as a safeguard from the dangers posed by technique. But can the law, even the laws protecting patient rights, guarantee freedom? To answer this question we must give new meaning to the basic terms *technique*, *freedom*, and *law*.

The rise of technical mastery over dying calls human freedom into question. The danger, however, does not lie in the proliferation of medical machinery, in the growing employment of medical practices at the deathbed, in any specific technique, or even in the accumulation of techniques. The danger of technical mastery lies not in techniques themselves but in the *rule of technique*.

All techniques enable humans to partially master a limited domain of their world. Although the use of specific techniques is always for the sake of mastery, techniques may be put in the service of ends that are *not* set to further achieve mastery. This was the case with the Methodist art of dying. Although the Methodists developed an art of mastering dying, it had the further purpose of achieving Christian perfection. In the holy art of dying, the techniques used to master death were not governed by the rule of technique but by a religious ethic.

At other times, however, the ultimate end of employing a technique *is* further mastery. The history of euthanasia reflects precisely this development. At first, euthanasia was offered as a medical practice limited to alleviating the pain and suffering of dying patients. But soon, this medical practice was employed to achieve further mastery, in the sense that euthanasia was incorporated into the larger framework of regulating biological processes. Thus euthanasia, as *a technique*, was subordinated to *the rule of technique*. Under the rule of technique, human beings are dominated by the desire to master their world for the sake of mastery alone. It is in this way that the rule of technique may undermine human freedom.

It is an important, perhaps paradoxical, aspect of the rule of modern technique that as a will to master, it produces techniques that are themselves in need of mastery. The problem of mastering dying thus gave rise to the problem of mastering medical technique. Law became involved in regulating the practice of medical euthanasia, determining the conditions under which it could take place. Law, in other words, became instrumental to the practice of medical euthanasia and became a technique in the service of a medical technique. At this point the management of dying passed from the province of medicine to the jurisdiction of positive law.

The first encounter between law and technique was, therefore, the employment of law as *a technique* to govern medical euthanasia. This was the first, although not the most essential way in which law became subordinated to the rule of technique. Nevertheless, the movement had begun; to govern the medical practice of euthanasia, law had first to abandon its unwavering position that euthanasia was murder. For this to happen, a shift within the law had to take place; the common-law tradition had to give way to legislation as the most authoritative source of law. Through this transition, law was prepared to take part in the rule of technique.

The incorporation of law into the rule of technique advanced with the rise of euthanasia as public policy. Euthanasia was promoted as a solution not only to the problem of dying but to other taxing cases of social suffering. Euthanasia became one among a variety of techniques aimed at managing biological resources. It is a central aspect of the *rule of technique* that the use of specific techniques, such as euthanasia, multiplies and spreads to new domains.

Thus, the second encounter between law and technique took place when this more developed form of euthanasia was advocated as a legal solution to social problems. It marked the rise of law as public policy. Law was no longer merely a technique in the service of medical technique but assumed the role of codifier of public policy.

Finally, through lethal dosing, the rule of technique approached completion. The rule of technique "completes" itself when it acquires the character of self-evidence and thus conceals its questionability. Indeed, what was striking about lethal dosing was precisely the way in which the law failed to state a position on the legality of the practice. Thus, the practice of lethal dosing eluded the law.

What these three movements have in common is that in every case, the law fails to distinguish itself from the rule of technique. In essence, this reflects the failure of modern humanity to develop nontechnical standards for judging technique. The inability of the law to develop a nontechnical framework for judging euthanasia has grave implications. In our private, individual lives, we may follow laws of tradition and faith, but as a society we have become defenseless in our confrontation with the technical laws governing the deathbed.

More recent developments, which include the rise of patient rights and Oregon's Death with Dignity Act, appear to suggest that the history of euthanasia has taken a turn away from the mastery of technique and toward patient autonomy and freedom. But while it is undeniable that important changes have taken place in the way Americans die, there has been confusion in understanding the significance of these changes. In light of the history of euthanasia, we cannot but suspect that these recent developments are not a break from the past but are merely variations on existing themes. In any event, one thing should be clear: patient autonomy should not be confused with freedom.

Human freedom depends on the existence of a law different than the rule of technique to govern the way we die. Absent such a law, human freedom is nothing other than the freedom to be subordinated to the rule of technique. To the extent that we moderns are unable to approach technique in nontechnical ways, this study of the history of euthanasia has confronted us with our lawlessness in facing technique.

If our aim were to ameliorate this condition we would be facing the desperate conclusion of the modern scholar:

> I've studied now Philosophy
> And Jurisprudence, Medicine,
> And even, alas! Theology
> All through and through with ardour keen!
> Here now I stand, poor fool, and see
> I'm just as wise as formerly.[10]

But since it is not in our power to ameliorate this condition, but only to make it visible, we may seek solace and hope in the wise words of an ancient king: "It is better to go to the house of mourning, than to go to the house of feasting; for that is the end of all men, and the living will lay it to his heart."[11]

Mercy Killing: Case History

NOTE: The following table includes reported cases of mercy killing between the 1920s and the early 1960s. The major source for these cases was the archive of the Euthanasia Society of America (PC). Several other sources have been used, including the *New York Times* archive, books, and articles. The cases are not in any particular order, and in some cases the full information could not be retrieved. They are divided into four different groups: acquitted (Q), committed suicide (S), attempted suicide and acquitted (AS), committed to a mental institution (C), punished (P). The distribution of the fifty-seven cases where the outcome is known are: Q=21, S=10, AS=11, C=3, P=12.

TABLE 2
Mercy Killings: Case History

Name	Year	Circumstances	Outcome
Dr. Howard Ellmer Blazer, Colo. physician	1926 Q	chloroforms his severely handicapped daughter	jury frees on grounds of temporary insanity
Lieutenant-Colonel William Dunn	1927 S	kills his invalid father and mother	commits suicide
Dr. Harold Blazer, Englewood, Colo.	1927 AS	chloroforms his incurably crippled daughter, being convinced that he was dying	attempts suicide
James Stenhouse[1]	1930 Q	chloroforms his two-year-old son, who suffered from an incurable brain disease	is acquitted, temporary insanity
Andrew Beers[2]	1930 C	kills his twenty-four-year-old mentally ill daughter	is committed to an asylum
R. B. Weimer[3]	1930	kills her sister to end grief	
High school student[4]	1932 P	kills foster mother, who suffered from an incurable disease	is sentenced to life in prison
Young Atlanta man[5]	1933 Q	smashes the head of his agonized aunt with a flower pot	is acquitted
J. Pera[6]	1934 S	shoots incurably ill son	commits suicide
Elizabeth Fiederer, 38, New Jersey[7]	1934 Q	kills husband and three children by gas, in fear of cancer	is accused of murder and found insane

Name	Year		Act	Outcome
M. S. Sevigny, nurse[8]	1935	Q	poisons a patient	grand jury refuses to charge, holds patient died from self-administered poison
Walsh sisters[9]	1935	Q	kill imbecile brother by administering gas and tablets	found insane
Carrie Bennet[10]	1935	P	provides poison for invalid husband	confesses as part of a plea bargain and sentenced to ten years
Frances Finkle, 20, Boston	1937	AS	offers mother opiates in a visit to the private hotel where she is staying	attempts suicide
Dr. Guy Shearman Peterkin, urologist[11]	1937	S	believing his son was suffering from an incurable malady, shoots the youth dead	kills himself in office
Dr. Guy Ueterkin, Seattle[12]	1937	S	kills son	commits suicide
Capt. Johan Stanton Stingfellow, 54[13]	1938	S	shoots his invalid wife in her flower-filled sickroom	commits suicide
Dr. Frances Tuttle[14]	1938	AS	offers an anaesthetic to her nine-year-old child	attempts suicide with the same poison
Kathleen Mumford, 40[15]	1938	P	puts her five-year-old imbecile son into the oven	is convicted of murder, but home secretary commutes sentence
Dorothy Sherwood, 27[16]	1938	P	walks into a creek until the waters are over the head of her hungry and cold child	has death penalty reversed by higher court, sending her back for a new trial; pleads guilty to a lesser charge and goes to prison
Harry C. Johnson, 65, Hewlett, L.I.[17]	1938	Q	kills his wife who suffered from cancer	is found temporarily insane

TABLE 2 (*cont.*)

Name	Year	Circumstances	Outcome
Josh Stephens, Atlanta[18]	1938 Q	batters the head of cancer-ridden aunt with a flowerpot	is exonerated
Ruth Steel[19]	1938 Q	shoots and kills sister, who was abandoned by her husband and kids and wished to die	is exonerated
G. Wreschler[20]	1938	kills mentally troubled wife	
Louis Repouille[21]	1939 P	chloroforms thirteen-year-old blind and bedridden son	is indicted for first-degree manslaughter, convicted of second-degree, and freed on suspended sentence of five to ten years
Louis Greenfield[22]	1939 Q	chloroforms his sixteen-year-old idiot son	acquitted of first-degree manslaughter on grounds of temporary insanity
Harry E. Johnson Hewlett, L.I.[23]	1939 Q	turns on gas to kill his cancer-stricken wife	is found temporarily insane
Joseph Saluto, 50 Union City, N.J.[24]	1939 S	kills infantile paralyzed son with razor	commits suicide by slashing his own throat
Margaret L. Cowan[25]	1939	kills sixty-seven-year-old sister, while visiting her in the state hospital	
J. Reichert[26]	1941 Q	murders brother	is acquitted and committed
Otto A. Fye[27]	1942	kills sister	pleads not guilty by reason of insanity (no more information available)

David McGibbon[28]	1942 C	kills sick wife	is committed to state hospital for terminal insane
Mary Bernett[29]	1942 P	strangles eight-year-old daughter	is sentenced to the Detroit House of Correction for five to fifteen years
Daniel W. Cahill, former mayor of Watertown, N.Y.[30]	1942 AS	strangles wife	attempts suicide
John F. Noxon Jr.[31]	1944 P	kills his six-month-old mongoloid son by electrocution	is convicted of first degree murder, a sentence of death in the electric chair had been stayed pending court action on the motion for a new trial
G. R. Long[32]	1946 P	gasses seven-year-old deformed imbecile daughter	pleads guilty and sentenced
Ella M. Haug[33]	1947 AS	murders her ill mother with sleeping pills	attempts suicide, is acquitted by jury
Robert Heye, 46[34]	1948 S	kills son with mixed poisons	commits suicide
Mrs. Blackford[35]	1948 AS	stabs husband	attempts suicide
Philop R. Athon[36]	1948 AS	shoots cancer-ridden wife	attempts suicide
Lucy Richart, 73[37]	1949 S	knifes her fifty-year-old invalid sister	commits suicide with the same pocketknife

TABLE 2 (*cont.*)

Name	Year	Circumstances	Outcome
Carol Paight[38]	1949 Q	kills her cancer-ridden father	is charged for second-degree murder and acquitted due to temporary insanity
Eugene Braunsdorf[39]	1949 Q	shoots daughter in institution, fearing her fate when he dies	attempts suicide, is found not guilty by reason of insanity
Dr. P. Klaft-Slaus[40]	1950 Q	kills incurable cripple with consent of mother	is released on mental irresponsibility pleas and committed to asylum
R. Henry[41]	1950	kills eight-year-old son crippled by polio	
J. G. Gilpatric[42]	1950 S	kills wife after discovering that she has cancer	commits suicide
John Moska[43]	1952	kills his eighteen-year-old invalid daughter with knife	is charged with murder
Shelton Hamlin, Bloomington, Ind., farmer[44]	1952 AS	shoots his wife, both in failing health	attempts suicide
Charles M. Collins, Belfast, Maine[45]	1952	shoots and kills insane son	
Lois Curtis, prominent athlete, Norwalk, Conn.[46]	1952 P	takes father's life by gas to end his suffering from cancer	attempts suicide, is found guilty of manslaughter
William R. Jones 62[47]	1953 AS	electrocutes diabetes-ridden wife	attempts suicide, convicted of second-degree murder and sentenced for a year and a day

Irvin C. Uhler, 51[48]	1953	kills wife, who suffered from neck and mouth ailment	is charged with murder (?)
Albert J. Sell, 44[49]	1953 Q	kills his five-year-old son, a cerebral palsy victim	a jury takes only six minutes to find him insane
Harriet Annuziata, 28[50]	1953	drowns her seven-month-old baby in a laundry tub	
Robert H. Matlock[51]	1953	kills suffering mother with a hammer	
Herman H. Nagle, 54, Arizo.[52]	1953 Q	shoots daughter	is charged with first-degree murder and acquitted by jury
John Petyo, 49[53]	1953 P	bludgeons and strangles his invalid wife	pleads no defense and is sentenced to four to ten years in state prison
Mrs. Elizabeth Wescott Fraps, 44[54]	1953 Q	administers sleeping pills to retarded daughter	is acquitted
Dr. S. Lawrence Woodhouse, Milroy, Pa.[55]	1953	shoots his adopted daughter, who suffered from a nerve and skin-tissue ailment	
Margaret Corkery Cannon, White Plains, N.Y.[56]	1954 C	shoots her husband to death at his request, because he believed he had cancer	is committed to Manhattan State Hospital for the Criminally Insane
Arthur Benies, St. Petersburg, Fl.[57]	1954 S	shoots to death his cancer-ridden wife	shoots himself
Raymond Wilson, Wisc.[58]	1954	kills his very ill wife	

TABLE 2 (*cont.*)

Name	Year	Circumstances	Outcome
Walter S. Mdore[59]	1955 P	terminally ends wife's life, who was paralyzed	jury finds guilty of first-degree murder but the judge delays sentencing to a later date
Mrs. Longevin[60]	1955	murders epileptic son	
J. S. Marples	1955	slays ill mother	is jailed and released
Bernard Ingerwald, 68[61]	1956	kills sister by cyanide poisoning	
W. S. Madon, retired contractor[62]	1956 AS	kills wife	attempts suicide
Grace Devoite, 32, Johnson City, Tenn.[63]	1962 AS	shoots sleeping six-year-old daughter	attempts suicide, is charged with first-degree murder
Dr. Carl Sander, Manchester, N.H.	Q		is acquitted
Harold Mohr[64]	P	kills blind cancer-stricken brother	is convicted, jury recommends mercy, is sentenced to three to six years imprisonment
Mr. Werner, 69	Q	suffocates hopelessly crippled, bedridden wife	court allows withdrawal of guilty plea
Hilton T. Howlett, 26	Q	shoots and kills hopelessly crippled idiot brother	is acquitted by reason of temporary insanity
Mr. Norberg, 31		kills mother suffering from tuberculosis	
Della True, 34, widow		kills two of her children by poisoning their milk	removed for observation, no later reports of the case

❖ Notes ❖

Introduction

1. The deathbed story that follows was published by Mrs. Hannah Howe's husband in "The Grace of God Manifested" *Methodist Review* 1 (1818): 22–25.

2. Hertzler, *The Horse and Buggy Doctor*, 125–126.

3. Thwing, "Euthanasia in Articulo Mortis."

4. Rilke and Mitchell, "Death."

5. Cowley, Young, and Raffin, "Care of the Dying."

6. More, *Utopia and Other Writings*.

7. Bacon, *The Works of Francis Bacon*, vol. 4.

8. Only a handful of historical studies of euthanasia go back to the nineteenth century. The most elaborate is a doctoral dissertation written by Stephen Louis Kuepper, "Euthanasia in America, 1890–1960: The Controversy, the Movement, and the Law" (Rutgers University, 1981). It has been an extremely helpful resource for chapters 3 and 4 of this study. Other less elaborate studies of the history of euthanasia are Emanuel, "The History of Euthanasia in the United States and Britain"; Fye, "Active Euthanasia"; Reiser, "The Dilemma of Euthanasia in Modern Medical History"; Van Der Sluis, "The Movement for Euthanasia, 1875–1975." A more recent book on the topic came out only after the completion of this study, Ian Dowbiggin's *A Merciful End: The Euthanasia Movement in Modern America*. Dowbiggin's book too, with the exception of a short introduction, begins in the twentieth century. In addition, the book focuses primarily on the euthanasia movement, whereas this study places the euthanasia debate and movement within the broader context of the history of dying.

9. The understanding of modernity as the world in which art has vanished and technique holds sway is grounded in the thinking of Martin Heidegger. This thought, so fundamental to Heidegger's work, cannot be located in any single text. For some of Heidegger's work that touches on the topic, see Heidegger's *Basic Questions of Philosophy; Poetry, Language, Thought;* and *The Question concerning Technology, and Other Essays;* and Heidegger and Fink, *Heraclitus Seminar, 1966/67*. A more detailed discussion of art and technique follows. It should be noted here that the common use of the word "technology" is inaccurate and misleading. It suggests that modern technique has self-knowledge, when this is clearly not the case. Whenever possible, I have substituted "technique" for "technology" and "technical' for 'technological."

10. A similar historical transformation from religion through medicine to public policy was documented in the study of cholera outbreaks in nineteenth-century America by Charles E. Rosenberg, *The Cholera Years*.

11. The distinction between different levels of historical accounts is captured nicely by the German language, which uses two different words for thinking about the past. The first, *Historie*, refers to the past as that which is no longer present and understands history as facticity, while the second, *Geschichte*, signifies the power of the past in the present, and understands history as destiny. For an elaborate discussion of this distinction, see Heidegger, *Basic Questions of Philosophy*.

12. *Oxford English Dictionary*, 2nd ed., S.V. "Euthanasy." The first appearance of the word "euthanasia" is in Aeschylus, *Agamemnon*, v. 1293.

13. Stephen Blanhard, *The Physical Dictionary: Wherein the Terms of Anatomy, the Names and Causes of Diseases, Chyrurgical Instruments, and their Uses, Are Accurately Described*, 5th ed. (London, 1708), 126, quoted in Fye, "Active Euthanasia."

14. For a more elaborate discussion of the *ars moriendi* tradition, see chapter 1.

15. Mather, "Euthanasia."

16. Quoted in Bodemer, *Physicians and the Dying: Passing Bell*.

17. Bodemer, "Physicians and the Dying," 831.

18. Novak, *The People's Welfare*.

19. Weber, "Religious Rejections of the World and Their Directions," in *From Max Weber*, 323–58.

20. Foucault, *The History of Sexuality*.

21. An example of a valuable discussion of the history of dying, which nevertheless focuses on the process of decline is Ariès, *The Hour of Our Death*. For an example of a historical study of euthanasia that focuses on the rise of bio-politics in the form of social Darwinism, see Emanuel, "The History of Euthanasia in the United States and Britain."

22. Hannah Arendt has also attempted to understand the inner relation between these two moments through what she has called the decline of politics and the rise of the social. Arendt, *The Human Condition*. The same problem has been more recently addressed in Agamben, *Homo Sacer*.

23. The notion that death can be beautiful appears already in Sophocles' Antigone, where Antigone explains to her sister that she has decided to bury her brother so he would not die a dishonorable death, which she describes in the words: οὐ καλῶς θανειν (to die with no beauty). Sophocles, *Antigone*, ed. Hugh Lloyd-Jones, v. 97.

24. Rothman, *Strangers at the Bedside*.

25. Becker, *The Denial of Death*; Ariès, *The Hour of Our Death*.

26. For a highly illuminating discussion of technique along similar lines, see Borgmann, *Technology and the Character of Contemporary Life*.

27. Weber, *Economy and Society*, 66.

28. For a careful study of the rise of pathology as a question of "life" in nineteenth century biology and medicine, see Canguilhem, *The Normal and the Pathological*.

29. Compare Nietzsche, *Will to Power*, trans. Kaufmann, section 916. I owe this revised translation to Philippe Nonet.

30. Franz Kafka as cited in Enright, *The Oxford Book of Death*, 96.

31. Heidegger, *The Question Concerning Technology, and Other Essays.*

Chapter One

1. The studies of eighteenth and early nineteenth century Methodism are numerous. This chapter relies on Baker, *From Wesley to Asbury*; Byrne, *No Foot of Land*; Dreyer, *The Genesis of Methodism*; Heitzenrater, *Wesley and the People Called Methodists*; Lyerly, *Methodism and the Southern Mind, 1770–1810*; Norwood, *The Story of American Methodism*; Nottingham, *Methodism and the Frontier*; Owen, *The Sacred Flame of Love*; Turley, *A Wheel within a Wheel.*

Discussions of death and dying during the period are less common. Some important studies are Ariès, *The Hour of Our Death*; Farrell, *Inventing the American Way of Death, 1830–1920*; Laderman, *The Sacred Remains*; McManners, *Death and the Enlightenment*. Some scholars have pointed out the importance of the early Puritan death to the formation of the American way of dying, but these studies have either focused on an earlier period, or did not address the Methodists in any specific way. E.g., Geddes, *Welcome Joy*; Stannard, *The Puritan Way of Death.*

Other scholars have written specifically about the Methodist way of dying but have limited their discussion to its importance for understanding Methodism. Chambers, "John Wesley and Death"; Holifield, *Health and Medicine in the Methodist Tradition*; Schneider, "The Ritual of Happy Dying among Early American Methodists"; Vanderpool, "The Wesleyan-Methodist Tradition."

No one, as far as I can tell, has tried to draw a connection between the Methodist way of dying and the modern way of dying, seeing the former not merely in contrast to the latter but also as its predecessor. More important, previous works have failed to capture important aspects of the modern way of dying that will be discussed in the following sections.

2. A brief overview of the *ars moriendi* tradition may be found in the introduction to this book, while a more elaborate discussion follows. For a compilation of the most important texts of the English *ars moriendi* tradition, see Atkinson, *The English Ars Moriendi, Renaissance and Baroque Studies and Texts*, vol. 5. For studies of the *ars moriendi* tradition, see Beaty, *The Craft of Dying*; O'Connor, "The Art of Dying Well."

3. For a detailed account of the evangelical revivals at the turn of eighteenth century America, known also as the "Second Great Awakening," see Mathews, "The Second Great Awakening as an Organizing Process, 1780–1830."

4. For a broader synopsis of religious views on medicine and death, which offers a brief overview of dying in the reformed tradition, see Vaux, *Health and Medicine in the Reformed Tradition*, 131–43. See also Marty, *Health and Medicine in the Lutheran Tradition*, 157–68. And compare with McCormick, *Health and Medicine in the Catholic Tradition*, 105–23.

5. Gaustad, *Historical Atlas of Religion in America*, 4–5.

6. The Methodists maintained this exponential growth rate and became 5.5 million in 1900. Ibid., 75–82. See also Vanderpool, "The Wesleyan-Methodist Tradition," 317–18.

7. Gaustad, *Historical Atlas of Religion in America*, 75–82. See also Farrell, *Inventing the American Way of Death*, 36.

8. Scholars who have studied religious life in America have pointed out the importance of recognizing regional differences within denominations, e.g., Lyerly, *Methodism and the Southern Mind*; Turley, *A Wheel within a Wheel*. The importance of regional variation notwithstanding, this study aims to focus on the continuation of the practice of dying among the Methodist communities during the turn of the nineteenth century. The striking resemblance in deathbed accounts, as well as the continuous reliance on John Wesley's theology, seems to justify minimizing the importance of regional differences for the purposes of this study.

9. Norwood, *The Story of American Methodism*, 17.

10. Hudson, "The Methodist Age in America."

11. Schneider, "The Ritual of Happy Dying among Early American Methodists," 352.

12. Farrell reintroduces this phrase on the basis of a late nineteenth-century editorial, "The Dying of Death," in *Review of Reviews*. According to the editorial, "the dying of death" signifies "the practical disappearance of the thought of death as an influence bearing upon practical life." Farrell, *Inventing the American Way of Death*, 4–5.

13. Under Wesley's guidance, Methodists viewed themselves as a movement within the Anglican Church. As a result of the successful assertion of American independence, Methodism became an independent church. Nottingham, *Methodism and the Frontier*, 5.

14. For a study of Methodism that emphasizes the continuity between Wesley and early American Methodism, see Baker, *From Wesley to Asbury*.

15. The story of Wesley's "pilgrimage" to Georgia has been told and retold by American Methodists and scholars who have studied their history. Ibid.; Heitzenrater, *Wesley and the People Called Methodists*; Nottingham, *Methodism and the Frontier*.

16. These events were recounted by Wesley in his journal on the following dates: 23 November 1735; 1 January 1736; 23 January 1736; 25 January 1736. The actual account of the storm is given on 25 January 1736 in Wesley and Outler, *The Works of John Wesley*, vol. 18.

17. "I have a sin of fear, that when I've spun / My last thread, I shall perish on the shore. . . . / Oh, who will deliver me from this fear of death? / What shall I do? Where shall I fly?" Wesley and Curnock, *The Journal of John Wesley*, 24 January 1738.

18. This observation was made more generally about the Puritans in Farrell, *Inventing the American Way of Death*, 22.

19. Some of Wesley's early sermons on death include "Death and Deliverance," sermon no. 133 in Wesley, Outler, and Heitzenrater, *John Wesley's Sermons*,

204–14; "On Mourning for the Dead," sermon no. 136, ibid., 236–43; "The Trouble and Rest of Good Men," sermon no. 109, ibid., pp. 533–41. Later sermons that address the issue include "On the Death of George Whitefield," sermon no. 53, *John Wesley's Sermons*, 325–47.

20. Holifield, *Health and Medicine in the Methodist Tradition*, 85.

21. See Wesley and Tyson, *Charles Wesley: A Reader*, 190–91, 362–71.

22. Ibid., 171.

23. See for example, Ariès, *The Hour of Our Death*.

24. There are several accounts in the literature of the Methodist understanding of death and dying. I have based my study on John Wesley's sermons, as well as on accounts of deathbed scenes that appear in his journals. In addition, I have examined the rich accounts of deathbed scenes found in the first twenty volumes of *Arminian Magazine* published between the years 1777 and 1797. Finally, I have had some more limited recourse to the works of Charles Wesley and particularly to his hymns and his theological debates with his brother.

25. Taylor and Stanwood, *Holy Living; and, Holy Dying*. For a summary of Taylor's teaching on holy dying, see Fitch, "Preparation for Death."

26. Wesley and Outler, *The Works of John Wesley*, 366–67.

27. Taylor and Stanwood, *Holy Living; and, Holy Dying*.

28. Beaty, *The Craft of Dying*; O'Connor, "The Art of Dying Well."

29. Chambers makes the same connection in Chambers, "John Wesley and Death," 154.

30. The name was, in fact, first given to the Methodists by their rivals but later proudly adopted by John Wesley. Heitzenrater, *Wesley and the People Called Methodists*, 45–47.

31. Beaty, *The Craft of Dying*, 198.

32. Ariès, *Western Attitudes toward Death*, 35–37.

33. Ariès makes this point more generally about a new variety of *artes moriendi*, which he names, "The New Arts of Dying," arguing that already in the sixteenth century, "the art of dying was replaced by an art of living." For Ariès, the emergence of these new "arts of dying" is a manifestation of the devaluation of the hour of death, which will ultimately lead to the modern denial of death, Ariès, *The Hour of Our Death* 300–305. However, Ariès is mistaken in interpreting this new approach to death as a disappearance of dying rather than as a truly new way of dying, which has positive content.

34. Taylor and Stanwood, *Holy Living; and, Holy Dying* 68.

35. Ibid., 69.

36. "Death and Deliverance," sermon no. 133 in Wesley and Outler, *The Works of John Wesley*, 4:206–14.

37. Job 3:17.

38. Sermon no. 133 in Wesley and Outler, *The Works of John Wesley*, 4:208.

39. Preaching to believers with the fires of hell was an old medieval tradition that persisted among American Puritans. See, e.g., Geddes, *Welcome Joy*, 1.

40. Nietzsche, Clark, and Leiter, *Daybreak*, 78.

41. Although John Wesley himself believed in the existence of hell, in his mature writings he preferred to emphasize the blessings of heaven. This fact stands in contrast (as one commentator has already pointed out) with the popular image of Wesley as a hellfire preacher, see Chambers, "John Wesley and Death," 152.

42. The letter was dated March 19, 1727 in Wesley and Outler, *The Works of John Wesley*, 25:214.

43. It seems that Wesley's motivation to ground Christian perfection on empirical grounds has to do with his scientific inclinations. These will be partially explored in what follows.

44. The Methodists were closer in their theology and practice to the Moravians than to the Puritans, who were mostly Calvinists, or to the Anglicans, who were not Evangelical. A recent and very important book on Methodist theology is Dreyer, *The Genesis of Methodism*, 106–16.

45. E.g., ibid; Heitzenrater, *Wesley and the People Called Methodists*.

46. Sermon no. 1 in Wesley and Outler, *The Works of John Wesley*, 1:122.

47. Heitzenrater, *Wesley and the People Called Methodists*, 77.

48. This event has become the most famous experience in the life of John Wesley. Wesley and Outler, *John Wesley, A Library of Protestant Thought*, 14.

49. Wesley and Outler, *The Works of John Wesley*, 18:249–50.

50. Later in his life, however, John Wesley would challenge the notion of one-step salvation and offer a two-stage process of justification and sanctification. Heitzenrater, *Wesley and the People Called Methodists*, 80; Wesley and Outler, *John Wesley*, 31.

51. Piette, *John Wesley in the Evolution of Protestantism*, 374.

52. The Methodists were not the only Protestant denomination that was concerned with the problem of dying, of course. A similar tradition of the art of holy dying and contemplating death can be found at the time among other denominations. For instance, in 1834, William B. Sprague, a prominent Albany Presbyterian minister published *Letters on Practical Subjects to a Daughter*. Appropriately, the book concludes with a chapter "Preparation of Death." Sprague felt that "the great majority of mankind manifests an absolute aversion to the contemplation of death. . . . But preparation for a Christian needed to go way beyond." See Farrell, *Inventing the American Way of Death*, 37.

53. From Becon's *Sick Mannes Salve*, quoted in Geddes, *Welcome Joy*, 174–75.

54. Ibid., 8. Indeed, there are instances in which Puritans rejected any claim for certainty in salvation. Thus, for instance, the American Puritans struggled from the 1580s to the 1660s to reform the Anglican Book of Common Prayer. They insisted that at burial services, the prescribed words "we therefore commit this body to the ground in sure and certain hope of resurrection to eternal life" were contrary to doctrine. After nearly a century of struggle, in 1661 they finally succeeded in having the words "sure and certain" stricken from the pages of the prayer book. Stannard, *The Puritan Way of Death*, 73.

55. Wesley and Outler, *The Works of John Wesley*, 25:318. Heitzenrater, *Wesley and the People Called Methodists*, 43.

56. Heitzenrater, *Wesley and the People Called Methodists*, 36.

57. Wesley and Outler, *The Works of John Wesley*, 25:177; "Christian Perfection," sermon no. 40 in Wesley and Outler, *The Works of John Wesley*, 4:99–124.

58. See also Schneider, "The Ritual of Happy Dying among Early American Methodists," 360.

59. There has been a long debate among Methodist scholars on the extent to which theology is central for understanding the Methodist life in general, and that of individual Methodists in particular. This debate has been quite misleading. One must distinguish between theology as a metareflection on religious experience and theology as the set doctrine, which every devoted Christian should affirm. While Wesley rejected the importance of theology in the latter sense, emphasizing the importance of one's state of heart and soul rather than one's state of mind, he gives tremendous importance to theology in the first sense. Yet in that capacity, it is only the concern of the few and by no means a necessary part of one's belief. For the scholar, on the other hand, the study of theology is central for understanding the ground of religious practice. See the discussion on Wesleyan theology in Dieter, "Wesleyan Theology."

60. The account of Welsey's death and the circumstances under which Miss Ritchie undertook their documentation can be found in John Wesley's journal in Wesley and Outler, *The Works of John Wesley*, 8:131–44. Compare to similar accounts of Charles Wesley's death in Wesley and Tyson, *Charles Wesley*, 480–81.

61. Wesley and Tyson, *Charles Wesley*, 132.

62. Leter from July 1768, in Wesley and Outler, *The Works of John Wesley*, 25:96.

63. Heitzenrater, *Wesley and the People Called Methodists*, 308.

64. Wesley and Outler, *The Works of John Wesley*, 8:143.

65. Ibid., 144.

66. For an exception see the death of Mr. Fletcher in *Arminian Magazine* (1793) 4.

67. See "Some Account for the Life and Death of Sarah Brough."

68. Ariès notes that the public aspect of the deathbed remains an essential characteristic of dying till the end of the nineteenth century. Ariès, *The Hour of Our Death*, 18. See also McManners, *Death and the Enlightenment*, 234.

69. Wesley and Outler, *The Works of John Wesley*, 21:307–8.

70. See "Memoir of Mrs. Mary Ann Peaco."

71. Schneider, "The Ritual of Happy Dying among Early American Methodists," 356.

72. A journal entry dated 21 March 1770 in Wesley and Outler, *The Works of John Wesley*, 22:357–61.

73. Ibid., 359.

74. Quoted in Geddes, *Welcome Joy*, 60.

75. The founding brothers of the Methodist Church argued profusely about the true nature of sanctification. For a detailed account of the various arguments, see Wesley and Tyson, *Charles Wesley*, 360–91.

76. Journal entry dated 18 July 1738 in Wesley and Jackson, *The Journal of the Rev. Charles Wesley*. See also Chambers, "John Wesley and Death."

77. Outler, *John Wesley's Sermons*, 32.

78. "Memoir of Mrs. Mary Ann Peaco," 276.

79. "The Recent Death of John Patrick," *Arminian Magazine* 20 (1797).

80. Ibid., 204.

81. Ibid., 205.

82. See "A Short Account of the Conversion and Death of Caster Garret: In a Letter to a Friend."

83. Ibid., 20.

84. Ibid., 20–21.

85. Journal entry dated 5 May 1757 in Wesley and Outler, *The Works of John Wesley*, 21:206–7.

86. See "The Life of Dr. Donne." See also a discussion in Fitch, "Preparation for Death."

87. Journal entry from December 1760 in Wesley and Outler, *The Works of John Wesley*, 21:425–27.

88. Ibid., 427.

89. Journal entry dated 21 March 1770 in ibid., 22:359.

90. Journal entry dated 5 May 1757 in ibid., 21:207.

91. Sermon no. 119 in ibid., 4:533–41.

92. Wesley, Outler, and Heitzenrater, *John Wesley's Sermons*, 533.

93. Journal entry dated 5 May 1757 in Wesley and Outler, *The Works of John Wesley*, 21:206.

94. Maddocks, "Health and Healing in the Ministry of John Wesley," 139.

95. Wesley, *Primitive Physic*.

96. Vanderpool, "The Wesleyan-Methodist Tradition."

97. Taken from Wesley's preface in Wesley, *Primitive Physic*.

98. Ibid., 26.

99. Ibid.

100. Nottingham, *Methodism and the Frontier*.

101 Thus, for example, one scholar has pointed out that "the liturgy and the prescribed hymns were entirely out of harmony with the type of Methodism that had been growing up in America since 1776. It was the *Discipline* rather than the *Sunday Service*—a manual for action rather than a manual of liturgy—that was to become the book that embodied the American Methodist spirit." Ibid., 7.

102. The following analysis of the decline of the Methodist *ars moriendi* relies heavily on secondary sources. The focus of the primary research is on the Methodist tradition prior to 1830.

103. Vanderpool, "The Wesleyan-Methodist Tradition," 333.

104. Ibid. See also Editorial, "The Medical Profession."

105. Vanderpool, "The Wesleyan-Methodist Tradition," 339.

106. Ibid., 344.

107. Holifield, *Health and Medicine in the Methodist Tradition*, 92.

Chapter Two

An earlier edited version of chapter 2 was published in the journal *Theoretical Inquiries in Law* (July 2003).

1. A discussion of the Birmingham Club and specifically its 1870 publication can be found in Editorial, "Essays of the Birmingham Speculative Club."

2. Williams, *Euthanasia*. For a more general discussion of the history of euthanasia and Williams's proposal, see Emanuel, "The History of Euthanasia in the United States and Britain." For a broader account, see the introduction.

3. Quoted in Williams, "Euthanasia."

4. See the introduction, as well as Emanuel, "The History of Euthanasia in the United States and Britain."

5. Goddard, "Suggestions in Favor of Terminating Absolutely Hopeless Cases of Injury and Disease"; Tollemache, "The Cure of Incurables." See more generally Emanuel, "The History of Euthanasia in the United States and Britain."

6. A good survey of euthanasia bills up to the 1970s can be found in Russell, *Freedom to Die*. The only euthanasia legislation that became effective in the United States is the Oregon physician-assisted suicide law. See Hendin, Foley, and White, "Physician-Assisted Suicide."

7. These proposals are called "physician-assisted suicide" in order to distinguish them from medical euthanasia proper.

8. The immediate responses to Williams proposal were Editorial, "The Doctrine of Euthanasia"; Editorial, "Essays of the Birmingham Speculative Club"; Editorial, "Euthanasia," *Popular Science Monthly*; Editorial, "The Euthanasia"; Editorial, "Euthanasia," *Medical Record* 28 (1885); Editorial, "The Limits of Euthanasia"; Editorial, "Permissive Euthanasia"; Hitchcock, "Annual Oration: Euthanasia"; and Tollemache, "The Cure of Incurables."

9. Editorial, "The Moral Side of Euthanasia," 382.

10. For a more elaborate discussion of the history of the term "euthanasia," see the introduction.

11. To avoid confusion, unless otherwise specified, the term "euthanasia" will be used in its strictly modern sense, signifying the medical and active hastening of death.

12. There are exceptions to this rule, most famously the recent enacted legislation in the Netherlands. The Dutch law does not make it mandatory that the patient be terminally ill; it is enough that the patient be in a state of great suffering. See Executive Summary, "Verbatim: Physician-Assisted Suicide and Euthanasia in the Netherlands."

13. Emanuel, "The History of Euthanasia in the United States and Britain."

14. For a general discussion of the history of death and dying in medicine, see Ackerknecht, "Death in the History of Medicine"; Bodemer, "Physicians and the Dying: A Historical Sketch"; Cowley, Young, and Raffin, "Care of the Dying."

15. For an elaborate discussion of the eighteenth-century "public panic over 'premature burials,' " see Pernick, "Back from the Grave."

16. Evidence for this behavior and its implications are offered in what follows.

17. For nineteenth century medical etiquette, see Baker, Porter, and Porter, eds., *The Codification of Medical Morality*. For its importance in promoting the esteem of orthodox medicine, see Coulter, *Divided Legacy*. For later codes, see Hamstra, "The American Medical Association Code of Medical Ethics of 1847."

18. Gregory, *Lectures on the Duties of a Physician*, 37.

19. The first use of "euthanasia" to signify the medical treatment of dying patient was by Paradys in a Latin text from 1794. Paradys, *Oratio De Euthanasia*. However Paradys's text does not manifest the new spirit of euthanasia as it appears in Marx's text and in what follows.

20. Cowley, Young, and Raffin, "Care of the Dying," 1478.

21. Bacon, *The Works of Francis Bacon*, 387.

22. Marx, "Medical Euthanasia."

23. It may be interesting to note that Marx had a great love for art, and was the first to systematically list and classify paintings of medical interest. Marx also published exhaustive studies on Herophilus, Blumenbach, Paracelsus, Leibnitz, and Schneider. See Garrison, *An Introduction to the History of Medicine*.

24. Ibid., 404–5.

25. Marx, "Medical Euthanasia."

26. See, e.g., Nuland, *How We Die*.

27. Marx, "Medical Euthanasia," 411.

28. Dendy, "On the Physiology of Death and the Treatment of the Dying," 121.

29. Marx, "Medical Euthanasia," 410.

30. Percival, *Percival's Medical Ethics*, 220–21.

31. Dendy, "On the Physiology of Death and the Treatment of the Dying," 122.

32. Marx, "Medical Euthanasia," 410.

33. On medicine in the nineteenth century in general, and on heroic medicine in particular, see Brieger, *Medical America in the Nineteenth Century*; Cassedy, *Medicine in America*; Castiglioni and Krumbhaar, *A History of Medicine*; Davis, *History of Medicine*; Rothstein, *American Physicians in the Nineteenth Century*.

34. Coulter, *Divided Legacy*, 53–54.

35. Rush, *Selected Writings of Benjamin Rush*, 315.

36. Cathell, *The Physician Himself and What He Should Add to His Scientific Acquirements*, 99.

37. Ibid.

38. Rush, *Selected Writings of Benjamin Rush*, 313.

39. Blanton, *Medicine in the Eighteenth Century*, 198–99, cited in Rothstein, *American Physicians in the Nineteenth Century*, 44.

40. Bigelow's famous article, "On Self-Limited Diseases," was originally delivered before the Massachusetts Medical Society in 1935.

41. Pernick, *A Calculus of Suffering*, 22. For a somewhat different account of the emerging medical trends of the time, see Warner, " 'The Nature-Trusting Heresy.' "

42. Kaufman, Galishoff, and Savitt, eds., *Dictionary of American Medical Biography*.

43. Some medical historians have ignored the importance of this distinction and hence have undermined the central place of the administration of hope in modern medicine. Most explicitly, Rothstein wrote, "The therapeutic value of hope and confidence exists solely because of the patient's faith in the physician. Therefore, any practitioner who inspires faith in his patients is the physician's equal in this regard. Indeed, lay healers, faith healers, Indian doctors, nostrum vendors, and the whole range of practitioners who relied largely on their charismatic qualities for their success were probably more successful than most physicians in inspiring hope and confidence in their patients." Rothstein, *American Physicians in the Nineteenth Century*, 10.

44. Hooker, *Physician and Patient*, 348.

45. Early in the century, Rush criticized this practice in medicine: "I know that the practice of predicting danger and death, upon every occasion, is sometimes made use of by physicians, in order to enhance the credit of their prescriptions, if their patient recover, and to save a retreat from blame, if they should die." Rush, *Selected Writings of Benjamin Rush*. For a general discussion of orthodox medicine and its relation to the different varieties of sectarian medicine, see Coulter, *Divided Legacy*.

46. Dendy, "On the Physiology of Death and the Treatment of the Dying," 121.

47. Ariès, *The Hour of Our Death*, 5–10.

48. Ibid, 583–93.

49. Hooker, *Physician and Patient*, 347.

50. Ariès, *The Hour of Our Death*, 559–67.

51. The term "repressive hypothesis" is borrowed from Foucault's critical discussion of nineteenth-century sexuality. Foucault argues that contrary to common wisdom, sexuality was not repressed by the Victorians but rather reinvented as subject to regulation by new techniques of power/knowledge. Here I wish to draw a partial analogy between sexuality and mortality only to emphasize the importance of acknowledging the productive power of the modern *ars moriendi* no less than that of *scientia sexualis*. See Foucault, *The History of Sexuality*.

52. Percival, *Percival's Medical Ethics*, 91.

53. Hooker, *Physician and Patient*, 350.

54. Ibid., 345.

55. Ibid., 345–46.

56. "As for the patient, as long as there is life, there is hope." Cicero, *Cicero in Twenty-Eight Volumes*, 9:10.

57. For an illuminating book on how to think in profound ways about emotions, see Katz, *How Emotions Work*.

58. Bigelow, "On Self-Limited Diseases," 106.

59. Oliver W. Holmes, cited in E. P. Buffet, "Pleasures of Dying," 240–41.

60. Ibid.

61. By the same token, in the contemporary context the hospital and the hospice, which are seen as two radically different way of dying, are merely divisions of labor within the modern way of dying. The same physicians who deny death are the ones who define it; the same physicians send their patients to the hospice.

62. One is tempted to say "from nature to the prerogative of man," but this is not the case. Medical man becomes a servant of technique rather than the other way around.

63. On the history of pain see, Pernick, *A Calculus of Suffering*; Rey, *The History of Pain*; Caton, "The Secularization of Pain"; Morris, "An Invisible History of Pain"; Moulin, "A Historical-Phenomenological Study of Bodily Pain in Western Man."

64. On the reaction of physicians to the discovery of ether, see Pernick, *A Calculus of Suffering*.

65. Quoted in Editorial, "A Medico-Literary Causerie: Euthanasia."

66. Ibid.

67. Over a century later, the pain and suffering of the dying patient is still a central concern in the treatment of dying. Pain is the most prevalent justification for the practice of physician-assisted suicide. Foley, "The Relationship of Pain and Symptom Management to Patient Requests for Physician-Assisted Suicide." This is so much the case that even opponents of physician-assisted suicide do not argue that the pain of dying is not the most important concern but rather that there are other ways for overcoming it. See, e.g., Justice O'Connor's position in *Vacco v. Quill*, 117 S. Ct. 2293 (1997); and *Washington v. Glucksberg*, 117 S. Ct. 2258 (1997).

68. Nuland, *How We Die*.

69. On the problem of understanding pain merely quantitatively, see Lavi, "The Problem of Pain and the Right to Die."

70. Moulin, "A Historical-Phenomenological Study of Bodily Pain in Western Man."

71. Elias, *The Civilizing Process*.

72. Mitchel, "Civilization and Pain." Compare Nietzsche, *On the Genealogy of Morals*, 46–49.

73. Munk, *Euthanasia or, Medical Treatment in Aid of an Easy Death*. By "euthanasia" Munk is not referring to the intentional killing of patients, as suggested by Williams, but rather to euthanasia in a more literal sense, i.e., the achievement of a good death.

74. Ibid., 7. Many medical works on death and dying arrive at a similar conclusion. A few examples are Philip, "On the Nature of Death"; Macdonald, *On Death and How to Divest It of Its Terrors*.

75. Munk, *Euthanasia*, 12–15.

76. Ibid., 20.

77. Quoted in Hitchcock, "Annual Oration: Euthanasia," 30.

78. See Hinohara, "Sir William Osler's Philosophy on Death."

79. For an elaborate discussion of Osler's approach to death, see Golden, "Sir William Osler."

80. Dendy, "On the Physiology of Death and the Treatment of the Dying," 118.

81. Such a representation of the dying process by the medical profession would surely be untenable today. As a contemporary physician referring to Osler's experiment has noted, "The last weeks and days of far more of my patients than Osler's one in five have been overfull with a plethora of purgatory, and I have been there to see it." Nuland, *How We Die*.

82. The last article of life has often been characterized as "the mortal agony" and a "death struggle" accompanied by "the pangs of death." Maeterlinck, *Death*.

83. For a rich historical account of attitudes toward pain, see Rey, *The History of Pain*.

84. Ibid.

85. This prevailing understanding of pain and its functions is summarized in Harold Balme, *The Relief of Pain*. A similar view of the functions of pain appears in more recent studies. See, e.g., Melzack and Wall, *The Challenge of Pain*, 11.

86. Pascalis, "Remarks on the Theory of Pain."

87. Baldwin, "The Natural Right to a Natural Death," 886.

88. *Oxford English Dictionary*, 2nd ed., S.V. "Euthanasy."

89. Marx, "Medical Euthanasia." A different tripartite process of dying was: mental death, somatic or corporeal death, and molecular death. Lange, "Modes of Dying," 27.

90. "All modes of death, with the exception of that from old age, may be regarded as more or less violent; but in considering their nature, we must not confound the last act of dying with the suffering which precedes it, and which is often no less when it terminates in recovery than in death, which equally relieves it; and as death in the usual acceptation of the word, from whatever cause it arises, consists in the loss of the sensorial functions alone, the act of dying is, in this respect, in all cases essentially the same." Philip, "On the Nature of Death," 174.

91. Lange, "Modes of Dying," 34.

92. "The state which immediately precedes the last act of dying, then, according to the common acceptation of the term, and sleep, depend on a failure of function in the same organs. In what, then, consists the difference of these states? The most evident is that the one is a temporary, the other a final failure; and it will appear, that in the only death which can strictly be called natural, the state of the sensitive system which immediately precedes death differs from its state in sleep in no respect but in degree." Ibid., 170.

93. Buffet, "Pleasures of Dying," 233.

94. Philip, "On the Nature of Death," 184.

95. For a similar argument, see Illich, *Medical Nemesis*.

96. Hitchcock, "Annual Oration," 32. In one of the earlier studies on the nature of death, Dr. Philip wrote, "I need not say that many advantages would arise from a correct knowledge of the immediate cause of death. . . . The most important would be, that it would give to the physician a clearer view of the tendencies of disease, and consequently of the indications of cure; but it would not be the least of its advantages, that it would tend to strip a change which all must undergo of the groundless terrors with which, we have reason to believe, the timid and fanciful have clothed it." Philip, "On the Nature of Death," 168.

97. Munk, *Euthanasia*, 54–55.

98. Ibid., 20.

99. Dendy, "On the Physiology of Death and the Treatment of the Dying," 119.

100. Munk, *Euthanasia*, 48.

101. Lange, "Modes of Dying."

102. Buffet, "Pleasures of Dying," 236.

103. Ibid., 239.

104. Munk, *Euthanasia*, 73.

105. Melzack and Wall, *The Challenge of Pain*, v. The birth of the pain clinic and the hospice, along with the developments of pain-control techniques in psychology, physiology, and clinical medicine, are manifestations of this growing concern.

106. Spender, *Therapeutic Means for the Relief of Pain*.

107. The choice of anesthetics should not be taken for granted. In fact, the possibility of using the electric chair, though not quite as popular, was also raised as a possible means of shortening the life of dying patients. Goddard, "Suggestions in Favor of Terminating Absolutely Hopeless Cases of Injury and Disease," 659. The appeal of death by anesthesia was precisely the way in which it could simulate falling asleep.

Chapter Three

1. For a similar discussion of the relation between law and other regulatory regimes, see Foucault, Burchell, Gordon, and Miller, *The Foucault Effect*.

2. For a fascinating and rich study of nineteenth-century common law in America and its transformation toward the end of the century, see Novak, *The People's Welfare*. A comprehensive account of antebellum legal reform can be found in Cook, *The American Codification Movement*. For a discussion of post–Civil War developments, see Nelson, "The Impact of the Antislavery Movement upon Styles of Judicial Reasoning in Nineteenth-Century America." For a more specific discussion of criminal law reform in England, see Hostettler, *The Politics of Criminal Law*.

3. Novak, *The People's Welfare*. For a nineteenth-century discussion of the binding power of English common law in the American territories and in the United States, see Goodenow, *Historical Sketches of the Principles and Maxims of American Jurisprudence in Contrast with the Doctrines of the English Common Law on the Subject of Crimes and Punishments*.

4. Untitled editorial, *Medical and Surgical Reporter* (1879).

5. Bell, "Has the Physician Ever the Right to Terminate Life?" 78.

6. For a discussion of religious objections to euthanasia and their limited influence, see chapter 4.

7. The place of religion in the modern euthanasia controversy, as well as the more specific question of whether the religious objections to euthanasia were truly as traditional as they appeared, will be further discussed in chapters 4 and 5.

8. Such a medical duty could be legally justified on the basis of the necessity defense. This hypothetical justification of euthanasia was not raised at the time. Compare, however, with more recent discussions, e.g., Williams, *The Sanctity of Life and the Criminal Law*.

9. Italics in original: Tollemache, "The Cure of Incurables," 225.

10. Bach, as quoted in Bell, "Has the Physician Ever the Right to Terminate Life?" 69.

11. For some turn-of-the-twentieth-century discussions, see Larremore, "Suicide and the Law"; Mikell, "Is Suicide Murder?" For a general overview of the legal history of suicide, see Burgess-Jackson, "The Legal Status of Suicide in Early America"; Marzen et al., "Suicide: A Constitutional Right?" For a general history of suicide, see Minois, *History of Suicide*.

12. Quoted in Bell, "Has the Physician Ever the Right to Terminate Life?" 69.

13. Bracton, *On the Laws and Customs of England*, 2:366.

14. Ibid.

15. Blackstone, *Commentaries on the Laws of England*, 4:189.

16. See discussion in Marzen et al., "Suicide: A Constitutional Right?" The co-writers found interesting variations among the different colonies.

17. Swift, *A System of the Laws of the State of Connecticut*, 2:304.

18. Ibid.

19. Interestingly, even after suicide could no longer be punished, it was still considered a crime, as a 1877 Massachusetts case suggests. *Commonwealth v. Mink*, 123 Mass. 422 (1877). See also the discussion in Marzen et al., "Suicide: A Constitutional Right?" 69.

20. In fact, there is evidence that in some law books, suicide was still considered a crime, at least nominally. Boehm, for instance, mentioned in 1895 that suicide was still present in the penal code of New York. Boehm, "The Right to Commit Suicide," 463.

21. Minois, *History of Suicide*.

22. Ibid., 462.

23. Blackstone, *Commentaries on the Laws of England*, 190.

24. The question of what, precisely, makes a suicide rational, was highly debated in the literature. It is interesting to note that the wish of the dying patient who is suffering from great pain to commit suicide was interpreted as both rational and irrational. This is a problem that to this day is at the center of the physician-assisted suicide and euthanasia debate.

25. From a strictly legal point of view, only rational suicide counted as suicide proper. Thus, for instance, when the question of life insurance came up, it was clear that the benefits of the policy could be contractually deprived only from a person who committed suicide while being of sound mind.

26. Foucault, *The History of Sexuality*, 138–39. See also Foucault et al., *Society Must Be Defended*.

27. Editorial, "Euthanasia and Suicide."

28. This is true even though the legal definition of assisted suicide implies that the "assistant" is not involved in the actual killing, whereas in the classic case of euthanasia the physician is responsible for hastening death. Nevertheless, the legal category of assisted suicide comes closest to describing both the suicidal aspect of euthanasia and the involvement of another party.

29. There was also the question of attempted suicide, which is less relevant to the discussion here and therefore is not fully explored.

30. There are, of course, alternative explanations as to why the law recriminalized assisted suicide. One possible explanation is that the law was still operating under the force of inertia, and since the prohibition on assisted suicide was centuries old, the law merely wished to maintain it in place. The reason why the legal status of suicide changed was because it was not punishable, and there was a growing realization that deterrence was ineffective. Since the modern criminal law understood the goal to be deterrence, suicide could no longer be recognized as a crime. This explanation is not very different from the one offered. It, too, recognizes a fundamental change in the role of law as a guardian of life.

31. Rosenberg and Aronstam, "Euthanasia—a Medicolegal Study," 110.

32. *Saturday Review*, 13 July 1872, quoted in Tollemache, "The Cure of Incurables," 230.

33. Ibid.

34. S. R. Wells, "Is 'Euthanasia' Ever Justifiable?" 4:5.

35. For an altogether different ground by which to distinguish euthanasia from suicide—based on social welfare—see discussion in the next chapter.

36. Tollemache, "The Cure of Incurables," 224.

37. Editorial, "A Medico-Literary Causerie: Euthanasia."

38. Rosenberg and Aronstam, "Euthanasia—a Medicolegal Study," 110.

39. This is part of a report delivered at a meeting of the South Carolina Medical Association. The report was given by a special committee on euthanasia that was asked to study the subject in its various aspects. Ibid.

40. Euthanasia is not offered, here, for handicaps and other "defectives." Indeed, Tollemache rejected this possibility up front. However, this possibility was raised by Charles Buxton, who seemed to have advocated such an idea.

41. Tollemache, "The Cure of Incurables," 222.

42. These latter questions are asked rhetorically. Wells, "Is 'Euthanasia' Ever Justifiable?" 10.

43. The constitutive power of law has become a focus of contemporary legal scholarship. The constitutive role of law is especially important with respect to legalization during the turn of the twentieth century, in the context of emerging welfare and public health legislation. Hunt and Wickham, *Foucault and Law*.

44. Popkin, *Materials on Legislation*, 20. In America, the New Deal legislation of the 1930s crowned the ascendancy of law by statute. Grad, "The Ascendancy of Legislation."

45. A similar bill was drafted in Iowa a few months later. Untitled editorial, *British Medical Journal* (1906). No record of the bill has been found in the Iowa legislature. Other scholars have been equally unable to trace the bill. Emanuel, "The History of Euthanasia in the United States and Britain."

46. Quoted Ibid.

47. Russell, *Freedom to Die: Moral and Legal Aspects of Euthanasia*.

48. *New York Times*, 29 January 1906.

49. Yale Kamisar, "Some Non-Religious Views against Proposed 'Mercy Killing' Legislation."

Chapter Four

1. The primary sources on the Euthanasia Society of America were kept in the society's archive, now managed by Partnership for Caring, Inc., and stored at the Lewis Associates, Baltimore, Md.; they are identified hereafter by "PC," followed by a reference to the specific box in the archive, e.g., PC-B4. The most elaborate secondary source on the society is a doctoral dissertation written by Stephen Louis Kuepper, titled "Euthanasia in America, 1890–1960: The Controversy, the Movement, and the Law." Another important study of the euthanasia movement in America has come out more recently, unfortunately only after the completion of this study: Dowbiggin's *A Merciful End: The Euthanasia Movement in Modern America*.

2. Potter, "Euthanasia Mercy Killing and Suicide," February 2, 1936 (PC-C4).

3. This chapter is based primarily on original research done in the archives of the Euthanasia Society in Baltimore. Other than the original ESA documents and other primary sources, such as newspaper articles, I have relied on the work of Stephen Kuepper, who has studied the society carefully. Kuepper, "Euthanasia in America, 1890–1960." Kuepper's dissertation, though highly thorough in gathering the materials, is weaker in proposing a framework for understanding the society's activity. Another dissertation that explores the American euthanasia society was written by Valery Garrett, "The Last Civil Right? Euthanasia Policy and Politics in the United States, 1938–1991." For a more general history of the euthanasia movement, see Emanuel, "The History of Euthanasia in the United States and Britain"; Fye, "Active Euthanasia"; Van Der Sluis, "The Movement for Euthanasia, 1875–1975"; Zucker, *The Right to Die Debate*.

4. Founding statement of the National Society for the Legalization of Euthanasia, 16 January 1938 (PC-C1).

5. For more details about Potter's biography, see Potter, *The Preacher and I.*

6. Potter statement (PC-C4). See also Kuepper, "Euthanasia in America, 1890–1960," 112–13.

7. Ibid., 112.

8. Jones also served for a time as the president of the International Birth Control Organization.

9. Similarly, Robert L. Dickinson, a noted gynecologist and medical researcher and another yet-to-be president of the ESA, was also highly involved in the birth-control movement.

10. Potter, in a release to the newspapers, 1938 (PC-C4).

11. For more on the struggle for birth control, see Chesler, *Woman of Valor.*

12. For more on the Comstock act, see Bates, *Weeder in the Garden of the Lord.*

13. For more on Sanger's life and her involvement in the birth-control struggle, see Chesler, *Woman of Valor*; Gray, *Margaret Sanger*; Sanger, *My Fight for Birth Control.*

14. Bates, *Weeder in the Garden of the Lord.*

15. *United States v. One Package of Japanese Pessaries*, 13 F. Supp. 334 (E.D.N.Y 1936), *aff'd* 86 F.2d 737 (2nd Cir. 1936).

16. Letter from Dr. Philbrick to Ann L. Mitchell, n.d. (PC-C1).

17. One of the leading advocates of birth control was also a supporter of euthanasia in England: Havelock Ellis. In 1934, Ellis wrote an article in *Esquire* magazine, where he explained the importance of birth control. He wrote: "Today, for the first time, we recognize both the direct and indirect influences that increase or diminish population, on the one hand by deliberate control of procreation, and on the other hand by undesigned factors of physiological, economic, or social nature" (PC-B1).

18. This suggestion was proposed in a board meeting sometime after 1947 (PC-C1).

19. "Involuntary euthanasia was also, at least theoretically, consonant with Potter's Humanism. His version of an ideal society was obviously one without defectives, and, as he had mentioned, the funds that supported the unfit could be diverted to developing the potentialities of those 'worth saving'" (PC-C4).

20. Potter, too, promoted birth control on both eugenic and humanitarian grounds. On the one hand, he argued there was "too large a proportion of defectives," while in the same breath he proclaimed that "couples should be allowed to space their offspring, so each child could receive adequate attention, and parents would not be strained with the burdens of oversized families" (PC-C4).

21. The emphasis on social engineering was perhaps more pronounced in America than in England. For example, in America, birth control was more likely to be justified as solving a social problem, whereas in England the concern was more about women's rights.

22. Numerous books and articles have been written on American eugenics. In what follows, I rely on Kevles, *In the Name of Eugenics*, and on Mehler, *A History of the American Eugenics Society, 1921–1940*.

23. It is hard to distinguish clearly between the birth-control and eugenic movements. The reason for discussing them separately is because they were separated institutionally. While the birth-control movement was focused primarily on legalizing the distribution of contraceptives, the eugenic movement had much broader goals and a wider array of practices, including contraceptives, sterilization, immigration restrictions, and euthanasia.

24. The term "defective" here and in what follows is taken from the literature of the time.

25. Francis Galton, *Inquiries into Human Faculty and Its Development*, quoted in Mehler, *A History of the American Eugenics Society, 1921–1940*.

26. Pernick, *The Black Stork*.

27. Pernick argues convincingly that the understanding of heredity and eugenics was not based only on scientific findings but also on a mutual interdependence of science and culture. From a cultural point of view (but also according to some scientists), only a transmission from parent to child—even if "environmental," such as syphilis—was considered "bad blood." Ibid.

28. Among the institutions that were founded in the spirit of the eugenic movement were the American Social Hygiene Association (1913), aimed at venereal diseases, and the child-labor-regulation compulsory-schooling movement. Ibid.

29. Kevles, *In the Name of Eugenics*, 92.

30. As early as 1896, Connecticut law prohibited marriage (as well as extramarital relations) to the eugenically unfit for women under forty-five. Violating these laws would carry the minimum penalty of three years. Ibid., 99–100. In 1914, thirty states enacted new marriage laws preventing the marriage of the mentally deficient.

31. Ibid. In the United States, most states did not generally enforce these rather extreme measures, and the number of sterilizations was seldom more than one hundred per year. Exceptions were California, where sterilizations averaged more than 350 cases per year, with a total of 9,931 by 1935, and some of the southern states, with fairly high sterilization rates relative to their populations.

32. Vasectomy is the surgical cutting of the male vas deferens tube; salpingectomy is a similar procedure applied to the female fallopian tubes.

33. *Buck v. Bell*, 274 U.S. 200, 205–6 (1927).

34. See Kuepper, "Euthanasia in America, 1890–1960," 62–63.

35. *New York Times*, 9 December 1936. To Goddard we owe the classifications of the mentally retarded into "idiots," "imbeciles," and "morons."

36. Ibid.

37. Kuepper, "Euthanasia in America, 1890–1960," 109.

38. *The New York Sun*, 31 March 1935. And yet this scientific finding was strongly questioned: "Without entering into the controversy on sterilization in any direct sense, let me state briefly the fundamental facts uncovered by the committee

of the American Neurological Association and its conclusions and recommendations. We find the claims of most eugenicists as to the incidence of mental disease and mental defect unwarranted. There is no evidence of an actual increase." (Abraham Myerson, M.D., chairman, American Neurological Association Committee for the Investigation of Sterilization, Boston, 10 March 1936).

39. Kuepper, "Euthanasia in America, 1890–1960," 108.

40. For a discussion of the treatment of deformed babies and its history see, Pernick, *The Black Stork*.

41. As in the case of euthanasia, this was not the first time in which the problem of infanticide was raised. It was a well-known practice, according to available sources in Sparta. But the topic reemerged side-by-side with euthanasia in the late nineteenth century. Thus, Baldwin, in the very same article in which he deals with euthanasia for the dying patient also discusses the possibility of offering it to the newly born. "As the old man has a right to a natural death, so has the unfortunate babe, that is born into the world with physical defects that, but for a surgical operation, would in a few hours or days take it out of it, when its surgical operation can only save the life, by making it a daily and hopeless misery. . . . Nature has her invariable laws. By one of them malformation, preventing the due exercise of any vital function, leads to death. The suffering will not be long. Man can throw his skill in the way of this law, and interrupt its course. He can attempt to reconstruct the body, where nature has failed." Baldwin, "The Natural Right to a Natural Death," *St. Paul Medical Journal* 1 (1899): 881–82. Baldwin, however, is speaking here of passive euthanasia. Similarly, the *Boston Medical and Surgical Reporter* discussed it in 1884: "The Journal has already noticed the assumption on the part of certain practitioners that a monstrosity should be put out of the way as soon as possible after birth, which proposal, though not (we are happy to say) generally 'recognized.'" Editorial, "Permissive Euthanasia," 19.

42. Pernick, *The Black Stork*, 3.

43. Ibid., 4.

44. Ibid., 3–4.

45. Ibid., 6.

46. See Kuepper, "Euthanasia in America, 1890–1960," 64–68.

47. Dr. Potter, reporting on a technique of mercy killing for babies: "The technique is simple. If, for instance, a baby is born a hopeless idiot, the doctor may go to the parents and say there is a delicate operation from which the baby has a 'chance in a thousand' of emerging. The father understands what he means, the nurses understand, the doctor understands. There is no one chance in a thousand." *New York Journal American*, 18 January 1938, quoted by Rev. McCormick in his pamphlet, "So-Called 'Mercy Killing'" (PC-B1). Potter, however, wasn't recommending this method, just pointing out the necessity of bringing euthanasia out into the open.

48. Kuepper, "Euthanasia in America, 1890–1960," 116. To be accurate, there were other social concerns that had nothing to do with control of life or death that were on the minds of ESA supporters. Thus Potter, in addition to his other

involvements mentioned above, was also concerned with the following: "conservation of natural resources, the extension of social insurance, the improvement of working conditions, the improvement of means of communication, the promotion of public health, the improvement and extension of educational facilities, the establishment of sexual equality, and the legalization of birth control" (PC-C4).

49. Cathell, *The Physician Himself and What He Should Add to His Scientific Acquirements*, 83.

50. Thwing, "Euthanasia in Articulo Mortis," 283.

51. Ibid., 284.

52. Tollemache, "The Cure of Incurables," 268.

53. Ibid., 219.

54. C. Killick Millard, quoting Mrs. Annie Besant, in ibid. Compare this with the different, more legalistic way of distinguishing the two practices noted in the previous chapter.

55. Dr. Ellsworth Huntington, eminent geographer and author, accepting membership on the board of the community (PC-C1).

56. Charles Potter (PC-C4). Similarly, Richardson wrote, "The sharpness of death removed from those who die, the poignancy of grief would be almost equally removed from those who survive, were natural euthanasia the prevailing fact." Richardson, "Natural Euthanasia," 618.

57. See chapter 2.

58. It is true that by the very raising of the question, the possibility of offering euthanasia to persons other than the dying was already present. Moreover, Lord Moynihan left open the possibility that with time the society would be willing to consider such cases as well. Yet the British society never seriously considered expanding the scope of euthanasia to other than dying patients, and whenever the question was raised it was quickly removed from the society's agenda.

59. Two other attempts to pass bills took place on 28 November 1950 and 25 March 1969.

60. Though the Nebraska bill was introduced before the ESA was founded, Philbrick had communicated privately with Potter, who was in the process of formulating similar euthanasia bills. Letter from Philbrick to Potter, 31 December 1936 (PC-C1).

61. *New York Times*, 14 February 1937.

62. Dr. A. L. Miller, the only physician member of the legislature and a fellow of the American College of Surgeons, declined to introduce the bill. He said he believed that the bill had merit but was "twenty-five years too soon." Reported by the *New York Times*, 14 February 1937.

63. *New York Daily News*, 3 February 1937.

64. However, if the child is fourteen or older, he must consent as well.

65. *New York Times*, 14 February 1937.

66. Letter from Philbrick to Potter, 20 December 1937 (PC-C1).

67. Potter, "The Case for Euthanasia," 27 February 1938 (PC-C4).

68. One could also locate in the ESA files the following finding by Dr. C.F. Williams, superintendent of the South Carolina State Hospital: "The net annual increase in mental patients in hospitals in the Untied States is 4-1/2 percent. The steady increase in mental diseases and the ever mounting costs are focusing attention of the public upon the question of prevention and those paying the bills are beginning to ask when they may expect some relief" (PC-C1).

69. PC-C1.

70. *Washington Post*, 19 April 1937.

71. Rabbi Sidney E. Goldstein was also a supporter of eugenics and birth control, and he urged the reform of family structure to include a more decisive role for women. He also worked on peace (the 1932 Geneva disarmament conference) and was a staunch backer of labor's right to organize.

72. Minutes from ESA executive meeting, 14 November 1939 (PC-C1). It is unclear, however, on what grounds Dr. Wolbarst based these figures.

73. PC-C4.

74. PC-C4.

75. PC-C3.

76. Letter from Millard to Mrs. Mitchell, July 19, 1938.

77. Kennedy, "Euthanasia: To Be or Not to Be," 1950 (PC-B3).

78. *Paducah (Kentucky) Sun Democrat*, 20 February 1938.

79. Dr. Goldenweiser, "Urges Killing Idiots" (PC-B2).

80. PC-B2.

81. These inmates, to wit, may have been idiots, but they certainly were not stupid.

82. Similarly, in 1942, when asked in a letter by Mitchell whether the euthanasia bill should be broadened "to include euthanasia for the imbeciles, the incurably insane and congenital monstrosities," Philbrick replied, "It seems to me we should be all inclusive in our *propaganda*; but there is so much *more* favorite opinion for euthanasia for sufferers from incurable disease than for defectives hopelessly insane that we restricted my bill to voluntary euthanasia. Should (which is *unthinkable!*) a legislature be sufficiently progressive to offer euthanasia for all the above members, an amendment can be introduced to make the bill more inclusive" (PC-C1).

83. Editorial, "Germany Executes Her Unfit."

84. There has been an attempt to "exonerate" the society, arguing that after the war it no longer supported euthanasia for the socially undesirable. Kuepper, "Euthanasia in America, 1890–1960," 158.

While it is true that the society as such did not openly promote euthanasia, neither did it make it clear that it objected to its practice. The point in what follows, however, is not to morally condemn the ESA, but rather to point out the ways in which the Society understood its role vis-à-vis the Nazi extermination.

85. A decision was made by the executive committee on 6 October 1942 to recommend to the board of directors that the work of the society be suspended for the duration of the war (PC-C1).

86. Letter from Mrs. Jones to members (PC-C1).

87. ESA newsletter, 1946 (PC-B2).

88. "Hitler personally ordered 'mercy killings' of insane persons, according to a former member of his Reich's Chancellery who gave evidence at a trial here today. The witness, named Allers, said that of 250,000 inmates of German asylums 70,000 were killed between 1939–1945." Editorial, "Mercy Killings Ordered by Hitler Witness Says," *Massachusetts Globe*, July 12, 1950. For a contemporary study, see Burleigh, *Death and Deliverance*.

89.McCormick, pamphlet on euthanasia, 1947 (PC-B2).

90. Board minutes, 7 April 1943 (PC-C1).

91. From a letter to the editor of the *New Republic*, mailed 13 June 1941 (PC-C1).

92. PC-C2.

93. A letter from Inez C. Phibrick to the editor of the *News* (PC-C1).

94. Thomas A. C. Rennie, a psychiatrist from New York Hospital, in a letter to Dr. Frank L. Meleney resigning from the society, dated 20 March 1951 (PC-C1).

95. ESA newsletter, 1952.

96. ESA newsletter, 1952.

Chapter Five

1. The bill presented before the House of Lords was titled Voluntary Euthanasia (Legalisation) [1 Edw. 8].

2. Excerpts of the speech appear in House of Lords, "Voluntary Euthanasia," 28 November 1950, 552–98.

3. There are numerous medical articles on the practice of lethal dosing. The practice, however, appears under different names. Some of the leading articles in the field are: J. A. Billings and S. D. Block, "Slow Euthanasia"; (1996); Cherny and Portenoy, "Sedation in the Management of Refractory Symptoms"; McGivney and Crooks, "The Care of Patients with Severe Chronic Pain in Terminal Illness"; Portenoy et al., "I.V. Infusion of Opioids for Cancer Pain"; Rousseau, "Terminal Sedation in the Care of Dying Patients"; Wanzer, Adelstein, and Canford, "The Physician's Responsibility Toward Hopelessly Ill Patients"; Wilson et al., "Ordering and Administration of Sedatives and Analgesics during the Withholding and Withdrawal of Life Support from Critically Ill Patients."

4. Council on Ethical and Judicial Affairs, "Euthanasia: Report C." Although lethal dosing uses the language of possibility ("may shorten life"), rather than certainty, it is not practiced on the basis of a calculated risk but rather with clear knowledge of the inevitable result.

5. Justice O'Connor in *Washington v. Glucksberg*, 117 S. Ct. 2258, 2303 (1997). For a discussion of this decision, see Burt, "The Supreme Court Speaks— Not Assisted Suicide but a Constitutional Right to Palliative Care."

6. In the scarce data available, the incidence of refractory symptoms among dying patients is controversial even in the limited case of advanced cancer patients. Enck, "Drug-Induced Terminal Sedation for Symptom Control." See also Cherny and Portenoy, "Sedation in the Management of Refractory Symptoms." The figures run all the way from 20 to 52 percent of dying cancer patients. The most common of the severe symptoms was reported to be shortness of breath (or dyspnea, suffered by thirty-three out of sixty-three patients), which is experienced by the patient as a sensation of suffocation. The second most common symptom was pain. Ventafridda et al., "Symptom Prevalence and Control during Cancer Patients' Last Days of Life."

7. The survey was conducted for the commission by Louis Harris and Associates.

8. Rosenberg and Aronstam, "Euthanasia—a Medicolegal Study."

9. Maeterlinck, *Death*, 21–22.

10. Williams, *The Sanctity of Life and the Criminal Law*.

11. Ibid., 326.

12. Congregation for Doctrine of the Faith, *Declaration on Euthanasia* (Washington, D.C.: United States Catholic Conference, 1980), 6; quoted in Kevin O'Rourke, "Pain Relief."

13. Ibid., 161.

14. The discussion of the doctrine of double effect has become prevalent in recent decades. On the history of the doctrine, see Managan, "An Historical Analysis of the Principle of Double Effect." See also Uniacke, "The Doctrine of Double Effect." For a more general study of the place of Catholic medical ethics, see Kelly, *The Emergence of Roman Catholic Medical Ethics in North America*. For a philosophical analysis, see Knauer, "The Hermeneutic Function of the Principle of Double Effect"; Bole, "The Theoretical Tenability of the Doctrine of Double Effect"; Finkelstein, "The Irrelevance of the Intended to *Prima Facie* Culpability."

15. Scholars have distinguished between *intending* a consequence and bringing it about *intentionally*. When an agent aims at an evil, it *intends* evil; and when an agent merely foresees that what it does will produce evil, it *intentionally* brings about evil that it did not intend. Finkelstein, "The Irrelevance of the Intended to *Prima Facie* Culpability," 338.

16. May, "Double Effect, Principle of." The formulation of the fourth condition of the doctrine is quite controversial. It is not clear whether Aquinas is suggesting a kind of moral balancing so that the good intended must outweigh the bad consequence or whether the fourth condition merely limits the bad consequence to the minimum necessary for achieving the good result.

17. The literature debating the applicability of the double effect doctrine to lethal dosing is vast, and includes Hooyman and Veremakis, "Relief from Pain and the Double Effect"; Quill, Dresser, and Brock, "The Rule of Double Effect."

18. It is on the basis of this doctrine, and specifically on the basis of its third principle, that a distinction is made between providing palliative care, knowing that it will have fatal side effects, and providing euthanasia. The intention of the

former is to relieve suffering despite the fatal side effect, while the intention of the latter is to cause death as the means by which relief of suffering is achieved.

19. Finkelstein, "The Irrelevance of the Intended to *Prima Facie* Culpability," 343.

20. Ibid.

21. As one scholar has noted, "It is altogether too artificial to say that a doctor who gives an overdose of a narcotic having in the forefront of his mind the aim of ending his patient's existence is guilty of sin, while a doctor who gives the same overdose in the same circumstances in order to relieve pain is not guilty of sin, provided that he keeps his mind steadily off the consequence which his professional training teaches him is inevitable, namely the death of his patient." Williams, *The Sanctity of Life and the Criminal Law*, 321–22.

22. Some physicians have found the doctrine of double effect senseless in the case of lethal dosing as well. Yet even those physicians do not object to the practice. Commonly, they hold that the practice of lethal dosing is morally not different from the euthanasia offered to dying patients and believe that both should be permitted.

23. As a famous legal scholar noted, "When a result is foreseen as certain, it is the same as if it were desired or intended. It would be an undue refinement to distinguish between the two." Williams, *The Sanctity of Life and the Criminal Law*, 322.

24. The criminal law occasionally does recognize a difference between intended and foreseen consequences, such as in the crime of treason, but in cases of homicide this distinction is clearly rejected.

25. Mich. Comp. Laws Ann. § 752.1027 (West 1994). Similar laws can be found in other states. For a comprehensive account and an original, though basically unconvincing, solution, see Cantor and Thomas, "Pain Relief, Acceleration of Death, and Criminal Law."

26. While this is clearly the case in the United States, matters may be somewhat different in other countries. Specifically, it seems that in England there is much more concern with the legitimacy of the practice of lethal dosing.

27. *Vacco v. Quill*, 521 U.S. 793, 117 S. Ct. 2293, 138 L. Ed. 2d 834.

28. Kass, *Assisted Suicide in the United States*.

29. For a discussion of the legal approach to the doctrine of double effect, see Brody, "Physician-Assisted Suicide in the Courts."

30. *Kansas v. Narmore*, 25 Kan. App. 2d 302 (1998).

31. Since the physician in this case was supplying a higher dosage than that necessary for relieving pain, his conduct may seem to constitute not lethal dosing but active euthanasia. However, there is good reason for considering this case as lethal dosing. The physician is justifying his action with the claim that he did not kill the patient (rather than that he justifiably killed the patient). This suggests the lack of causal connection between the action and its consequence that characterizes lethal dosing, as we shall see. The case is cited in the *Hastings Center Report* 22, no. 2 (1992): 8.

32. For a comprehensive overview, see Melzack and Wall, *The Challenge of Pain*.

33. Cherny and Portenoy, "Sedation in the Management of Refractory Symptoms."

34. On the introduction of the morphine pump to medical treatment in the 1980s, see Gaylor and Coombs, "New Technology: Morphine Pump." While the morphine drip is the most common technique for achieving terminal sedation, it is not the only way for doing so. See Quill, "Palliative Options of Last Resort." More important, the morphine drip is not used only for lethal dosing; it is commonly used in the ordinary treatment of pain, for example, in the process of recovering from surgery. In any event, the practice of lethal dosing usually takes place when all other treatments are useless. See Cherny and Portenoy, "Sedation in the Management of Refractory Symptoms."

35. Here, I am indebted to an argument made in a powerful book by Griffiths, Bood, and Weyers, *Euthanasia and Law in the Netherlands*.

36. "By training, physicians are concerned with causation and consequence. Although intent is important in law, in medicine we assume our intent is to benefit patients, and it is otherwise of peripheral relevance in a scientific endeavor. Applying a legal and ethical principle to a medical practice produces cross-cultural [i.e., disciplinary] dissonance." Quill, "The Ambiguity of Clinical Intentions."

Chapter Six

1. *Windsor (N.Y.) Standard*, May 18, 1939.

2. A detailed list of mercy killings appears in the appendix. The list is based on reported cases of mercy killings in the *New York Times* and in the archives of the Euthanasia Society of America. The list is, of course, not comprehensive. A significantly shorter list of mercy killings appears in Sanders "Euthanasia: None Dare Call it Murder," 351. It is interesting to note that I was not able to locate any detailed descriptions of mercy killings prior to the 1920s. This is not to suggest that such killings did not take place but only that they did not capture public attention. The earliest known case of mercy killing that was brought to trial is the *Roberts* case to be discussed later on. For a new and fascinating book that discusses mercy killings, see Burt, *Death Is That Man Taking Names*.

3. Silving, "Euthanasia: A Study in Comparative Criminal Law."

4. Sanders, "Euthanasia: None Dare Call It Murder."

5. Editorial from the *New York World-Telegram*, distributed by the ESA as a pamphlet (PC-B2).

6. Kuepper, "Euthanasia in America, 1890–1960," 121; Potter, "Mercy Deaths You Don't Hear About, or Secret Euthanasia," 1939 (PC-C4), dated by reference to the *Greenfield* case.

7. See above editorial from the *New York World-Telegram*.

8. Defense attorney Leibowitz, quoted in *New York Times*, 9 May 1939.

9. *Washington Times*, 12 May 1939.

10. "Taking Life Legally," *Magazine Digest* (March 1947) (PC-B2).

11. According to Dr. Sarah Hirsdansky, a child specialist for the Board of Education (PC-B2).

12. "Taking Life Legally," *Magazine Digest* (March 1947) (PC-B2).

13. Wolbarst, "The Case for Voluntary Euthanasia" (PC-B3).

14. *Birmingham (Ala.) Age Herald*, 13 May 1939.

15. Wolbarst, "The Case for Voluntary Euthanasia" (PC-B3).

16. *Los Angeles Shreveport Journal*, May 17, 1939.

17. The *Beers* case was reported in the *New York Times*, 13, 14, 17, and 22 July 1930.

18. See Shrift, *The Logic of the Gift*.

19. *People v. Roberts* (1920), 178 N.W. 690, 211 Mich. 187, 13 A.L.R. 1253.

20. In the *Braunsdorf* case, a father took his twenty-nine-year-old daughter out of a sanitarium and shot and killed her because he feared for her future should he die. He then attempted suicide by shooting himself twice in the chest. He was found not guilty by reason of insanity. *New York Times*, 23 May 1950.

21. Maguire, *Death by Choice*, 25.

22. Kamisar, "Some Non-Religious Views against Proposed 'Mercy Killing' Legislation," 1020.

23. *New York Times*, 20 April 1942.

24. *ESA Bulletin* 4, no. 10 (March-April 1954); *New York Herald Tribune*, 20 March 1954 (PC-B3).

25. (PC-B3) 22 December 1962.

26. In *Commonwealth v. Noxon*, 391 Mass. 495, 66 N.E.2d 814 (1946). See also Sanders, "Euthanasia: None Dare Call it Murder"; *New York Times*, 16 November 1944.

27. The *Repouille* case was reported by the *New York Times*, 14 October 1939.

28. See, e.g., Calabresi and Bobbitt, *Tragic Choices*.

29. *Philadelphia Bulletin*, 20 September 1947.

30. See appendix.

31. *Santa Barbara (Calif.) New-Press*, 19 July 1953.

32. *ESA Bulletin* 4, no. 7 (September–October 1953).

33. *Denver Post*, 20 February 1949.

Epilogue

1. Norman Cantor, "Twenty-Five years after Quinlan," *Journal of Law, Medicine and Ethics* 29, no. 2, 182–96.

2. Emanuel, "The History of Euthanasia in the United States and Britain."

3. Death with Dignity Act, Ore. Rev. Stat. § 127.805 s.2.01, 127.880 s.3.14.

4. Similar proposals have been put on the ballot in Washington and California but did not receive the required majority.

5. Oregon act § 127.805 s.2.01.

6. For a more elaborate analysis of the use of freedom to regulate human behavior, see Nikolas Rose, *Powers of Freedom: Reframing Political Thought* (Cambridge: Cambridge University Press, 1999).

7. See chapter 2.

8. I owe this insight to Thomas Laqueur.

9. The idea of constructed autonomy appears in other end-of-life decision processes. Thus for example, the legal mechanism of living wills that was introduced in the late 1970s, was meant to encourage patients to form a clear set of desires with respect to the time and manner of their dying.

10. Goethe, *Faust*, trans. George Madison Priest (New York: Encyclopaedia Britannica, 1988).

11. Ecclesiastes 7:2.

Appendix

1. *New York Times*, 16 and 31 January 1933.

2. *New York Times*, 13, 14, 17, and 22 July 1930.

3. *New York Times*, 16 September 1930.

4. *New York Times*, 25 April 1932.

5. *New York Times*, 16 December 1932.

6. *New York Times*, 26 January 1934.

7. *Herald Tribune*, 27 January 1934(?), could be 1935.

8. *New York Times*, 17 and 18 December 1935; 1 February 1936.

9. Associated Press, 22 September 1935.

10. *Grand Rapids (Mich.) Herald*, 22 March 1945.

11. *New York Times*, 24 July 1937.

12. *Austin (Minn.) Herald*, 7 February 1938.

13. *Washington Post*, 23 May 1938.

14. *Newsweek*, 31 January 1938; *Time*, 31 January 1938.

15. *Watertown (N.Y.) Times*, 30 December 1938.

16. *NYC Bronx Record and Time*, 19 May 1939.

17. Ibid.; *New York Times*, 2, 12, 16, and 19 October 1938.

18. *New York Times*, 8 December 1933; *NYC Bronx Record and Time*, 19 May 1939.

19. Ibid.

20. *New York Times*, 4 November 1938.

21. *New York Times*, 13, 14, and 16 October 1939; 8 May 1940; 6 June 1941; 6, 10, and 25 December 1941; 6 December 1947.

22. *Washington Times*, 12 May 1939; *New York Times*, January 13, 1939; January 14, 1939; January 18, 1939; January 19, 1939; April 19, 1939; May 9, 1939; May 10, 1939; May 11, 1939; May 12, 1939; *Hartford Courant*, 15 May 1939; *New York Times*, 11 and 12 May 1939.

23. *New York Times*, 2, 12, and 19 October 1938.

24. *New York Mirror*, 28 January 1939.

25. *New York Times*, 16 August 1939.

26. *New York Times*, 4 December 1941; 27 June 1942; 2 and 3 July 1942.

27. *Oakland Tribune*, 12 January 1942.

28. *Brooklyn (N.Y.) Eagle*, 10 March 1942.

29. *Detroit Times*, 11 February 1942.

30. *New York Times*, 21 April 1942.

31. *New York Times*, 28 and 29 September 1943; 29 October 1943; 7 July 1944; 16 October 1947; 15, 25, and 30 December 1948; 4 and 15 January 1949; 8 August 1949; 16 November 1944. See also how the Massachusetts Supreme Court affirmed the trial court's decision and denied Noxon's request for a new trial, based on technical grounds in *Commonwealth v. Noxon*, 319 Mass. 495, 66 N.E.2d 814 (1946).

32. *Time*, 2 December 1946; *New York Times*, 10 October 1946; 23 and 29 November 1946.

33. *Philadelphia Bulletin*, 20 September 1947.

34. *New York Times*, 8 February 1949.

35. *New York Times*, 2 June 1948.

36. *Cincinnati Times Star*, 26 February 1948.

37. *New York Post*, 12 August 1949.

38. *New York Times*, 24, 25, and 26 September 1949; 2, 12, and 14 October 1949; 24, 26, 27, and 28 January 1950; 1, 2, 3, 4, and 8 February 1950; 2 April 1950; *Newsweek*, 13 February 1950; *Time*, 6 February 1950.

39. *New York Times*, 25 June 1949; 23 May 1950; *Time*, 5 June 1950.

40. *New York Times*, 23 March 1950.

41. *New York Times*, 2 November 1950.

42. *New York Times*, 9 July 1950.

43. *New York Herald Tribune*, 27 August 1952.

44. *ESA Bulletin* 4, no. 3 (September–October 1952).

45. Ibid.; *New York Times*, 5 and 6 May 1952.

46. *ESA Bulletin* 4, no. 3 (September–October 1952).

47. *Time*, 27 July 1953; *Santa Barabara (Calif.) New-Press*, 19 July 1953.

48. *Lansford (Pa.) Record*, 2 February 1953; *Harrisburg (Pa.) Patriot*, 5 February 1953.

49. *New York Times*, 30 March 1953; April 4, 1953; *New York Herald Tribune*, 18 April 1953.

50. Ibid.

51. *Riverside (Calif.) Enterprise*, 31 February 1953.

52. *New York Times*, 7 September 1953; 24 December 1953; *New York Herald Tribune*, 24 December 1953; *San Bernardino (Calif.) Telegram*, 7 September 1953.

53. *New York Times*, 26 October 1953; *New York Herald Tribune*, 20 March 1954.

54. *Los Angeles Times*, 17 February 1953.
55. *ESA Bulletin* 4, no. 7 (September–October 1953).
56. *ESA Bulletin* 4, no. 10 (March–April 1954). *New York Times*, 23 February 1954; 2 March 1954; March 26, 1954.
57. *ESA Bulletin* 4, no. 10 (March–April 1954).
58. *ESA Bulletin* 4, no. 12 (November–December 1954).
59. *ESA Bulletin* 4, no. 15 (September–October 1955).
60. *New York Times*, 2 November 1955.
61. *ESA Bulletin* 5, no. 17 (March–April 1956).
62. Ibid.
63. *New York Times*, 23 November 1962.
64. *New York Times*, 12 March 1950; 4, 8, 11, and 28 April 1950.

⟡ Bibliography ⟡

Ackerknecht, Ervin H. "Death in the History of Medicine." *Bulletin of the History of Medicine* 42, no. 1 (1968): 19–23.

Agamben, Giorgio. *Homo Sacer: Sovereign Power and Bare Life*. Stanford, Calif.: Stanford University Press, 1998.

Arendt, Hannah. *The Human Condition*. Chicago: University of Chicago Press, 1998.

Ariès, Philippe. *The Hour of Our Death*. New York: Knopf, 1981.

———. *Western Attitudes toward Death: From the Middle Ages to the Present*. Johns Hopkins Symposia in Comparative History. Baltimore: Johns Hopkins University Press, 1974.

Atkinson, David William. *The English Ars Moriendi*. Renaissance and Baroque Studies and Texts, vol. 5. New York: Lang, 1992.

Bacon, Francis. *The Works of Francis Bacon*, vol. 4. London: Longman, 1860.

Baker, Frank. *From Wesley to Asbury: Studies in Early American Methodism*. Durham, N.C.: Duke University Press, 1976.

Baker, Robert, Dorothy Porter, and Roy Porter, eds. *The Codification of Medical Morality*. Dordrecht: Kluwer Academic, 1993.

Baldwin, Simeon E. "The Natural Right to a Natural Death." *St. Paul Medical Journal* 1 (1899): 875–99.

Balme, Harold. *The Relief of Pain: A Handbook of Modern Analgesia*. London: Churchil, 1936.

Bates, Anna L. *Weeder in the Garden of the Lord: Anthony Comstock's Life and Career*. Lanham, Md.: University Press of America, 1995.

Beaty, Nancy L. *The Craft of Dying: A Study in the Literary Tradition of the Ars Moriendi in England*. New Haven: Yale University Press, 1970.

Becker, Ernest. *The Denial of Death*. New York: Free Press, 1973.

Bell, Clark. "Has the Physician Ever the Right to Terminate Life?" *Medico-Legal Studies* 5 (1898): 66–78.

Bigelow, Jacob. "On Self-Limited Diseases." In *Medical America in the Nineteenth Century: Readings from the Literature*, edited by Gert H. Brieger. Baltimore: Johns Hopkins University Press, 1972.

Billings, J. A., and S. D. Block. "Slow Euthanasia." *Journal of Palliative Care* 12, no. 4 (1996): 21–30.

Blackstone, William. *Commentaries on the Laws of England*, vol. 4. Chicago: University of Chicago Press, 1979.

Bodemer, Charles W. "Physicians and the Dying: A Historical Sketch." *Journal of Family Practice* 9, no. 5 (1979): 827–32.

Boehm, G. "The Right to Commit Suicide." *Bulletin of the Medico-Legal Congress* (1895): 462–64.

Bole, T. J. "The Theoretical Tenability of the Doctrine of Double Effect." *Journal of Medical Philosophy* 16, no. 5 (1991): 467–73.

Borgmann, Albert. *Technology and the Character of Contemporary Life: A Philosophical Inquiry.* Chicago: University of Chicago Press, 1984.

Bracton. *On the Laws and Customs of England.* Cambridge, Mass.: Harvard University Press, 1968.

Brieger, Gert H. *Medical America in the Nineteenth Century: Readings from the Literature.* Baltimore: Johns Hopkins Press, 1972.

Brody, H. "Physician-Assisted Suicide in the Courts: Moral Equivalence, Double Effect, and Clinical Practice." *Minnesota Law Review* 82 (1998): 939–63.

Buffet, E. P. "Pleasures of Dying." *New Englander and Yale Review* 55 (1891): 231–42.

Burgess-Jackson, Keith. "The Legal Status of Suicide in Early America: A Comparison with the English Experience." *Wayne Law Review* 29 (1982): 57–85.

Burleigh, Michael. *Death and Deliverance: "Euthanasia" in Germany c. 1900–1945.* Cambridge and New York: Cambridge University Press, 1994.

Burt, Robert A. *Death Is That Man Taking Names: Intersections of American Medicine, Law, and Culture* (Berkeley: University of California Press, 2002).

———. "The Supreme Court Speaks—Not Assisted Suicide but a Constitutional Right to Palliative Care." *New England Journal of Medicine* 337, no. 17 (1997): 1234–36.

Byrne, Donald E. *No Foot of Land: Folklore of American Methodist Itinerants.* Metuchen, N.J.: Scarecrow, 1975.

Calabresi, Guido, and Philip Bobbitt. *Tragic Choices.* New York: Norton, 1978.

Canguilhem, Georges. *The Normal and the Pathological.* New York: Zone, 1991.

Cantor, Norman. "Twenty-Five Years after Quinlan." *Journal of Law, Medicine and Ethics* 29, no. 2 (2001): 182–96.

Cantor, N. L., and G. C. Thomas. "Pain Relief, Acceleration of Death, and Criminal Law." *Kennedy Institute of Ethics Journal* 6, no. 2 (1996): 107–27.

Cassedy, James H. *Medicine in America: A Short History.* The American Moment. Baltimore: Johns Hopkins University Press, 1991.

Castiglioni, Arturo, and E. B. Krumbhaar. *A History of Medicine.* New York: Knopf, 1958.

Cathell, Daniel W. *The Physician Himself and What He Should Add to His Scientific Acquirements.* New York: Arno, 1972.

Caton, Donald. "The Secularization of Pain." *Anesthesiology* 62 (1985): 493–501.

Chambers, Wesley A. "John Wesley and Death." In *John Wesley: Contemporary Perspectives.*, edited by John Stacey, 150–61. London: Epworth, 1988.

Cherny, N. I., and R. K. Portenoy. "Sedation in the Management of Refractory Symptoms: Guidelines for Evaluation and Treatment." *Journal of Palliative Care* 10, no. 2 (1994): 31–38.

Chesler, Ellen. *Woman of Valor: Margaret Sanger and the Birth Control Movement in America*. New York: Anchor, 1993.

Cicero, Marcus Tullius. *Cicero in Twenty-Eight Volumes*, vol. 9. Cambridge: Harvard University Press, 1912.

Cole, Thomas R. *The Journey of Life: A Cultural History of Aging in America*. Cambridge and New York: Cambridge University Press, 1992.

Cook, Charles M. *The American Codification Movement: A Study of Antebellum Legal Reform*. Westport, Conn.: Greenwood, 1981.

Coulter, Harris L. *Divided Legacy: A History of the Schism in Medical Thought*. Washington, D.C.: Wehawken Book Co., 1973.

Council on Ethical and Judicial Affairs. "Euthanasia: Report C." In *Proceedings of the House of Delegates of the AMA*. Chicago, 1988.

Cowley, Tad L., Ernle Young, and Thoumas A. Raffin. "Care of the Dying: An Ethical and Historical Perspective." *Critical Care Medicine* 20, no. 10 (1992): 1473–82.

David, Morris B. "An Invisible History of Pain: Early Nineteenth-Century Britain and America." *Clinical Journal of Pain* 14 (1998): 191–96.

Davis, Nathan S. *History of Medicine*. Chicago: Cleveland, 1907.

De Moulin, Daniel. "A Historical-Phenomenological Study of Bodily Pain in Western Man." *Bulletin of the History of Medicine* 48, no. 4 (1974): 540–70.

Dendy, Walter C. "On the Physiology of Death and the Treatment of the Dying." *Journal of Psychological Medicine and Mental Pathology* 1 (1848): 112–24.

Dieter, Melvin E. "Wesleyan Theology." In *John Wesley: Contemporary Perspectives*, edited by John Stacey, 162–75. London: Epworth, 1988.

Dowbiggin, Ian. *A Merciful End: The Euthanasia Movement in Modern America*. New York: Oxford University Press, 2003.

Dreyer, Frederick A. *The Genesis of Methodism*. London: Lehigh University Press, 1999.

Editorial. *Medical and Surgical Reporter* (1879): 479–80.

———. *British Medical Journal* 1 (1906): 817.

———. "The Doctrine of Euthanasia." *Medical and Surgical Reporter* 41 (1879): 479–80.

———. "The Dying of Death." *Review of Reviews* 20 (1899): 364–65.

———. "Essays of the Birmingham Speculative Club." *Saturday Review*, 1870, 632–34.

———. "Euthanasia." *Popular Science Monthly* 3 (1873): 90–96.

———. "The Euthanasia." *Medical and Surgical Reporter* 29 (1873): 122–23.

———. "Euthanasia." *Medical Record* 28 (1885): 322.

———. "Euthanasia and Suicide." *Journal of the American Medical Association* (1904): 897.

———. "Germany Executes Her Unfit." *New Republic*, May 5 1941, 527–28.

———. "The Limits of Euthanasia." *Spectator* 46 (1873): 240–41.

———. "The Medical Profession." *Methodist Quarterly Review* 47 (1865): 100–15.

————. "A Medico-Literary Causerie: Euthanasia." *Practitioner* (1896): 631–35.

————. "Mercy Killings Ordered by Hitler, Witness Says." *Massachusetts Globe*, July 12 1950.

————. "The Moral Side of Euthanasia." *Journal of the American Medical Association* 5 (1885): 382–83.

————. "Permissive Euthanasia." *Boston Medical and Surgical Journal* 60, no. 1 (1884): 19–20.

Elias, Norbert. *The Civilizing Process.* Oxford: Blackwell, 1978.

Emanuel, Ezekiel J. "The History of Euthanasia in the United States and Britain." *Annals of Internal Medicine* 121, no. 10 (1994): 793–802.

Enck, R. E. "Drug-Induced Terminal Sedation for Symptom Control." *American Journal of Hospice and Palliative Care* 8, no. 5 (1991): 3–5.

Enright, D. J. *The Oxford Book of Death.* Oxford: Oxford University Press, 1983.

Executive Summary. "Verbatim: Physician-Assisted Suicide and Euthanasia in the Netherlands: A Report to the House Judiciary Subcommittee on the Constitution." *Issues in Law and Medicine* 14 (1998): 30.

Farrell, James J. *Inventing the American Way of Death, 1830–1920.* American Civilization. Philadelphia: Temple University Press, 1980.

Finkelstein, Claire. "The Irrelevance of the Intended to *Prima Facie* Culpability: Comment on Moore." *Boston University Law Review* 76 (1996): 335–46.

Fitch, John A. "Preparation for Death." *Theology* 66 (1963): 445–53.

Foley, K. M. "The Relationship of Pain and Symptom Management to Patient Requests for Physician-Assisted Suicide." *Journal of Pain Symptom Management* 6, no. 5 (1991): 289–97.

Foucault, Michel. *The History of Sexuality.* New York: Pantheon, 1978.

Foucault, Michel, Mauro Bertani, Alessandro Fontana, François Ewald, and David Macey. *Society Must Be Defended: Lectures at the Collège de France, 1975–76.* New York: Picador, 2003.

Foucault, Michel, Graham Burchell, Colin Gordon, and Peter Miller. *The Foucault Effect: Studies in Governmentality.* London: Harvester Wheatsheaf, 1991.

Fye, W. Bruce. "Acive Euthanasia: An Historical Survey of Its Conceptual Origins and Introduction into Medical Thought." *Bulletin of the History of Medicine* 52, no. 4 (1978): 492–502.

Garrett, Valery. "The Last Civil Right? Euthanasia Policy and Politics in the United States, 1938–1991." Ph.D. diss., University of California, Santa Barbara, 1998.

Garrison, Fielding H. *An Introduction to the History of Medicine.* Philadelphia: Saunders, 1929.

Gaustad, Edwin S. *Historical Atlas of Religion in America*, rev. ed. New York: Harper and Row, 1976.

Gaylor, M. S., and D. W. Coombs. "New Technology: Morphine Pump." *Psychiatric Medicine* 5, no. 3 (1987): 219–34.

Geddes, Gordon E. *Welcome Joy: Death in Puritan New England.* Studies in American History and Culture, no. 28. Ann Arbor, Mich.: UMI Research Press, 1981.

Goddard, C. E. "Suggestions in Favor of Terminating Absolutely Hopeless Cases of Injury and Disease." *Medical Times and Hospital Care* 29 (1901): 656–59.

Golden, Richard. "Sir William Osler: Humanistic Thanatologists." *Omega* 36, no. 3 (1998): 241.

Goodenow, John M. *Historical Sketches of the Principles and Maxims of American Jurisprudence in Contrast with the Doctrines of the English Common Law on the Subject of Crimes and Punishments.* Ohio: printed by James Wilson, 1819.

Grad, Frank. "The Ascendancy of Legislation: Legal Problem Solving in Our Time." *Dalhousie Law Journal* 9 (1985): 228–60.

Gray, Madeline. *Margaret Sanger: A Biography of the Champion of Birth Control.* New York: Marek, 1979.

Gregory. *Lectures on the Duties of a Physician.* 1809.

Griffiths, John Alex Bood, and Heleen Weyers. *Euthanasia and Law in the Netherlands.* Amsterdam: Amsterdam University Press, 1998.

Hamstra, Kenneth W. "The American Medical Association Code of Medical Ethics of 1847." Ph.D. diss., University of Texas, 1987.

Heidegger, Martin. *Basic Questions of Philosophy: Selected "Problems" of "Logic."* Bloomington: Indiana University Press, 1994.

———. *Poetry, Language, Thought.* New York: Harper and Row, 1971.

———. *The Question concerning Technology, and Other Essays.* New York: Harper and Row, 1977.

Heidegger, Martin, and Eugene Fink. *Heraclitus Seminar, 1966/67.* Tuscaloosa: University of Alabama Press, 1979.

Heitzenrater, Richard P. *Wesley and the People Called Methodists.* Nashville: Abingdon, 1995.

Hendin, Herbert, Kathleen Foley, and Margot White. "Physician-Assisted Suicide: Reflections on Oregon's First Case." *Issues in Law and Medicine* 14 (1998): 243–70.

Hertzler, Arthur E. *The Horse and Buggy Doctor.* New York: Harper, 1938.

Hinohara, S. "Sir William Osler's Philosophy on Death." *Annals of Internal Medicine* 118, no. 8 (1993): 638–42.

Hitchcock, Frank E. "Annual Oration: Euthanasia." *Transactions of the Maine Medical Society* 10 (1889): 30–43.

Holifield, E. Brooks. *Health and Medicine in the Methodist Tradition: Journey toward Wholeness,* Health/Medicine and the Faith Traditions. New York: Crossroad, 1986.

Hooker, Worthington. *Physician and Patient.* New York: Baker and Scribner, 1849.

Hooyman, T. A., and C. Veremakis. "Relief from Pain and the Double Effect." *Journal of the American Medical Association* 268, no. 14 (1992): 1857–58.

Hostettler, John. *The Politics of Criminal Law: Reform in the Nineteenth Century.* Chichester: B. R. Law, 1992.

Hudson, Winthrop S. "The Methodist Age in America." *Methodist History* 12 (1974): 2–15.

Hunt, Alan, and Gary Wickham. *Foucault and Law: Toward a Sociology of Law as Governance*, Law and Social Theory. London and Boulder, Colo.: Pluto, 1994.

Illich, Ivan. *Medical Nemesis: The Expropriation of Health*. Ideas in Progress. London: Calder and Boyars, 1975.

Kamisar, Yale. "Some Non-Religious Views against Proposed 'Mercy Killing' Legislation." *Minnesota Law Review* 42 (1958): 969–1042.

Kass, Leon. *Assisted Suicide in the United States, Hearing before the Subcommittee on the Constitution for the House Committee on the Judiciary*. 104th Cong., 2d sess., 1996, 368.

Katz, Jack. *How Emotions Work*. Chicago: University of Chicago Press, 1999.

Kaufman, Martin, Stuart Galishoff, and Todd L. Savitt, eds. *Dictionary of American Medical Biography*. Westport, Conn.: Greenwood Press, 1984.

Kelly, David F. *The Emergence of Roman Catholic Medical Ethics in North America: An Historical-Methodological-Bibliographical Study*. Texts and Studies in Religion, vol. 3. New York: Mellen, 1979.

Kevles, Daniel J. *In the Name of Eugenics: Genetics and the Uses of Human Heredity*. Cambridge, Mass.: Harvard University Press, 1995.

Knauer, Peter. "The Hermeneutic Function of the Principle of Double Effect." *Natural Law Forum* 12 (1967): 132–62.

Kuepper, Stephen Louis. "Euthanasia in America, 1890–1960: The Controversy, the Movement, and the Law." Ph.D. diss., Rutgers University, 1981.

Laderman, Gary. *The Sacred Remains: American Attitudes toward Death, 1799–1883*. New Haven: Yale University Press, 1996.

Lange, J. Chris. "Modes of Dying." *Pittsburgh Medical Review* 3 (1889): 27–34.

Larremore, Wilbur. "Suicide and the Law." *Harvard Law Review* 17 (1904): 331.

Lavi, Shai J. "The Problem of Pain and the Right to Die." In *Pain, Death, and the Law*, edited by Austin Sarat. Michigan: Michigan University Press, 2001.

"The Life of Dr. Donne." *Arminian Magazine* 2 (1779): 436–68.

Luker, Kristin. *Abortion and the Politics of Motherhood*. California Series on Social Choice and Political Economy. Berkeley: University of California Press, 1984.

Lyerly, Cynthia Lynn. *Methodism and the Southern Mind, 1770–1810*. New York: Oxford University Press, 1998.

Macdonald, Keith Norman. *On Death and How to Divest It of Its Terrors*. Edinburgh: Maclachlan and Stewart, 1875.

Maddocks, Morris. "Health and Healing in the Ministry of John Wesley." In *John Wesley: Contemporary Perspectives*, edited by John Stacey, 138–49. London: Epworth, 1988.

Maeterlinck, Maurice. *Death*. New York: Dodd, Mead, 1912.

Maguire, Daniel C., *Death by Choice*. Garden City, N.Y.: Doubleday, 1974.

Managan, Joseph T. "An Historical Analysis of the Principle of Double Effect." *Theological Studies* 10 (1949): 41–61.

Marty, Martin E. *Health and Medicine in the Lutheran Tradition: Being Well*, Health/Medicine and the Faith Traditions. New York: Crossroad, 1983.

Marx, Carl F. H. "Medical Euthanasia: Thesis." *Journal of the History of Medicine and Allied Sciences* 7 (1952): 403–16.

Marzen, T., M. O'Dowd, D. Crone, and T. Balch. "Suicide: A Constitutional Right?" *Duquesne Law Review* 24, no. 1 (1985): 1–242.

Mather, Cotton. "Euthanasia: A Sudden Death Made Happy and Easy to the Dying Believer." Boston: Kneeland, 1723.

Mathews, Donald G. "The Second Great Awakening as an Organizing Process, 1780–1830: An Hypothesis." *American Quarterly* 21 (1977): 23–43.

May, William. "Double Effect, Principle of." *Encyclopedia of* Bioethics, New York: Macmillan, 1978.

McCormick, Richard A. *Health and Medicine in the Catholic Tradition: Tradition in Transition*, Health/Medicine and the Faith Traditions. New York: Crossroad, 1984.

McGivney, W. T., and G. M. Crooks. "The Care of Patients with Severe Chronic Pain in Terminal Illness." *Journal of the American Medical Association* 251, no. 9 (1984): 1182–88.

McManners, John. *Death and the Enlightenment: Changing Attitudes to Death among Christians and Unbelievers in Eighteenth-Century France.* Oxford: Oxford University Press, 1981.

Mehler, Barry Alan. *A History of the American Eugenics Society, 1921–1940.* Ph.D. diss., University of Illinois, Champaign, 1988.

Melzack, Ronald, and Patrick D. Wall. *The Challenge of Pain.* New York: Basic Books, 1983.

"Memoir of Mrs. Mary Ann Peaco." *Methodist Magazine* 1 (1818): 272–77.

Mikell, W. "Is Suicide Murder?" *Columbia Law Review* 3 (1903): 379–94.

Minois, Georges. *History of Suicide: Voluntary Death in Western Culture.* Medicine and Culture. Baltimore: Johns Hopkins University Press, 1999.

Mitchel, S. Weir. "Civilization and Pain." *Journal of the American Medical Association* 18 (1892): 108.

More, Thomas. *Utopia and Other Writings.* New York: New American Library, 1984.

Morris, David B. "An Invisible History of Pain: Early Nineteenth-Century Britain and America." Clinical Journal of Pain 14 (1998): 191–96.

Munk, William. *Euthanasia; or, Medical Treatment in Aid of an Easy Death.* New York: Arno, 1887.

Nelson, William E. "The Impact of the Antislavery Movement upon styles of Judicial Reasoning in Nineteenth-Century America." *Harvard Law Review* 87, no. 3 (1974): 513–66.

Nietzsche, Friedrich W. *On the Genealogy of Morals*, Cambridge: Cambridge University Press, 1994.

———. *Will to Power*, translated by Walter Kaufman. New York: Random House, 1967.

Nietzsche, Friedrich W., Maudemarie Clark, and Brian Leiter. *Daybreak: Thoughts on the Prejudices of Morality.* Cambridge: Cambridge University Press, 1997.

Norwood, Frederick A. *The Story of American Methodism: A History of the United Methodists and Their Relations.* Nashville: Abingdon, 1974.

Nottingham, Elizabeth K. *Methodism and the Frontier: Indiana Proving Ground.* New York: Columbia University Press, 1966.

Novak, William J. *The People's Welfare: Law and Regulation in Nineteenth-Century America,* Studies in Legal History. Chapel Hill: University of North Carolina Press, 1996.

Nuland, Sherwin. *How We Die.* London: Chatto and Windus, 1996.

O'Connor, Mary C. *The Art of Dying Well: The Development of the Ars Moriendi.* New York: Columbia University Press, 1942.

O'Rourke, Kevin. "Pain Relief: Ethical Issues and Catholic Teaching." In *In Birth, Suffering and Death,* 157–69. Dordrecht, Netherlands: Kluwer Academic Publishers, 1992.

Outler, Albert C. *John Wesley's Sermons: An Introduction.* Nashville: Abingdon, 1991.

Owen, Christopher H. *The Sacred Flame of Love: Methodism and Society in Nineteenth-Century Georgia.* Athens: University of Georgia Press, 1998.

Paradys. *Oratio De Euthanasia.* Leiden: n.p. 1794.

Pascalis, Felix. "Remarks on the Theory of Pain." *North American Medical and Surgical Journal* 1 (1826): 79–89.

Percival, Thomas. *Percival's Medical Ethics.* Baltimore: Williams and Wilkins, 1927.

Pernick, Martin S. "Back from the Grave: Recurring Controversies over Defining and Diagnosing Death in History." In *Death: Beyond Whole-Brain Criteria,* edited by Richard M. Zaner, ix, 276. Boston: Kluwer Academic, 1988.

———. *The Black Stork: Eugenics and the Death of "Defective" Babies in American Medicine and Motion Pictures since 1915.* New York: Oxford University Press, 1996.

———. *A Calculus of Suffering: Pain, Professionalism, and Anesthesia in Nineteenth-Century America.* New York: Columbia University Press, 1985.

Philip, A. P. W. "On the Nature of Death." *Philosophical Transactions,* no. 124 (1834): 167.

Piette, Maximin. *John Wesley in the Evolution of Protestantism.* New York: Sheed and Ward, 1938.

Popkin, William. *Materials on Legislation.* New York: Foundation, 1993.

Portenoy, R. K., D. E. Moulin, A. Rogers, C. E. Inturrisi, and K. M. Foley. "I.V. Infusion of Opioids for Cancer Pain: Clinical Review and Guidelines for Use." *Cancer Treatment Reports* 70, no. 5 (1986): 575–81.

Potter, Charles Francis. *The Preacher and I: An Autobiography.* New York: Crown, 1951.

Quill, Timothy E. "The Ambiguity of Clinical Intentions." *New England Journal of Medicine* 329, no. 14 (1993): 1039–40.

Quill, Timothy E. "Palliative Options of Last Resort: A Comparison of Voluntarily Stopping Eating and Drinking, Terminal Sedation, Physician-Assisted Suicide, and Voluntary Active Euthanasia." *Journal of the American Medical Association* 278 (1997): 2099.

Quill, Timothy E., R. Dresser, and D. W. Brock. "The Rule of Double Effect—A Critique of Its Role in End-of-Life Decision Making." *New England Journal of Medicine* 337, no. 24 (1997): 1768–71.

"The Recent Death of John Patrick." *Arminian Magazine* 20 (1797): 203–6.

Reiser, Stanley J. "The Dilemma of Euthanasia in Modern Medical History: The English and American Experience." In *The Dilemmas of Euthanasia*, edited by John A. Behnke and Sissela Bok. Garden City, N.Y.: Anchor, 1975.

Rey, Roselyne. *The History of Pain*. Cambridge, Mass.: Harvard University Press, 1995.

Richardson, B. W. "Natural Euthanasia." *Popular Science Monthly* 8 (1869): 617–20.

———. "The Painless Extinction of Life in Lower Animals." *Popular Science Monthly* 26 (1884–85): 641–52.

Rilke, Rainer M., and Stephen Mitchell. "Death." In *The Selected Poetry of Rainer Maria Rilke*, 145–46. New York: Random House, 1982.

Rose, Nikolas. *Powers of Freedom: Reframing Political Thought*. Cambridge: Cambridge University Press, 1999.

Rosenberg, Charles E. *The Cholera Years: The United States in 1832, 1849, and 1866*. Chicago: University of Chicago Press, 1987.

Rosenberg, L. J., and N. E. Aronstam. "Euthanasia—a Medicolegal Study." *Journal of the American Medical Association* 36 (1901): 108–10.

Rothman, David J. *Strangers at the Bedside: A History of How Law and Bioethics Transformed Medical Decision Making*. New York: Basic, 1991.

Rothman, Sheila M. *Living in the Shadow of Death: Tuberculosis and the Social Experience of Illness in America*. New York: Basic, 1994.

Rothstein, William G. *American Physicians in the Nineteenth Century: From Sects to Science*. Baltimore: Johns Hopkins University Press, 1972.

Rousseau, P. "Terminal Sedation in the Care of Dying Patients." *Archive of Internal Medicine* 156, no. 16 (1996): 1785–86.

Rush, Benjamin. *Selected Writings of Benjamin Rush*. New York: Philosophical Library, 1947.

Russell, O. Ruth. *Freedom to Die: Moral and Legal Aspects of Euthanasia*. New York: Human Sciences, 1975.

Sanders, Joseph. "Euthanasia: None Dare Call It Murder." *Journal of Criminal Law, Criminology and Police Science* 60, no. 3 (1969) 351.

Sanger, Margaret. *My Fight for Birth Control*. New York: Farrar and Rinehart, 1931.

Schneider, A. Gregory. "The Ritual of Happy Dying among Early American Methodists." *Early American Methodists* 10 (1982): 348–63.

Schrift, Alan D. *The Logic of the Gift: Toward an Ethic of Generosity*. New York and London: Routledge, 1997.

"A Short Account of the Conversion and Death of Caster Garret: In a Letter to a Friend." *Arminian Magazine* 10 (1787): 18–21.

Silving, Helen. "Euthanasia: A Study in Comparative Criminal Law." *University of Pennsylvania Law Review* 103, no. 3 (1954): 350–89.

"Some Account for the Life and Death of Sarah Brough." *Arminian Magazine* 3 (1780): 592–601.

Sophocles. *Antigone; The Women of Trachis; Philoctetes; Oedipus at Colonus*, edited and translated by Hugh Lloyd-Jones. Cambridge, Mass.: Harvard University Press, 1994.

Spender, J. K. *Therapeutic Means for the Relief of Pain*. London: Macmillan, 1874.

Stannard, David E. *The Puritan Way of Death: A Study in Religion, Culture, and Social Change*. New York: Oxford University Press, 1977.

Swift, Zephaniah. *A System of the Laws of the State of Connecticut*, vol. 2. New York: Arno, 1972.

Taylor, Jeremy, and P. G. Stanwood. *Holy Living; and, Holy Dying*. Oxford: Oxford University Press, 1989.

Thwing, E. P. "Euthanasia in Articulo Mortis." *Medico-Legal Journal* 6 (1888): 282–84.

Tollemache, Lionel A. "The Cure of Incurables." *Fortnightly Review* (1873): 218–30.

Turley, Briane K. *A Wheel within a Wheel: Southern Methodism and the Georgia Holiness Association*. Macon, Ga.: Mercer University Press, 1999.

Uniacke, Suzanne M. "The Doctrine of Double Effect." *Thomist* (1984): 188–218.

Van Der Sluis, I. "The Movement for Euthanasia, 1875–1975." *Dedalus* 66 (1979): 131–72.

Vanderpool, Harold Y. "The Wesleyan-Methodist Tradition." In *Caring and Curing: Health and Medicine in the Western Religious Traditions*, edited by D. W. and R. L. Numbers Amundsen, 317–53. New York: Macmillan, 1986.

Vaux, Kenneth L. *Health and Medicine in the Reformed Tradition: Promise, Providence, and Care*. Health/Medicine and the Faith Traditions. New York: Crossroad, 1984.

Ventafridda, V., C. Ripamonti, F. De Conno, M. Tamburini, and B. R. Cassileth. "Symptom Prevalence and Control during Cancer Patients' Last Days of Life." *Journal of Palliative Care* 6, no. 3 (1990): 7–11.

Wanzer, Sidney H., S. James Adelstein, and Ronald E. Canford. "The Physician's Responsibility toward Hopelessly Ill Patients." *New England Journal of Medicine* 310, no. 15 (1984): 955–59.

Warner, John H. " 'The Nature-Trusting Heresy': American Physicians and the Concept of the Healing Power of Nature in the 1850s and 1860s." In *Perspectives in American History*, edited by Donald Fleming. Cambridge, Mass.: Harvard University Press, 1978.

Weber, Max. *Economy and Society: An Outline of Interpretive Sociology*. Berkeley: University of California Press, 1978.

———. *From Max Weber: Essays in Sociology.* New York: Oxford University Press, 1958.

Wells, S. R. "Is 'Euthanasia' Ever Justifiable?" *Transactions of the Medico-Legal Society for the Year 1906–74* (1907): 1–14.

Wesley, Charles, and Thomas Jackson. *The Journal of the Rev. Charles Wesley.* London: Wesleyan Methodist Book-Room, 1849.

Wesley, Charles, and John R. Tyson. *Charles Wesley: A Reader.* New York: Oxford University Press, 1989.

Wesley, John. *Primitive Physic; or, An Easy and Natural Method of Curing Most Diseases.* London: Printed by G. Paramore, 1792.

Wesley, John, and Nehemiah Curnock. *The Journal of John Wesley.* New York: Capricorn, 1963.

Wesley, John, and Albert Cook Outler. *John Wesley*, A Library of Protestant Thought. New York: Oxford University Press, 1964.

———. *The Works of John Wesley.* Nashville: Abingdon, 1984.

Wesley, John, Albert Cook Outler, and Richard P. Heitzenrater. *John Wesley's Sermons: An Anthology.* Nashville: Abingdon, 1991.

Williams, Charles B. "Euthanasia." *Medical Record* 70 (1894): 909–11.

Williams, Glanville. *The Sanctity of Life and the Criminal Law.* New York: Knopf, 1957.

Williams, Samuel D. *Euthanasia.* London: Williams and Norgate, 1872.

Wilson, W. C., N. G. Smedira, C. Fink, J. A. McDowell, and J. M. Luce. "Ordering and Administration of Sedatives and Analgesics during the Withholding and Withdrawal of Life Support from Critically Ill Patients." *Journal of the American Medical Association* 267, no. 7 (1992): 949–53.

Zucker, Marjorie B. *The Right to Die Debate: A Documentary History*, Primary Documents in American History and Contemporary Issues. Westport, Conn.: Greenwood, 1999.

❖ Index ❖